Formerly a lawyer in London, two years ago Jamie Ivey decided to give up office life and commuting, and moved to the South of France with his wife, Tanya, where they rented an old farmhouse outside Lourmarin. His first book, *Extremely Pale Rosé*, about their search for the palest rosé in the country, was published in 2006 and won the Gourmand Award 2006. The following year Jamie wrote *La Vie en Rosé* in which he recounts how they ran the first rosé bar in France. Visit his website at www.extremelypalerose.com.

By Jamie Ivey

Extremely Pale Rosé
La Vie en Rosé
Rosé en Marché

Rosé en Marché

JAMIE IVEY

PHOENIX

A PHOENIX PAPERBACK

First published in Great Britain in 2008
by Weidenfeld & Nicolson
This paperback edition published in 2009
by Phoenix,
an imprint of Orion Books Ltd,
Orion House, 5 Upper Saint Martin's Lane,
London, WC2H 9EA

An Hachette UK company

1 3 5 7 9 10 8 6 4 2

Text © Jamie Ivey 2008
Illustrations © Neil Ashworth 2008

A CIP catalogue record for this book
is available from the British Library.

ISBN 978-0-7538-2586-0

Typeset by Deltatype Ltd, Birkenhead, Merseyside

Printed in Great Britain by CPI Mackays, Chatham, ME5 8TD

The Orion Publishing Group's policy is to use papers that
are natural, renewable and recyclable products and
made from wood grown in sustainable forests. The logging
and manufacturing processes are expected to conform to
the environmental regulations of the country of origin.

www.orionbooks.co.uk

For Elodie

Only in France

The Provençal town of Apt, capital of the Luberon National Park, rests in a cradle of pine-filled hills. It's a pretty, but not arresting place, and a photograph of the centre would rarely make it into anyone's holiday album, always being passed over like a plain girl at a ball in favour of the more gaudy delights of Roussillon, Bonnieux and Gordes. A handful of cafés are scattered where the main street finally breaks the banks of surrounding shops, and here people sip on short black coffees and watch the bustling crowd. Apt is nearly always busy. Hazard lights wink like chains of Christmas illuminations, particularly around the main square – the home of the *sous-préfecture* of the Vaucluse. This mighty instrument of government pulls in thousands of people a year in pursuit of the multitude of licences so intrinsic to life in France. Today my wife, Tanya, and I have joined the magnetised throng.

We are waiting in a seminar room in one of the many administrative buildings. About twenty plastic seats are arranged round a large U-shaped table, but demand for the course we are attending is such that several people have to stand. In front of us there's a whiteboard covered with confusing acronyms. They stretch from the ceiling to the floor in five eye-blurring columns. There's also an overhead projector displaying an intimidating flow chart. The air in the room is hot, wet and soporific. The two-hour programme hasn't even begun and I've already had several disturbing flashbacks to the dead hours I spent imbibing banal facts at school.

There's a single window, with the blind pulled half down. Outside, it is still sheeting with rain. The muffled progress of a marker pen across the whiteboard and the incessant thump of raindrops on thin glass are the only sounds. Looking across at Tanya, I see that water is dripping from her blonde hair on to the virgin sheets of her notepad. Our clothes are soaked through as a result of the miserable half-hour we've spent traipsing the streets trying to find the right location, stumbling into doctors' surgeries and insurance offices before alighting on the non-descript building that is the Salle d'Anpe. Tanya has a perplexed look on her face as she etches slowly in capitals on her paper. The lead smudges as she completes the phrase 'THIS BETTER BE WORTH IT' and underlines it three times. Bored, I swing on my chair, just catching myself as the legs begin a backwards cartwheel.

Finally the organiser of the course finishes writing on the board. He's a young man in his mid- to late thirties, perhaps a couple of years older than us. His hair has been shaved to a gossamer layer, which emphasises his angular nose and long, thin face. After laying a battered briefcase on the table – made of the type of aged leather favoured by Oxbridge academics – he smiles warmly and introduces himself in French as Gautier. 'I hope today's course can be as interactive as possible. I really want to encourage people to speak about their projects.'

The word 'interactive' induces immediate fear. Despite nearly a year in France, my French is still somewhat limited and humiliation beckons. In the past my mistakes have included mixing up mobile phones and drinking water – 'portable' and 'potable' – and mispronouncing 'orage' and 'orange': I thought I was making small talk about a storm; the shopkeeper thought I was trying to buy some oranges. Some days I felt I could speak the language reasonably, but on others my confidence deserted me. Today I knew my limit and addressing a room full of people in French was definitely beyond me, so I looked across at my wife.

Tanya's mother had been brought up in Montreal and spoke fluent French. From an early age she'd talked to her children in the language, and although Tanya sometimes forgot vocabulary, she spoke nearly faultlessly. Unfortunately Tanya is also a mimic, a tease and endlessly mischievous.

At that moment these were qualities I could have lived without.

'I'm not saying a word,' she whispered.

I kicked her under the table and gave an imploring look.

She grinned and mouthed, 'It will be good for you.'

Gautier removed a wooden conductor's baton from his briefcase and pointed it with a flourish at the girl two to my left. 'Now, if everybody can explain why they are here.'

The chosen girl must have been barely twenty and her skin flushed red with nerves as she began to talk. The more she spoke, the more confused I became. The presentation touched on issues like sourcing a cheap supply of essential oil, the age profile of the potential clientele and the availability of a loan to purchase a €5,000 table. After she finished, I wrote a message to Tanya – 'A masseuse??'

Before I could read Tanya's reply, Gautier waved his baton with the flair of a maestro and randomly selected the next person, another girl. This time the subject was aromatherapy. Using herbs and nut extracts from the Luberon, the girl had built up a range of products that she used to cure people's allergies. A half-hour session with her cost about €30, but she promised to be able to treat maladies ranging from hay fever to insomnia.

I looked down at my notepad, where Tanya had written, 'Are you *sure* this course is for market traders?'

I'd thought that at the end of the morning we would be free

to work in any market from Cannes to Calais, but with every passing second I was becoming more doubtful – why would the morning need to be interactive? Were we going to role-play selling a kilo of vegetables or dealing with customer complaints? And what about the aromatherapist and the masseuse? Either this session would witness the birth of a new breed of spa markets or it was time to collect our notepads and leave.

Unfortunately it was too late. Gautier's baton was already dancing in the air. It wavered like a divining stick between Tanya and myself, offering us both the opportunity to speak. 'I see you are English. Are you setting up a *gîte*?' he asked.

Just breathe, I advised myself in my head as I began to speak.

But within seconds I'd made my biggest mistake, and it wasn't grammatical – naïvely I started at the beginning of our complex story, leaving me a full ten minutes of difficult dialogue before I could hope to stop. After twenty seconds most of the other people on the course were ignoring me and taking down the information on the whiteboard. At the minute mark there were only two people still listening: Tanya and Gautier. After two minutes Tanya was doodling and Gautier was aimlessly twirling his baton.

My aim at the outset had been to summarise just how Tanya and I came to be in the room. Two years ago we'd been undistinguishable from any other professional couple in London. I worked as a lawyer at a large London firm, and Tanya in marketing in the entertainment industry. From the beginning of my legal career the long hours and dreary documents drained me of enthusiasm and I couldn't escape the feeling that my life was somehow pre-packaged. Provided I worked super-humanly hard and sacrificed most of my personal life, material wealth would accrue. I could of course have changed jobs within the City, but that was like being forced to select from a limited range of ready meals, knowing that whatever choice I made it would be bland and unexciting.

Fortunately Tanya had a solution – from an early age she'd been fascinated by the south of France. The strong smells of lavender, wild herbs and sticky pines, the luscious blue of the sky and the fragile clarity of the light. Since our relationship began, we'd holidayed amid the olive trees and the vines, soaking up the song of the cicadas and drinking rosé. To us, there had always been something magical about a glass of pale-pink wine in the sunshine. It was synonymous with long, lazy afternoons filled with idle conversation, tables sagging with cold meats and cheeses, tarts and fresh fruit, where only the curtain of darkness separated one meal from another. And so two years ago we'd taken a sabbatical from our careers and had hared around France trying to win a bet and find the palest rosé in the land, but when autumn had arrived, we'd returned to London and the dissatisfaction had crept back into our lives.

Gradually an idea evolved – we wanted to set up a bar that offered a wine list composed exclusively of rosés. It would be called La Vie en Rosé, and it would be the first bar of its type in France. Work would become a pleasure. The challenges of sourcing different wines and then creating an atmosphere where people could enjoy them began to dominate my thinking. Without realising it, I was falling deeper and deeper into the world of wine. Every new bottle I tasted was a journey – picturing the heat-baked soil or the squall of rain before the harvest, which manifested itself in that touch of extra acidity as I sipped. Life in the wine industry offered new discoveries each day, and where better to enjoy them than the home of rosé – Provence. Against the advice of our friends, we gave up our jobs, finally quit our secure life in London and headed to France to try to make this dream a reality.

We spent the summer holding small rosé festivals on the terraces of various bars in Provence and the Côte d'Azur, serving Sancerre to the jet set as they idled on sun loungers or persuading the locals to relinquish their pastis and replace it with rosé. While our contemporaries sweated their way to work in London, we meandered through shady cobbled streets, wheeling trolleys of new stock to the latest bar. Rather than look out of the window at another glass-clad office block, we marvelled at the sympathetic curves of the archways in Uzès, or the blue canvas of the sea framed by the multicoloured parasols of the Cannes beach clubs.

When we weren't working, we were busy looking for our own bar, hunting in the pine-clad hills of the Var and the Luberon, always dreaming of discovering a run-down property we could convert into our future. But as purchase after purchase fell through, our thoughts turned to returning home. The cost of running a bar proved to be much higher than we'd anticipated. Alcohol licences retailed at about €20,000, and legislation prohibited any new bar from being established within 50 metres of an existing one. Unfortunately the prices for existing bar businesses were invariably hugely inflated.

Finally we discovered a place that seemed perfect – a derelict bar high in the hills on the edge of the Luberon National Park. There was a crumbling terrace with panoramic views over the surrounding valleys and an old house in which we could live. The price was surprisingly cheap. Retrospectively it was obviously too good to be true, but it was only after we had put down a deposit that we discovered plans to build a sewage farm at the bottom of the land. We pulled out of the purchase.

Just as we were on the verge of giving up and returning home, we realised our idea could work on a much simpler level – in the markets. There was a market in one village or another every day of the week, and in the summer they were busier than a pre-Christmas high street. There were no requirements for an alcohol licence, and the price for a 2-metre pitch was €2. We would never make a fortune, but it seemed perfectly possible to create a reasonable life for ourselves touring the village markets and making a name as wine merchants who specialised in rosé.

And what locations to work in – under the shade of century-old plane trees, or in the lee of medieval châteaux, always looking up at the unique blue of the region's skies.

Despite our disappointments, it was too exciting a prospect to give up and so two days ago, on a sunny late-September morning, we'd driven a car full of wine into Apt with the intention of selling it in the town's market. We'd been told by the traders that all we needed to do to secure a pitch was to turn up at 7 a.m. and speak to the *police municipale*.

We'd made our way through the market, past the other vendors, who were already snapping apart table legs and laying out boards on which to display their wares. Vans were parked across the street with their boots raised so that we could make out all sorts of neatly stacked goods inside – wicker tubs of olives, brightly coloured Provençal linen precisely folded into neat creases, boxes full of *saucissons* and rows of pesto jars. Each successive vehicle held a new palate of colours and assortment of aromas. To our left, a narrow street bent away towards the church. Amid the shadows cast by the encroaching buildings, traders had laid out ornate rugs and assorted furniture carved from dark woods. Spice sticks had been lit and lanterns, with the carved casings of the Orient, hung over the cobbles.

Nearer the centre of town, the road widened into a large square in front of the *sous-préfecture* – an imposing building bedecked with French flags. Two grand balustraded staircases led up to oak doors with heavy wrought-iron handles. We passed the mobile *boucheries* and *fromageries*, which were arranged in a semicircle at the base of the stairs, and spotted the small cubbyhole office of the *police municipale*. Having knocked on the door, we entered.

Minutes later we'd been disabused of the notion that market trading in France would be easy. The police had asked for our trading licence, our social security numbers and proof of insurance. I'd rather lamely handed over my passport in the hope that the rules might be different for foreigners, but instead of a place in the market we'd been handed an enrolment form for this course.

'And so,' I concluded, 'I think the gendarme must have given us the wrong form.'

'No,' said Gautier, 'you're in the right place, though the course is not just for market traders; it's to help people set up new businesses. But selling wine is tough. How will it work?'

The question was sympathetic, but Gautier might as well have been a medieval torturer tightening a thumbscrew. I had to speak again. Glancing sideways at Tanya, I saw she was grinning at my ordeal as I began my explanation.

Traditionally pink wine had been seen as a poor cousin to red and white wines. Vignerons had kept their rosé in a forgotten vat at the back of the *cave*, periodically chucking in some sulphur to prolong its life. As a result rosé had become synonymous with head- and stomach aches. Hardy hunters swigged it in bars early in the morning, but no one was foolish enough to drink it with food, except of course the tourists.

In the last five years, however, the reputation of rosé had changed dramatically. Vignerons noted that those vineyards which produced good pink wine sold out quickly. In a stagnant wine market, making an excellent rosé could help ensure the survival of the family business. And as the quality of rosé improved, so demand increased. We'd discovered that it was not unusual for sommeliers at Michelin-starred restaurants to recommend rosé to accompany meals. Pink wine had suddenly become trendy – superstars like Kate Moss were pictured swigging it on the beach, and teenagers sipped it from straws in nightclubs.

Then there was our visit to the newest and hippest of Saint-Tropez's beach clubs – Nikki Beach. Surrounded by dazzling white umbrellas and staff straight from a film set, we observed bottle after bottle being drained. The demand for rosé was such that the bar didn't even sell red or white wine. By the end of the afternoon the bottles were so large that the waitresses had to bend on one knee and hoist the rosé on to their elfin shoulders to pour.

'If we can just get the formula right, then rosé will sell,' I finished.

'*Bon,*' said Gautier, still unconvinced, and pointed dramatically with his baton at the next person. Perhaps his way of relieving boredom was conducting an imaginary symphony in his head.

For the next hour we sat and listened as everybody in the room outlined their plans. Gautier then explained the tax implications of setting up a business in France, which was very expensive – before we even sold a bottle of wine, the government would expect us to pay over €2,000 in social security contributions – and the list of grants we could apply for, if, that is, we were under twenty-five, or had been born within the environs of the Luberon National Park, or were selling produce we'd made ourselves, or had a carbon-neutral business. Everybody in the room managed to fit themselves into one category or other except us.

This was followed by a discussion about our social responsibilities as small-business owners. Most of the vocabulary was beyond me and for the last ten minutes of the session I followed the path of raindrops down the window, amusing myself by guessing whether they would turn right or left. A yawn from Tanya triggered the same response from me. The air grew stickier and my head repeatedly dropped, only to jerk back up like a yo-yo. Finally it happened – I fell asleep, lurching forwards and scattering paper everywhere as my head hit the table. Two minutes later the other attendees filed out and I woke myself up with an enormous snore.

Leaving me in an embarrassed daze, Tanya gathered up the various papers and forms we'd been given and approached Gautier. Despite the intensive two-hour interactive course, we were still no clearer about how to get our market-trading licence.

'You're supposed to apply in Avignon, but you can get the right papers through the basement window opposite the Caisse d'Epargne.'

'So we didn't need to come on this course?' asked Tanya.

'No.'

We both glanced across at the whiteboard full of information about the taxation of small businesses and the confusing acronyms detailing the various subsidies to which we weren't entitled.

'At least you had a nice sleep,' consoled Tanya, as we walked away.

Outside, the rain had stopped, but streams still ran through the gutters. Passing cars kicked waves of water on to the pavement, and pedestrians glanced anxiously skywards, waiting for the next deluge. Splashing our way back to the *sous-préfecture*, we stopped as advised opposite the Caisse d'Epargne. We'd just been discussing how surreal our lives had become – from city slickers to seminars about the medicinal properties of Luberon pine-nut oil – unaware that things were about to become even more perverse.

In front of us was a queue of people, and at its head, despite the weather and the slippery streets, a man was lying flat on the pavement. He was dressed in army fatigues, and on the ground next to him was a long canvas bag that appeared to house a shotgun. The man was fumbling in his pockets for something. In London I would have presumed we were witnessing a botched hold-up, but the locals walking past showed not the slightest bit of interest. Apparently this type of behaviour had become quite normal.

Joining the queue, we learnt that two weeks ago the majority of the administrative functions of the *sous-préfecture* in Apt had been transferred to Avignon. This meant that everybody who, for example, needed a hunting or a driving licence theoretically had to travel an hour to Avignon. The government had, however, underestimated the determination of the Provençaux, particularly since it was September and the hunting season had just begun. All around us the Luberon hills echoed to the report of gunfire, and as well as offering cigarettes, *tabacs* now also sold *munitions de chasse*. There were wild boar in the hills waiting to be killed, and somebody had noticed that while the relevant office in Apt might have closed, the staff could be reached in another way.

The system worked like this: a metal railing divided the street from the administrative building, and only the topmost part of a large basement window could be reached through the fence. To speak to the civil servants, either one had to squat or lie on the pavement. Given the average length of a consultation, lying was proving to be the more popular. Old or young, the procedure was the same – you stood against the wall, queued in the shadow of the building and then lay flat on the ground and poked the necessary papers through the railings.

After twenty minutes it was our turn. Following my performance in the seminar, I decided to let Tanya take the lead. With her head resting in her hand, and her elbow planted in a crack in the pavement, Tanya began talking through the grille. The civil servant dealing with us was a woman with short-cropped black hair, a knitted jumper and a calf-length skirt. The woman's eyes were concealed behind thick-framed glasses. She might have looked terribly officious were it not for the fact that she was standing on a table, one leg planted precariously either side of a computer keyboard, as she struggled to hand pieces of paper through the window.

Another mitigating factor was her complete disorganisation. Just as she was passing a leaflet upwards, she changed her mind, jumped back down from her desk and crossed to a filing cabinet laden with piles of paper. Each stack was held down with the help of a piece of fruit used as a paperweight. Whether this was part of an innovative staff health campaign or just an expedient way of using one's lunch remains unclear to me.

In any event the woman lifted an apple and an orange out of the way and retrieved various pieces of paper. Then halfway back to the window, she changed her mind, replaced one form underneath the orange (I could have sworn this initially came from the apple pile) and instead lifted up a pear. Back wobbling on her table, she patiently explained the documents we would need to produce to get our market licence: our marriage certificate (dated within the last three months), a copy of the lease for our house, a copy of an electricity bill under three months old, a copy of an electricity bill over six months old, our passports and a letter from our landlord approving our proposed activity.

We had of course heard stories of the French penchant for unnecessary bureaucracy but it was still hard to understand the purpose of each particular bit of paper. There were also some requirements that we would be unable to meet. We'd only just moved into our house and hadn't yet received our first electricity bill, so would we really have to wait until we had a bill that was six months old? And what of the requirement to produce our marriage certificate, dated within the last three months? Our certificate was six years old.

Now wasn't the time to get into a discussion. Tanya was shivering on the ground, and more dark clouds were rushing over the hills. We thanked the woman and resolved to return to our house and see what documents we could produce.

To sensible people, the previous three hours would have served as a warning – starting a legal relationship with the French state wasn't to be undertaken lightly. But sensible people didn't give up their jobs in London, make presentations in barely intelligible French about their fledgling rosé business and then lie on the pavement in a puddle, surrounded by dog *merde* while trying to obtain a market licence. Sensible people woke up every morning, got on the Tube and went to work in a well-paid job.

At least we knew where we stood. Regardless of bureaucracy, we wanted to become market traders as quickly as possible.

2

Les Pignons

Our home village of Lourmarin is not a place you just happen upon. Protected by the broad sweep of the river Durance to the south, it shelters on the Mediterranean side of the Luberon. During our travels through France Tanya and I had passed close on a number of occasions. We'd visited vineyards in the immediate environs, we'd observed the pastiche of mismatched houses unified into a picturesque whole by the towers of the two churches and the salt-shaker-shaped belfry, but we'd never had time to stop and explore. The road network, it seemed, conspired to sweep away the hurried or uninquisitive – the main regional cities of Marseille and Aix are reached by crossing the Durance in Cadenet, 5 kilometres away, and because Apt is accessible from Lourmarin only by taking a sinuous track through the hills, most motorists enter the northern Luberon via Cavaillon to the west or Manosque to the east.

As a result we'd dreamed of setting up our rosé business in any number of villages – Gordes and Goult, which are close neighbours to Apt, the for ever chi-chi Saint-Rémy and the sleepily Mediterranean La Cadière d'Azur – but Lourmarin had never been mentioned. Then three weeks ago, at the beginning of September, after our final attempt to buy a bar had fallen through and we'd almost given up hope of finding somewhere to live in France, the phone had rung. Within minutes of seeing the suggested property we'd suffered what the French refer to as a *coup de coeur*, or blow to the heart.

Our house, or more accurately apartment, is 2 kilometres outside Lourmarin. It's approached by a bumpy road, to the left of which is a grove of immaculately groomed olive trees. To the right, there is a field full of lush vines, with a conical-shaped stone building known as a *borrie* in one corner. Traditionally a peasant would construct a *borrie* to store his tools or shelter from the mistral, safe in the knowledge that in the absence of wind or work he could always use it to hide from his wife.

There's a natural ramp in the road that takes a chunk out of the undercarriage of the car every time we pass. The track then bends round the back of a sprawling farmhouse, which appears to be on the verge of crumbling away. The front of the building is dominated by a large arch, through which you can walk into a shady courtyard. There's a pond full of fish, a pump to a well that was sunk by the Romans and a shady porch for long lunches. This south-facing part of the property is where our landlords, Madame and Monsieur Bernardi, live.

Whenever we pass they stop work and wave. They are usually involved in tending the olive trees – spraying them with pesticide, weeding between the roots or picking off diseased olives. Monsieur is about fifty years old. He hides the remains of his grey hair under a weathered baseball cap, which he frequently removes to wipe his brow. He is as thin and wiry as his wife is round and homely. They wear simple clothes – her a flowery dress, him a rough shirt and patched trousers – and like the French peasants of popular imagination, they drive an old Renault van. We first met them at the estate agent's office to sign the lease. This apparently simple procedure turned into a time-consuming exercise to convince the Bernardis to trust two foreigners. There were a lot of disgruntled head-shaking and hurried conversations. Tanya commented afterwards that it was as if we wanted to adopt their child, rather than pay them rent. Luckily the estate agent had strategically started at 11 a.m. and after an hour stomachs were rumbling, watches were consulted and a decision had to be made.

Typically we will leave the landlords sweating over a particularly recalcitrant weed and continue round behind the *mas*, or farmhouse, halting opposite a long, narrow outbuilding. The windows of this outhouse are opaque and cracked, and the wooden lintels are sagging and rotten. Inside, there are rows and rows of old metal stalls where the farmer used to keep his pigs, and where on first viewing – such was our distrust of local estate agents and pessimism about our budget – Tanya and I assumed we might be living. Instead, the old pig house, the *cochonnière*, forms part of our view as we look out from our apartment. For three weeks now we've lived in four newly renovated rooms at the back of the farmhouse. There's a double-height living area, a bathroom, a couple of bedrooms, plenty of large windows opening on to the surrounding countryside, and most importantly a *cave* to store the wine.

Looking north, the old *cochonnière* is in the foreground, surrounded by the puffy branches of olive trees. At sundown its terracotta-tiled roof, which is bowed in the middle like the hull of a boat, glows a balmy orange. Behind the *cochonnière* is a row of cypresses, and seen from the house, their angular tips only just reach higher than the green slopes behind. The gentle curve of these interlocking pine-filled hills is occasionally broken by a seam of bare rock, and at the summit the odd lone tree stands silhouetted against the sky. As night falls, their sentinel shapes are the last things we see before darkness consumes the hills.

So far we've had few visitors to the house. On our first night as we sat outside, struggling to identify the various star constellations that hung vividly above us, a family of black cats crept on to the terrace, pressing their bodies stealthily to the ground and starting at every movement. We agreed to be friendly but never to feed them, yet within days I'd weakened, leaving out a little milk, and now three healthy somnolent cats are permanently curled outside. Their peaceful existence is disrupted only by the arrival of the two stray dogs we have christened Scruffy and Gentle. Scruffy is a black spaniel puppy who is always covered in dirt and loves nothing better than to jump excitedly and muddily all over us. Gentle is an Alsatian-Labrador cross who wears a look of permanent exasperation at the antics of his young companion.

Our only other visitor has been the postman. Leaving the engine of his bright-yellow car running, he poked his head into each of our rooms and told us that if we wanted to know anything about Provence, he was our man – hornets in the postbox or vipers in the grass, he could deal with any eventuality. Take scorpions, for instance – all we had to do was put a little lavender essence in the water when we mopped the floor and we wouldn't have a problem. These days we hoot as we pass each other on the road, but there's been no follow-up visit.

As well as our fleeting acquaintance with the postman, we are starting to be noticed in the village. To begin with, we must have blended in with the legion of red-kneed tourists, but as September progressed, and we continued going to the *boulangerie* on a daily basis and having a lunchtime drink in the cafés, the residents realised we were a more permanent fixture. The shopkeepers and waiters greet us with a familiar '*Bonjour. Ça va?*' every morning, and we respond cheerily with the textbook '*Ça va bien, merci*'. At least it's a start. Doubtless people are still expecting us to disappear come the winter; after all, there are still plenty of reasons to explain our continued presence – perhaps a month-long art or language course – and while there are plenty of retired British people living in the area, there's nobody our age.

Because the village is going to form such an important part of our life, we have approached cautiously, gently cultivating a relationship. Viewed from the outside, Lourmarin is an attractive place. To the south, the foreground is filled by a field of vines and cherry trees, and from the far side of this orchard the old stone buildings of the village rise. A trinity of towers presides over the residents – a belfry, the peaked roof of the Protestant temple and the green-tiled spire of the Catholic church. Each guides the eye ever upwards to the immensity of the hills and the rich blue sky. From the west, the view is dominated by the fifteenth-century château, with its stocky buttresses and foundations built into solid rock. And then there's the vista I like best. As we approach every morning from the east, the spire of the church and the belfry gradually rise above us and the rest of the village emerges, revealing itself building by building, almost coquettishly.

On our first trips to the village we were drawn to the main thoroughfare – the cobbled road that runs through the centre, past the *boulangerie* and the *tabac*, before widening and bending at exactly the appropriate point, providing space for three cafés, each with its own distinctive livery – the green of Café l'Ormeau, the blue of Café Gaby and the beige of Café de la Fontaine.

Past the cafés, the road comes to a junction. Continuing straight on takes us out of the village on to a modern *place*, which used to house the *cave* cooperative, where the local vignerons brought their grapes to be made into wine. Now the *place* has been cleared and young plane trees planted, which in twenty years' time will provide wonderful shade. Rows of smart shops fringe the sides of the square, and a set of steps lead down to an avenue of older plane trees, through the branches of which the dark-green hills and the squat structure of the château are visible.

It was here in our first week that the village put on its party frock. The *fête du village* celebrated the end of the long summer season. Lights were strung in waves from the branches of the trees, and a dance floor was improvised in the centre of the road. We'd been subjected to some of the worst music in the world at previous festivals we'd attended, including dreadful French covers of songs such as 'Another Brick in the Wall' and 'Sunday, Bloody Sunday', all interwoven with bursts of techno. But Lourmarin surprised us. A jazz band played gentle standards and people waltzed under the full moon, with one particularly relaxed reveller smoking his pipe as he guided his wife around the dance floor. Later, fireworks exploded over the rooftops in fountains of light and we toasted our new life with champagne.

With each trip to the village we discovered a new facet. Moving away from the main street, we climbed up narrow cobbled alleys, filled with artists' studios and hidden restaurants. We frequented the quiet *place* by the church, where a fountain of water gurgled in the shade and an old lady rested on a wooden chair outside her front door. If we visited at dusk, we would encounter children playing football, using the buildings on either side of the street as goal posts and recklessly shredding flowers from pots as they tried to curl the ball round the keeper. A cacophony of horns at six o'clock became a familiar sound, as people left their cars blocking the street and ducked into the *tabac* to get their cigarettes before it closed. Hikers with ski poles and serious expressions replaced the louche rosé-quaffing summer tourists, and gradually as autumn took hold the streets became quieter and we decided it was time to start our social life and allay our landlords' fears, which had been so obvious at the estate agent's, by inviting them round for a drink.

Monsieur and Madame Bernardi were the people we were going to be living next door to for at least a year. We would probably see them three or four times a day and it was imperative we got on. Rather than offer just a few peanuts and crisps, we opted to prepare some food – goat's cheese on a circle of puff pastry, sprinkled with pine nuts and splashed with a little olive oil. In fact our nibbles – in particular the choice of pine nuts – had the opposite of the intended impressive effect.

We'd given ourselves the whole morning to organise the drinks, which was lucky because we'd perfected the difficult trick – one which I think is the special preserve of the city-dweller living in the country – of being permanently busy while achieving absolutely nothing. We would try to post letters or go shopping at midday, which, as anybody familiar with France knows, is the start of lunch and therefore not just a stupid thing to do, but also an affront to the country's cultural mores. We would visit the *mairie*, the mayor's office, in the afternoon and discover it was only open in the morning. In short if there was something to do, we would attempt to do it during the only hours when it was impossible. Our memories were so poor that we lived in our own mini version of Groundhog Day, repeatedly visiting the same places until we got lucky.

Thankfully my trip to the local supermarket to buy the ingredients for our nibbles coincided with opening hours.

'Why do you need to buy pine nuts?' asked the cashier, as if I was trying to source some outlandish ingredient.

I explained; she shrugged, to indicate they didn't stock them, and said I should try one of the delis in Pertuis, the nearest town. Once there, I was directed to another shop and so on. Eventually, and for no other reason than I had tried everywhere else, I ended up in the butcher's. He gave a big, slightly patronising smile, which I later realised he must reserve for idiots and tourists, went upstairs to his flat and left me squeamishly inspecting a collection of brains, heads and testicles, which were so drained of blood they'd faded to a bleached white. Around here real men ate sweetbreads, not pine nuts, I reasoned, as I tried to slip away. Before I could leave, the butcher returned with a bag of nuts. It looked like he'd fetched them from his larder, but I gratefully paid, managing to resist the temptation of asking for a side order of testicles to restore my masculinity. As I turned to shut the door, the butcher was ruefully shaking his head.

At precisely midday our landlord and landlady arrived.

Monsieur Bernardi knocked on the door, took off his cap, bowed his head and asked permission to enter. Shaking hands with me, he apologised for the dirt running along the lines of his palms and under his nails. '*Je suis un paysan*,' he said, shrugging.

Madame followed, her eyes moving swiftly around the interior of the apartment, taking in all the changes we'd made and scanning for damage.

Both Tanya and I were a little nervous. The meeting at the estate agent's had been a tense affair and we wanted to break down the barriers between us, move on to first-name terms and switch from the formal '*vous*' to the friendly '*tu*'. I'd filled the fridge with good wine and I now removed a bottle and asked whether they would like a glass. They examined the label.

'Do you have any pastis?' asked Monsieur Bernardi.

I shook my head.

'Any whisky?' asked Madame.

Again I shook my head. Having spent a summer trying to set up a rosé bar, we should have been prepared. Although the English tend to treat wine as a drink for any occasion, the same isn't true in France. In polite society good wine is only drunk with meals. Other wines, classed as *vin de soif*, or wines for thirst, were acceptable as aperitifs, but because of their questionable quality, people often preferred spirits. The bottle of cold Petit Chablis I'd removed from the fridge, although appropriate for an aperitif in England, was the wrong choice in France. It was perfect for accompanying fish and white meat, but not as a pre-lunch drink and so Monsieur returned to the other side of the house to fetch whisky and pastis. At 12.05 p.m. these drinks should – and I say 'should' – have carried enough alcoholic punch to smooth the wrinkles in our French and ease any awkwardness from the conversation.

Madame spoke with the clarity of a primary-school teacher. Each syllable was perfectly enunciated and she deliberately chose simple words, emphasising each point with an appropriate hand gesture. Monsieur Bernardi was, however, practically unintelligible, speaking with the heaviest of Provençal accents, to which our ears were just not attuned. While Tanya and Madame discussed culinary matters – how to make homemade foie gras by splitting the raw liver, adding a little salt and pepper, boiling in a bain-marie and then leaving to set in the fridge – I struggled to interest Monsieur.

Our friendship mission would definitely have fared better had our roles been reversed. Tanya is such a natural conversationalist that I sometimes feel she missed her calling in life and should have been a chat-show host. She instinctively divines people's favourite subject and her innate curiosity leads her from one topic to the next. On the other hand, I am totally self-conscious – wondering what to say next, half listening to the other conversation across the table or suddenly remembering I've forgotten my mother's birthday and completely losing track.

Within minutes of sitting down Madame was smiling happily as Tanya played the eager sous-chef anxious to grasp every nuance of the recipes being imparted. In the brief pauses in the conversation, the two of them munched happily on the goat's cheese and pine-nut tarts, and in a moment of true bonding Madame even asked Tanya how she'd made them.

Across the table, things were not progressing as smoothly. During an interminable half-hour I was forced to ask Monsieur to repeat nearly every sentence as I tried to decipher a language that sounded nothing like French. Eventually I gave up and smiled encouragingly as he narrated the history of pastis, while continually glancing at his watch. No doubt Monsieur was wondering what was for lunch and whether his new tenant was as much of an imbecile as he appeared. Through sign language and guesswork I learnt that the Ricard we were drinking was slightly less alcoholic than Pernod 51, which was usually served in bars. Both brands were now manufactured by the same company, but they had originally started out as competitors. According to Monsieur, if I really wanted to taste a proper pastis, I should try one of the artisan brands or, better still, some local moonshine, which as well as anise was loaded with herbs from the *maquis*, or scrubland.

I mixed another Ricard – five parts water to one part spirit – and, to distract Monsieur from his grumbling stomach, offered around the tarts. He looked suspiciously at the plate and eventually accepted. Trying another solid masculine conversation, I asked whether he hunted. It was another faux pas. He shook his head. 'It's a sport for drunks. The hunters are as likely to kill each other as an animal. The boars come looking for water and they pass right by the house, so you must be careful – where there are boar, there are hunters.'

I couldn't find anything else to say. Subjects flitted into my mind but I lacked the confidence to broach them in a foreign language and so we sat in silence sipping our drinks, looking at the hills. No doubt, like me, Monsieur was wondering how we would survive the coming year. The drinks party that was supposed to have soothed his suspicions was in all probability having the opposite effect.

In contrast to my juddering wreck of a conversation, Tanya was chattering animatedly away about how to make the perfect truffle omelette, prompting Madame to reveal the secrets of her kitchen. Every Christmas the Bernardis would buy a truffle from the local market and then leave it in a glass jar with some eggs throughout the festive period. The truffle was tenderly wrapped in a piece of cloth, which needed to be changed each day, and then to round off a week of oysters and foie gras, Madame would make a plain omelette with the eggs. Even to jaded taste buds, the flavour of the truffle, which was infused into the eggs by its close proximity, was sensational. '*Il faut essayer. C'est merveilleuse*,' concluded Madame with a smile, as she finished the last of Tanya's goat's cheese nibbles.

'How are you getting on with the locals?' asked Monsieur, desperately trying to involve everyone.

Tanya explained that so far everyone in the village had been very welcoming. The Bernardis glanced at each other. 'Those aren't the real locals; they're the Parisians who own businesses down here.' Madame explained that she'd been born in the house we now lived in and then pointed to a house hidden among the pines high in the hills. 'And that was where my grandmother was born, but we lived in Sisteron for twenty years and to the locals that makes us foreigners and as bad as the Parisians. We're ignored in the bars, and in the streets they even vandalised the building equipment when the house was being renovated.' We must have looked confused because Madame continued, 'Perhaps it's easier to be English. Then you are a proper foreigner, but you still have to be careful – to people who were born here and who haven't moved since birth, you are a threat.'

We finished our drinks and Monsieur rose from the table clearly delighted that it was finally lunchtime. Emboldened by the hour we'd spent in each other's company, and keen to emu-late Tanya's effortless success, I made one final effort at conver-sation, explaining how hard it had been for me to find pine nuts and asking Madame where to buy them. It seemed a sensible question and one that would appeal to her obvious love of food, but instead of answering, she glanced at her husband and raised both her eyebrows. Turning away from us, she walked off into the field.

Somehow I'd undone all the good work. My mind turned to the cashier in the supermarket and the butcher, who'd both re-acted in a similar way. Returning seconds later, Madame showed us a large pine cone. She cracked it against a nearby rock and a handful of golden nuts spilled out. We all laughed. What else was there to do? Laugh and feel inadequate and realise that I was completely the wrong person to be living in the middle of the French countryside.

3

La Vie en Rouge

At the beginning of October we travelled back to Apt to try to get our market licence. Ridiculous as it might seem, an official with a penchant for using fruit as a paperweight and a genetic inability to balance on her table stood between us and our future. We'd gathered together our dossier but still lacked two of the key requisite documents – a six-month-old electricity bill and a marriage certificate dated in the last three months – but there was nothing more we could do to obtain them.

We'd phoned our vicar and asked for a recently dated copy of our marriage certificate, but when we'd confessed – lying to a priest is difficult – to still having the original, he refused. Rather than repeatedly visit the *sous-préfecture* in Apt and face the dry-cleaning bills resulting from recumbent chats through the pavement-height window, we'd then phoned government call centres all over France, explaining again and again that wedding certificates were issued in a different way in England. In the end we gave up; after all, there was no way of getting round our lack of a suitably dated electricity bill, so what did it matter?

As we waited in the queue outside the *sous-préfecture* with our incomplete dossier, we discussed our one available but nonsensical legal option – wait for six months for the utility bill and use the intervening time to get divorced and remarried, updating our marriage certificate in the process. Our other alternatives were illegal: forgery – a neat job with a photocopier and a felt-tip pen – or bribery – a couple of €50 notes slipped between the pages. Such practices had to be common in the face of a bloated bureaucracy, but there was also doubtless a peculiarly French way of bypassing officialdom with favours repaid years or even decades later. Tempted as we were, any clumsy attempts to cheat the system would probably end up with us in court, which left us either with divorce or accepting defeat.

Eventually it was my turn and I squatted down on the pavement and passed our papers through the grille to the basement office, explaining that we were still missing several key documents. The civil servant wobbled back off her desk, clamped our dossier under an orange, selected a red marker pen and drew a line through the troublesome papers. She had approved our application. All the worry and the phone calls had apparently been a waste of time. Elation quickly replaced any sense of irritation as I realised that we could be trading in a couple of days' time.

Or so I thought. Clambering on to her desk and pushing her thick glasses back on her head, the official explained that she would now lodge our dossier with the Chamber of Commerce in Cavaillon. We should wait two weeks and then ask for the registration papers of our micro-enterprise.

At least we'd got past the first hurdle, and so while the gargantuan bureaucratic wheels creaked, we decided to start buying some stock. During our trips around France we'd learnt plenty about rosé. We'd started out as wide-eyed amateurs amazed that a field half the size of a football pitch could produce 10,000 bottles of wine, and we'd assumed, like plenty of other people, that the unique colour of rosé was achieved by mixing together red and white wine.

It was only when we saw the dark, inky skins of the red grapes that we appreciated how they lent their colour to the wine. As countless vignerons explained to us, leave the clear juices of a red grape to macerate on the skins for a short period of time and you'll get a rosé, leave it too long and you'll end up with a red wine. Little by little we'd become rosé connoisseurs, selecting examples from across the country to sell in our bar and now on our stall – Marsannay from Burgundy, Sancerre from the Loire, the exceedingly dark clairet from Bordeaux and wonderfully pale rosé from the coast between Toulon and Saint-Tropez. There were also some little-known vinous gems we'd discovered that I wanted to rotate on our list from time to time, such as Champagne's Rosé de Riceys – a still wine with such fortifying properties that it was the choice of Louis XIV's stonemasons when they built Versailles. It was made only in exceedingly hot years, when the grapes were so heavy with juice that a press was unnecessary. Unlike most rosés, it improved with age and could be cellared for decades, making it an attractive wine for us to buy.

But there was a problem – with winter approaching, the rosé season had nearly finished. The coldest weather on record in the Luberon occurred in 1956, when the severity of the frost killed all the olive trees, and according to our landlords, it was not uncommon to get snowed in. The nearest ski resort was only just over an hour away, and the balmy summer climate would soon be blown away by bitter winds. Come November, people would retreat inside, stoke a fire and sip on warming Côtes du Rhône. We would have to sell red wine.

Despite our travels, we both felt a little apprehensive about selling red. Just like learning a language, the more we discovered, the more the subject expanded and the more impossible it appeared ever to become an expert. Some minds can recite all 154 classed-growth estates of Bordeaux, cope with the bewildering array of small Burgundy producers and remember every good vintage since the turn of the century, but mine is not one of them. On our trips we'd sipped soft and velvety

Gevrey-Chambertins, rich Pomerols, smooth Saint-Emilions and the luscious, deep Bandols. I'd appreciated, if not mastered, the art of tasting – examining the colour of a wine and mentally feeling my way towards the grape variety and type of growing conditions before I even put the glass to my lips. Gradually my palate was improving and with it the ability to distinguish the technical nuances of winemaking – the vivid vanilla of a wine stored in an old oak barrel or the concentrated power released by a judicious percentage of Cabernet Sauvignon.

Even so, other than by price I still struggled to tell a very good wine from just a good one, and in blind tastings embarrassingly often I preferred the purportedly inferior bottle. The one area I remained poor at was describing wines. While teams of experts could eulogise about broad-hipped wines that nevertheless had long legs, all I usually resorted to was 'It's delicious, thank you.' I consoled myself with the fact that for me a bottle of wine was a drink, and while a French vigneron could make straight-faced analogies between his wine and the female form, I'd just sound ridiculous.

Tanya was slightly more successful in picking the supposedly better wines at tastings, but only slightly. Aware of our shortcomings, we approached our upcoming foray into the red-wine business with caution. We did at least have one advantage, or so we thought. For the last two decades the wine business in France had been lurching from crisis to crisis and buyers were now in a position of unparalleled strength.

On average, French winemakers were forced to spend the same amount per bottle on bureaucracy as New World producers did on advertising, with the result that French wine was overpriced and poorly marketed. Australian, South African and Chilean wine exports to major territories like the UK had increased, while those from France fell. Nevertheless the French government had continued to offer subsidies for planting more vines, while at the same time insisting on archaic regulations that hamstrung vignerons. In Bordeaux, for example, vignerons were forbidden from putting the grape variety on the front label. Consumers were supposed to know that if the wine came from the left bank of the Gironde, then Cabernet Sauvignon would predominate in the mix, and if it came from the right bank, the reverse would be true and Merlot would predominate. Unsurprisingly the unsophisticated Merlot-loving punter would just plump for a New World wine – at least he would know what he was buying.

Adding to the problem, the domestic market in France began to contract as a result of a nationwide health campaign. If there is one thing that the French love more than food, it is talking about being ill. Ailments can be discussed for hours, and in a nation of hypochondriacs, where a common cold is a life-threatening event and the queue at the pharmacy is always longer than at the *boulangerie*, posters and TV ads targeting the ill effects of alcohol were particularly effective.

More recently the gendarmerie began to focus on drink-driving. Gone were the days when a hunter could return from the *chasse* at ten in the morning, enjoy a carefree couple of glasses of wine or pastis in the local bar and then obligingly be directed out of his parking spot by a white-gloved policeman. Now the same gendarme would have a breathalyser in the boot.

The result of the shrinking domestic and export market was a massive wine surplus. Every year thousands of litres of unwanted wine were tipped down drains or subjected to hare-brained but environmentally well-intentioned schemes such as conversion into fuel. In the local paper, *La Provence*, I'd read about one famous nearby vineyard being ripped up and developed. There were pictures of the grim-faced mayor and the vigneron sitting round a table persuading the assembled residents and journalists that an eighteen-hole golf course and driving range was in the best interests of the local community. In fact, there was such a glut of wine in France that the government had reversed its policy and was now paying vignerons to uproot the same vines that they'd just subsidised them to plant.

Even winemakers who were determined to resist the trend were in trouble. Unable to sell all their stock, a backlog was building up in their cellars, with the result that the only people reputed to be doing well in the trade were manufacturers of the large stainless-steel *cuves* used to store the excess. If there was ever a time to be buying red wine, it was now. We couldn't ask for a better negotiating position and I was convinced we would be able to buy top-quality wine at knockdown prices. The only question was where to start. We wanted to sell wine from across France, but to begin with at least it was important to include the top local vineyards on our list.

In the end we decided to visit Château la Dorgonne first, which was located just outside the village of La Tour d'Aigues, about 20 kilometres up the road from us. The vigneron was called Bauduin Parmentier, a diminutive former banker from Belgium. We'd served the château's pink wine at our rosé festivals the previous summer and on our last visit Tanya and Bauduin had formed an immediate understanding, thanks to their shared love of the sights and smells of the south of France.

The two of them had wandered through the fields of vines pausing to inhale the scent of pine and cypress. During our time in France we'd met plenty of former bankers turned vignerons – the type who'd once competed to drive the fastest Porsche in the Square Mile and now wanted to own the biggest château – but Bauduin was the only ex-City worker we'd encountered to have seriously considered becoming a lavender farmer rather than a winemaker. He enthused about the soothing aroma and medicinal uses of the plant in a way that would have had the average banker kicked off the trading floor, and he appeared to be motivated by love of the land rather than ego.

His château was located on top of a hill overlooking the slopes of the Grand Luberon. Horses grazed in the grounds, lavender was planted in immaculately tended rows, and completing the idyll, mature olive trees circled a swimming pool that had been sunk into an old water basin. Because of the vineyard's height, harvesting could take place late, starting at the end of September and continuing into October. These extra few weeks of late-summer sun helped concentrate the flavour of the grapes, and the vineyard was renowned for producing some of the best local wine.

As we arrived, we were greeted by the acrid smell of ferment-ing grapes. The large double doors to the *cave* were open, and a team of workers were busily plucking stalks, leaves and dam-aged grapes from a conveyor belt. This process of hand selection ensured that only the best grapes were used to make the wine. Heading round behind the *cave*, we traipsed into the fields to look for Bauduin. The earth was solid and dusty from a dry summer, and cracks as wide as our feet made walking hazardous.

Eventually we came across a huddle of harvesters. They sat on the floor, hugging the limited shade offered by the vines, as they smoked and waited for their exacting labour to begin again. There were plenty of youngsters, some probably taking part in their first *vendange*, but also old men and women who'd doubtless harvested when a horse and cart, not a tractor, took the grapes in from the field. Without exception their clothes were bedraggled and stained with grape juice. They looked exhausted and hung their heads in their hands, struggling to say even a word to each other. I could sympathise. When Tanya and I had taken part in the *vendange* two years ago, we'd spent the following week nursing our aching backs and grazed knees, and we'd only completed a day's work, not the month or so it usually took to harvest an average vineyard.

Still, despite the extra effort and cost involved, most good winemakers preferred to harvest by hand, arguing that the machines for harvesting needed to be booked months in advance, meaning that the *vendange* started when the machines arrived, not when the grapes were ready. And because of the machines' lack of precision, the skins of the grapes tended to be bruised and split in the harvesting process, causing the fermentation to start in the hot sun and not in the carefully controlled conditions of the *cave*. Hand-harvesting, by contrast, was gentler, and the pickers were able to discard unwanted grapes as they went. The end result was that wines made from a *vendange à main* were of consistently better quality.

That, at least, was the reasoning I'd heard on countless occasions. Personally I loved the romance of drinking a hand-harvested bottle of wine, picturing the vines and the soil, and appreciating the care that had gone into creating the wine. But in a blind tasting would I, or the average consumer, always select a hand-harvested wine over a machine-harvested one? It was not a debate to enter into with the forlorn workers struggling to their feet and looking down the barrel of another endlessly straight row of vines.

A tractor pulling a trailer laden with grapes chugged towards us. High in the seat, looking like a modern-day feudal lord, was Bauduin's nephew, Nicolas. He wore a pressed shirt and chinos, topping the outfit off with a straw panama, which would not have been out of place in the pavilion at Lord's. Nicolas took off his hat, mopped his brow and jumped down to meet us.

As we strolled back towards the *cave*, we discussed our plans for the year. Tanya and I chatted excitedly about the markets we would work in and the different wines we wanted to sell. We knew Château la Dorgonne made a deep ruby-red 100 per cent Cabernet Sauvignon, which was classed as a *vin de pays* because it didn't comply with the strict rules of the Appellation d'Origine Contrôlée, the French body responsible for categorising wines, as well as two other AOC reds, and we wanted to conduct a tasting to compare prices and decide which would work best for us. After the tasting I intended to negotiate as much as 50 per cent off the price of the wine. I say 'intended' because haggling with vignerons over the cost of a bottle didn't appeal to either of us; nevertheless if we were going to make a living, we had to get used to this side of the business.

Nicolas paused in the shade of a stone wall. 'Did you not get my phone message?'

I shook my head.

'Ah, I talked with my uncle about your plans and I am afraid that we cannot let you have any Dorgonne wine.'

I glanced at Tanya, checking that I had understood correctly, but she too was looking quizzically at Nicolas. Our relationship with the château was excellent, and as a start we were planning to buy 300 bottles.

'Let me explain. The reputation of our red wine is excellent and we must be very careful where the wine is sold. At the moment we only supply retailers who agree not to sell any other competing wines. You are going to be selling other wines and you'd also be selling the wines in markets, which I am not sure is the right place.'

'But ... but,' I stuttered, astounded that in such a competitive market a vineyard could afford to take such a position.

'We completely understand,' said Tanya, steering me towards the car.

Nicolas shook hands with us both. 'I must get back to the harvest, but when you have settled into your new house, come over for lunch.'

With an empty boot we headed back home. We passed vineyard after vineyard, including one that we knew was selling off old stock for €1 a bottle. Tempting as it was to purchase some and then multiply the price by five in the market, we were determined to sell only good wine. We stopped and bought a copy of the local paper. The forecast for the next couple of days was more blisteringly hot weather, followed by storms.

As Tanya drove, I flicked through the news stories, including a piece about a football tournament held between teams representing all the Michelin-starred restaurants in the area. The matches had taken place at Olympic Marseille's stadium – the Stade Vélodrome – and over half the article was given over to a description of the food at the post-tournament dinner, including details of the wine served with each course. The main dish was a *filet de boeuf rossini* and the accompanying red was from Domaine de la Brillane, just outside Aix.

'What do you think, shall we try some?' I said to Tanya.

Twenty minutes later we pulled up outside an imposing ochre-coloured building. Surrounded by vines, it faced south towards the imperious ridges of Mont Sainte-Victoire. This kilometre-long wall of rock, which in the past had inspired painters such as Cézanne and Matisse, dominated the skyline, and Tanya and I stood enjoying the view and the warm sun on our faces.

A tall, slim man with receding dark hair and the round glasses of a classroom swot bounded up to us like an overenthusiastic puppy and addressed us in English. 'What can I do for you?'

'We'd like to taste,' said Tanya.

'Well, you've come to the right place. My name's Rupert Birch,' he said, placing an arm on each of our shoulders and guiding us at a running trot towards the building. 'Let's get some coffee and tour the *cave*.' Rupert rattled off three double espressos from a machine on his desk and then guided us, coffee in hand, through a set of double doors. Once again we were assaulted by the acrid smell of fermentation.

We'd visited enough vineyards to know that the *cave* was where a vigneron's sales pitch began. Usually they would grab a couple of glasses and a long pipette – known in the business as a 'thief' – and lead you among the *cuves*, stopping here and there to uncork a barrel and suck up some wine to taste with the pipette. At harvest time there was also one show-stopping routine they commonly tried, encouraging people to stick their head into a vat of fermenting wine and breathe in. Both Tanya and I had fallen for this trick before and emerged gasping for breath as the giggling vigneron explained that the fermenting grapes gave off carbon dioxide and that if a person fell in a vat, they would be dead within two minutes.

Old hands that we were, we were prepared for Rupert's spiel but not the enthusiasm and speed with which he delivered it. Gulping his coffee, he resembled a mad professor who'd been working too hard on some crazy experiment. His eyes were red and bloodshot, his hair dishevelled and his glasses askew. In ten minutes we learnt that Rupert had owned the *domaine* for five years and in that time had built the modern building we were standing in, opened an associated bed and breakfast, and started producing wine to the highest standards. Everything was done according to strict organic principles, was harvested by hand and the grapes were fermented in modern stainless-steel *cuves* because, according to Rupert, the *terroir* didn't support oaky wines.

Grabbing a hose, Rupert scrambled up a ladder and affixed the end to the top of a *cuve*. 'We pump the wine from the bottom to the top to introduce oxygen and encourage the fermentation. It also breaks the layer of grape skins that rests on top of the liquid. The more times you do it, the better the wine,' Rupert explained. 'Of course, some people just drain the juices off and make a rosé, but I can't abide the stuff.'

Tanya and I glanced at each other but said nothing.

'Now, I need another coffee and you need to taste the wine.'

As we followed Rupert into the tasting room, he revealed the reason for his manic behaviour. 'I haven't slept for two days. We've got to harvest the grapes before the weather breaks.'

With the coffee machine chugging away in the background, Rupert poured the first of the estate's wines, Domaine de la Brillane, made from a mixture of Grenache, Cinsault, Cabernet Sauvignon, Counoise and Carignan. It was a rich, luscious purple colour with an almost luminous surface layer. We swilled the wine round in our glasses, sniffed and tasted.

'It's delicious,' I said, resorting to my old tried and tested description.

'Absolutely delicious,' Tanya backed up.

The wine was much less viscous than some of the region's reds I'd tasted, but in the mouth it had a depth of flavour that outclassed anything we'd tried so far.

'And now Cuvée Flora, named after my daughter,' announced Rupert, as he furiously rubbed his eyes to keep himself awake. 'It's the top *cuvée* of the *domaine*, made from Cabernet Sauvignon and Grenache.'

The wine was much deeper in colour and lacked some of the luminosity of the Brillane. Tanya and I took a sip, expecting great things. It too was delicious, but to me, it lacked the subtlety of the first wine. It was overpowering, whereas the first wine had been gentle. Once again I liked the cheaper wine better. It might have been good for my bank balance, but it did nothing for my confidence in my taste buds. I looked at Tanya and could see she agreed.

'It's delicious,' we chorused like a couple of idiots, which at least was preferable to the other description that popped into, and thankfully remained in, my head – 'round-buttocked'. I'd clearly been spending too much time with French winemakers.

It was time for business. We had to negotiate a good price before Rupert fell asleep. Tanya began to explain our plans for the year and as Rupert listened a massive grin spread across his face. At last we'd found a kindred spirit.

'Let me get this right,' said Rupert. 'You two are going to sell wine in the markets. Have you any idea just how tough that is? Of course, none of the locals are going to buy anything – they just drink wine in a box, at two euros a litre. Even vignerons find it hard to sell stuff in markets. I've done plenty. You get up at seven, sit there all morning and, if you are lucky, shift half a dozen bottles. I don't think you'll last the winter.'

'We will – we have to,' said Tanya.

'Do you know how cold it gets? And do you have any idea how quiet it is in January? I did the local market in Rognes and the people next to me were up at two in the morning to bake biscuits. They drove two hours from Gap, sat in the market from seven till one, sold ten euros' worth, then drove two hours home. It's a mug's game.'

'Ah, but it's busy in the summer and that's when we'll make our money. Until then we'll just tick over, but we need to buy your wine at a good price.'

'Look,' replied Rupert, grinning at the absurdity of our idea, 'I'd love to help you, I really would, but you must appreciate how much time and effort goes into the marketing of the wine. Look at our label. I spent hours with a graphic designer trying to achieve the right combination of simplicity and elegance. I've travelled across France ensuring that our wine is on all the right wine lists. Now Domaine de la Brillane is a name that people know and recognise. I am really, really sorry and I wish you all the luck in the world, but I can't let you sell it in the market.'

Back at home, Tanya and I sat in the garden sipping the complimentary wine that Rupert had given us. The setting was perfect, we were surrounded by olive trees, the sun was dipping behind the hills, and we had a luxurious wine to savour, but the disappointment of the day overshadowed everything. We'd started out full of hope and vigour, trying to find some really good local wine, which we'd expected to buy at an excellent price, but for whatever reason two of the area's best vignerons had refused to let their red wine be sold in a market. We couldn't help but conclude that there was an element of snobbery involved. It was as if they'd invested their wines with a personality and thought that we were going to defame them. No wonder the industry was in crisis.

4

An Unlikely Conversion

A s it turned out, our problems with the *sous-préfecture* in Apt had only really been a preliminary skirmish – a sort of light war game to warm us up and get us battle-ready for the heavy battalions the French government were going to throw at us. Clearly the last thing that the Parisian plutocrats wanted was for a couple of Brits to set up a business, and their weapon of choice to prevent such an outcome was the Cavaillon Chamber of Commerce. The first volley arrived in the form of an official letter demanding our presence.

We duly reported to the office in Cavaillon. Sitting at a desk in front of us was a middle-aged woman with peroxide-blonde hair. She wore a shiny blouse with a plunging neckline and decorative frills. Behind her was a large cabinet. The doors were flung wide open and the hundreds of hanging files resembled the teeth of a monster. Ignoring us, the woman rose and started flicking idly through them. Her short skirt was overly tight, and the backs of her legs were stained with what I presumed was fake tan. She tottered back to her desk, lit a cigarette and pretended to notice us for the first time.

In our experience there are two types of civil servant in France: those who realising that we are English make an exceptional effort to be friendly, understood and helpful, and those who do the exact opposite. In Cavaillon, I knew we were in trouble before I even opened my mouth.

It took us five minutes to explain why we were there. At every step the bureaucrat feigned misunderstanding and responded with rapid staccato sentences. Doubtless our pronunciation wasn't quite correct, but at the same time it was clear what we wanted. After ten minutes we eventually managed to persuade her to find our dossier and outline the problem.

'*C'est pas bon*,' she said, shoving a copy of our marriage certificate towards us and telling us that we had to have a copy dated within the last three months.

Patiently Tanya explained that the *sous-préfecture* in Apt had said it was fine, but in mid-sentence the woman took a call on her mobile and swung round in her chair to discuss where she planned to eat for dinner that evening.

It was hard not to lose our tempers. We weren't applying for a skilled or sensitive job; all we wanted was the right to stand side by side in a market and sell wine. I'd once seen a programme about the traders in Borough Market in London, where the sole requirement to be awarded a pitch was to pay £10. If only life were that simple in France. Much as I would have liked to get into an economic debate about the crippling effects of over-regulation, the peroxide on the phone was too worried about her supper and was chatting away about the preferred venue. Oblivious to our presence, she was oscillating between two cafés, one of which did the better *steak tartare*, the other the better *tarte tatin*. At least we knew where we stood on her list of priorities.

Turning back to us, she smiled a thin-lipped smile and declared, 'No certificate no market licence.'

We had of course heard stories about the intractability of the French civil service, but until this point I'd always assumed they were exaggerated. We'd been trying to get our papers in order for over a month and it felt like we were further away than ever.

At least she'd been too busy thinking about supper to notice that our electricity bill was not the requisite six months old. Tanya smiled at the official, tugged on my arm and pulled me outside into the warm sunshine.

'I've got an idea for the certificate – we'll call Peter.'

'Why?'

'If anyone can charm the vicar, he can.'

Peter Tate had been our companion on our first two trips around France. He was a fixer with such enthusiasm for life that people invariably liked him within seconds and after half an hour in his company they felt like his best friend. In conversation he would often grin at totally inappropriate points, but there was such an infectious joy to his *bonne humeur* that others invariably joined in. He frequently started sentences with a laugh, and if you knew him well enough, you could trace the passage of the thought from his mind to the wide smile that spread across his face, then the laugh with its slightly wicked undertone. By the time he expounded whatever wild idea had just occurred to him, whoever was listening was already predisposed to agree.

He was also a total Francophile and shared with the French their love of food and wine. It had been his original idea to set up a rosé bar and now he was a great supporter of our plan to become market traders. It was an idea that had caused deep concern to my parents and no doubt secret delight to their middle-class friends – 'My son's a lawyer. What does yours do?' – but to Peter it was a terrific plan.

At the end of last summer he had even lent us his old BMW convertible, which he called Betty, to use until we could find a suitable French car. Betty, it turned out, was almost as eccentric as her master, developing an array of faults almost the moment that Peter left, including an electrical malfunction that at random moments emptied the entire contents of the wiper-fluid reservoir. Invariably, and much to the enjoyment of other motorists, it happened when the roof was down, leaving us drenched. At other times the locks refused to work and the electric windows failed. Such was the frequency of the problems we began to wonder whether Betty was pining for Peter.

At least the temperamental nature of his car meant that we'd been keeping him up to date with our progress, and during the last phone call he'd promised to visit soon, 'even sooner, if my wife insists on keeping me on a diet'. If anybody could persuade our vicar to issue an illicit marriage certificate, it was Peter. Even if he wasn't personally successful, he wouldn't give up. One of his mantras in life was 'help is only three phone calls away', which meant that in the event he couldn't fix something he believed that with just three calls he could find someone who could.

Tanya dialled Peter's number on our mobile. We were about to put him to the test.

'It's you two,' I heard him bellow down the line. 'Great to hear from you. Marvellous, absolutely marvellous.'

Even with Peter on the case, I wasn't optimistic. The vicar had been just as adamant as the French civil servant, and although I was convinced there had to be another solution, it wasn't an obvious one. Scant consolation that it was, at least we didn't have to worry about our lack of red-wine stock.

While we were waiting for news, winter encroached on the Luberon. It should have been an enchanting time of the year, but our inability to start work made me acutely conscious of the passage of time. Row by row the vines began to change colour. Some turned the rich orange hue of the setting sun, others a lustrous yellow, while a minority still clung to their greenery. The patterns appeared totally random, with auburn swirls enveloping some fields and leaving adjacent ones untouched. The trees too began to shed their summer foliage, and after one particularly cold, clear night, we awoke to a landscape dominated by a golden spectrum. All the vines had turned, as had the local oak, cherry and almond trees, and only the evergreen pines and the olive grove around our house remained as promises of a distant heat.

The streets of Lourmarin became quieter and Tanya and I began to feel more and more self-conscious as we strolled through the village. Whereas before we'd been one of a multitude of foreigners, now there were but a few, and we were the newest of the contingent. When the two of us walked along the main street, our mutual companionship insulated us, but whenever one of us was alone, we always sensed we were being stared at.

One afternoon we were passing the local school. All the children had emptied out on to the street. They were wearing their white art smocks and were crouched in the centre of the road colouring in cartoon characters – enormous bunny rabbits, ducks and dogs – that had been sketched by a teacher. It was picking-up time and the parents sat on benches as their children autographed their particular creation. Apparently it was an annual event because, looking closely, I could make out the faded remnants of last year's efforts. As we weaved our way through the pictures, the children looked quizzically up at us and it was easy to imagine a question in their wide eyes – 'What are they doing here?'

Thankfully our insecurities vanished at the weekend, when the Parisians arrived at their *maisons secondaires*. It was impossible to feel self-conscious amid the ensuing parade. The women waltzed up and down the narrow cobbled streets dressed as if they were on an excursion to a dinner party in the Marais, rather than the village *boulangerie*. Men in pressed shirts followed behind as if they and not the obligatory poodle were the ones on the lead. Some creations bordered on the comic, and we wondered whether the septuagenarian who strutted around with 'Miss Universe' printed in gold lettering on the back of her jeans could possibly be serious.

In the cafés bottles of wine, rather than *pichets*, became the norm, and outrageously large diamonds glinted on Parisian fingers as hands were arrogantly raised for service. But on Sunday afternoon on the stroke of four the streets cleared and people scurried anxiously to their cars. Such was the intensity of the exodus that Tanya and I half expected some fairytale curse to descend – perhaps at 4.01 p.m. all the glittering jewels turned to stone – but the reality was more prosaic: they were all rushing to catch the last TGV from Aix to Paris.

Back at our apartment, we were blending in about as well as the Parisians in the village. After Monsieur Bernardi's warning about drunken hunters who were as liable to shoot us as a wild boar, this was at least partly deliberate. Tanya had already had one close encounter with a *chasseur* when she had woken in the early hours of the morning and looked out of the window into the moonlit countryside. Unfortunately she'd neglected to put on her dressing gown, and strolling casually across our courtyard with his gun broken over one arm and his dog at heel, a twilight hunter had casually waved at her as if she was an acquaintance passing in the street.

We learnt quickly that the Luberon hills had a remarkable amplifying effect, with the crack of a gunshot ricocheting off every crevice. If a lone hunter took a couple of pot shots at a fleeing hare, it sounded to us like a regiment of trigger-happy Marseillais was sweeping down the valley in a pincer move-ment. And so whenever we walked in the countryside, I donned the luminous roadside jacket that legally we were required to keep in the back of the car. Even the most short-sighted *chas-seur* couldn't mistake me for prey, but just in case whenever the Gatling gun-esque echoes erupted around us, Tanya started singing at the top of her voice, '*Je ne suis pas un sanglier. Je suis une dame anglaise.*'

It was at just such a moment when we were turning the final corner back to our home that we encountered Monsieur Bernardi. Tanya was in full cry, and in my luminous-yellow regalia I looked like I'd just stepped off a building site. Our landlord waved in a friendly way, but he also took off his hat and scratched his head. I quickly discarded the jacket and hid it behind my back.

'As long as you stay on the tracks, you'll be just fine,' Monsieur Bernardi reassured us in a deadpan way, but there was mirth in his eyes and I could already imagine him in the village bar with a rapt audience, telling the story of the petrified promenading *anglais*.

Our next faux pas was to buy bedding trays of the brightly coloured flowers that were beginning to proliferate in the local shops. They had gentle, delicate petals that looked like they would be shredded by the first frost, but we assumed that given the frugal reputation of the locals, they must last until early December. We arranged them neatly on the terrace and enjoyed them on a daily basis. So delighted were we with them that we called Madame Bernardi over to show her. She'd been working amid the olive trees. Her complexion was red, there was sweat on her brows, and she gave a big, broad smile when she saw the array of colour.

Accepting a glass of water, she took a big gulp, gathered her breath and started to laugh. 'You do know they are flowers for the dead. It's the Saints' Day soon and you're supposed to put them on graves to ward off evil spirits.' She walked away chuckling – first the pine nuts and now this.

Despite such moments, our first month in our new house had largely been a happy one. We'd achieved our dream of living in France, and it was so satisfying to open the door in the morning and see the olive trees waving in the light wind. Apart from the odd heavy thunderstorm, the weather was still wonderful – reaching the mid-twenties by lunchtime and then dipping sharply as the light faded at around six o'clock. Behind the idyll, however, there was always a nagging worry – what if we couldn't make our idea work? What if we had to return to London? To begin with at least, we'd decided not to buy a television and so we had plenty of time to sit and talk through our options. Whenever we discussed going back to England, the conversation turned to the horrific cost of living, the crammed commute on the Tube, the ever-present threat of terrorism and the folly of a life eaten away by the demands of work. But then we would return to our current dilemma – just how to get started. The longer we waited, the more frustrating it became.

With the tourists long gone, roadside signposts were covered with posters advertising local events: *vides-greniers*, the French version of a car-boot sale; *bourse vélos*, second-hand bike sales; and festivals for ancient vegetables. We never witnessed the posters going up, but they were updated on a daily basis and served as a sort of village semaphore alerting everyone to events within a half-hour radius. Trying to ignore our bureaucratic headaches, we participated as fully as we could.

I tracked the progress of the nearest *bourse vélos* in Cadenet. To begin with, the organisers declared that they expected over five hundred bikes to be available for sale, but after five days this figure had more than trebled, and each increase was announced with a new poster. Full of good intentions and mental pictures of ourselves cycling through the hills, Tanya and I traipsed along to the *bourse*, a word also used for the Paris Stock Exchange. We struggled to park and, having arrived late, made our way to the sale, passing a succession of happy kids with new bikes. They wobbled this way and that, reminding me of newborn foals trying to find their legs.

The *bourse* was held round the village athletic track, which was circled with stands full of bikes. Most of the attendees had come in full cycle regalia – overly tight Lycra, a small peaked cap bearing sponsors' logos, a pair of wraparound sunglasses and a water bottle filled with an energy drink. It didn't seem to matter that they lived in the village and that the most exercise they were likely to do was a lap of the track: the *bourse* was an opportunity to display their kit.

In retrospect, it was inevitable that we were going to make a poor purchase. There we were amid a nation of cycle enthusiasts, people who could name makes, chassis type and gear combinations from a fleeting glance of a passing *peloton*. The French dedication to the sport made English trainspotters look like balanced individuals, and it was indisputable that everyone knew their stuff. Crouching on the floor and checking the mountings of the chain and the brakes, these were people who could price a bike to the nearest euro.

Then there was us – Londoners to whom bikes were for couriering things and a method of transport that I had always seen as one careless motorist away from a trip to casualty. Neither of us could remember when we had last ridden, but overcome by our new life in the country, we'd fooled ourselves into thinking it was time.

We stopped at the first stand, pedalled enthusiastically round the track a couple of times and purchased at an inflated price. Within days I had a puncture and Tanya's brakes had ceased to work. I had vague childhood memories of taking the tubing off a tyre and placing it in a bath of water to isolate the puncture, but with Tanya's bike also broken, it seemed a lot easier to visit the bike shop. There we were greeted by a tall, lean individual with a shaved head. No doubt this was to aid his aerodynamic profile when he was in the saddle. We showed him our forlorn bikes, and in return he showed us pictures of his father competing in the Tour de France in the 1950s, an era, he hastened to point out, when there were no support cars and competitors had to repair punctures by themselves. Suitably chastened and feeling even more like outsiders, we left the bikes to be fixed.

Fortunately – despite an initial mishap when we arrived at the wrong village and had to drive around looking for a poster on a lamp-post to redirect us – we fared better at the next local festival we attended – the *vide-grenier* in Puget. These 'empty attic' sales could have been specifically designed for people like Tanya and myself who'd just moved into a new house. People laid out all their unwanted belongings and spent the day nattering to neighbours about who was throwing out what. The majority of goods on sale were a load of old rubbish – ancient printers, computers from the 1980s and lights and televisions from the 1970s, all of which looked like they might fuse an entire village – but there were lots of attractive pieces hidden in the confusion. In fact *vides-greniers* had become so popular with antique hunters that the *brocante*, or second-hand, merchants were beginning to complain. Anything sold at a *vide-grenier* was effectively tax-free, and as well as locals from the village, lots of unofficial dealers had turned up in Puget. There were stalls full of the rusted sickles and hammers that tended to adorn the walls of tourist houses, as well as collections of old furniture and household goods, including an antique ice-making machine that some Corsicans were trying to sell for a ludicrously expensive €300.

As much as the professional *brocante* dealers complained, *vides-greniers* were also a wonderful resource for them. Teams of them scoured people's possessions before the stands had been properly set up. A collection of old boules was only worth a few euros at a *vide-grenier*, but an unsuspecting tourist could easily be persuaded to part with ten times the price on a Sunday market at L'Isle-sur-la-Sorgue.

Despite the late hour and the competition from dealers, we managed to buy decorative posters of Pernod bottles and village houses with flaking walls, and still-life oil paintings of bowls of fruit and broken baguettes. The prices were low, and in a bargain-hunting rush we came away with a huge chest of drawers for our spare bedroom. It was the type of fair that Peter would have adored and we picked him out a set of six coloured Napoleonic brandy glasses, for which we paid the princely sum of €2. The whole event made me feel a lot better about the bikes and momentarily helped me forget that we were just passing time waiting for news.

Then, on a sunny warm day in late October, we received two phone calls. The first was from Rupert Birch, the insomniac vigneron we'd visited near Aix.

'It's Rupert. I've been thinking about your little project and I want to let you have some wine.'

Images of Rupert gulping his umpteenth coffee of the day, scrambling up a ladder to check on the fermentation while trying to talk to us on the phone came to mind.

'There's just a few conditions – I'd prefer it if you didn't sell the wine in Aix. We're in a lot of restaurants there and it might look a bit strange having it in the market. Also, what other wines are you going to be selling? It's important that they are of a similar quality to the Brillane.'

'Just yours at the moment.'

'What? Why?' Rupert's voice was incredulous.

I didn't want to bore him by going over our problems with the French administration. I was sure we would find some more good red wine soon, but until we had our licences there was no great urgency. Instead I let the silence on the phone extend, hoping that Rupert would fill it with some recommendations.

'I'll give you some addresses. Côtes du Rhône, Bordeaux, what do you need?'

I replied that they would both be useful and the phone snapped down as Rupert either rushed off to find them or fell off his ladder. Moments later he returned with the contact details.

'Now, how many of my bottles do you need? Don't tell anyone else but I'll give you export price – can't have you starving to death. You probably will anyway, but at least it won't be my fault. Either that or you'll freeze. There are easier ways to earn a living, you know.'

I got the feeling that each sentence was out of Rupert's mouth before he could evaluate whether it was rude or not, but his enthusiastic doom-mongering was strangely comforting. Beneath the humour I sensed he desperately wanted us to succeed.

'Can we hold off on the number of bottles for the moment? We haven't got our market licences yet.'

'What?' exclaimed Rupert with the disbelief of a man who had built a profitable vineyard in just five years. 'Why not? What are you living off? At least let me come round and give you some wine.'

Moments after I had finished on the phone with Rupert, Tanya took a call from Peter.

'Lovely fellow your vicar. Turns out he used to play rugby for Redhill. We might even have played against each other once. Big chap. Must have made a good second row. Redhill always had good second rows. Not like England these days.'

Tanya coughed politely.

'How's my car, by the way? I must come and get it sometime. I forgot to tell you – if the lights on the dashboard stop working, just give the plastic a whack. Works a treat.'

'Peter, what about the—'

'The wedding certificate? Ah, yes, I was coming to that. Did I tell you that the vicar scored ten tries in just four seasons? That's pretty impressive for a second row.'

'Peter—'

'It's in the post,' he said, punctuating the sentence with a trademark laugh and a puff on a cigar. 'I sent it registered, so you should have it in a day. Do you want to know something strange? He even talked me into going back to church. Haven't been for years. Anyway, as I was saying, if you have any prob-lems with the dashboard, just give it a whack.'

It had been quite some day. Peter had found God, we'd found some wine, and the last real obstacle to us receiving our market licence had been removed. By 1 November we would be ready to trade.

5

Love and Cold Water

During the course of the last couple of summers we'd stopped at hundreds of vineyards and tasted thousands of wines. The experience of seeing the gnarled vines burrowed deep into the soil, sand or rock, searching for moisture, helped us understand and describe a wine. And so with the updated marriage certificate in the post, we'd decided to make an overnight trip to Bordeaux to expand our range of reds.

There are times and places to taste wine. At the very least a sensible trade buyer approaches a tasting with a clean palate and he or she will probably insist on a glass of water and some plain crackers between each new glass. Then there are grander tastings, where groups of chefs and vignerons combine to display their talents, matching combinations of wine and food into many-coursed banquets, with each different mouthful choreographed to allow the wines to dance down the throat. Events like this are rare. Even rarer still, if not unique, was the tasting that Tanya and I conducted in Bordeaux.

Vineyard trips rarely disappointed us. Discovering a new wine was always interesting, and in our experience vignerons were some of the happiest people on the planet. Typically they were relaxed and self-fulfilled, and the majority had slightly quirky senses of humour, which they'd probably adopted to deal with the multitude of disasters that fate might visit on their vineyard – disease, hailstorms that wiped out a year's work in minutes and, most trying on the patience, the arrival of professional – well, semi-professional in the case of red wine – buyers such as Tanya and myself sucking cough sweets.

Somewhere between Provence and the small hamlet of Fronsac, just kilometres from Pomerol and Saint-Emilion, we'd caught dreadful colds. As we stepped out of our car into a squall of rain, our eyes were streaming, our nostrils were red, inflamed and flared like an angry horse's, and our throats felt as if a maze of barbed wire had been laid across them. In the last hour we'd consumed over a packet of super-strength cough sweets and we'd both become addicted to this drip-fed anaesthetic, popping pastille after pastille. Yet we'd travelled over 500 kilometres for the meeting and there was no point in going back home. We knocked on the door of a thin-walled outbuilding at the Château Villars vineyard and entered, unaware that our handicapped taste buds would prove a surprising advantage.

The vigneron, Thierry Gaudrie, was a small man with round glasses whose vision kept being blocked by the splash of way-ward dark hair that broke over his forehead. He sat behind a desk piled high with papers. Above his head was a map of the Bordeaux wine-producing area and various framed awards for his wines. On the floor were assorted boxes containing wine labels, price lists and shipping details. Outside, the weather was dreadful. Walls of rain swept across the vines and slammed against the thin window of the office. To the side of his desk was a small electric fire chugging out heat. We sat in front of the three glowing orange bars with tissues in hand, and as Thierry talked to us about his wines, we did our best not to scatter his papers with each new sneezing fit.

'I think I ought to be offering you whisky rather than wine.' He smiled, passing a fresh box of tissues. 'As I was saying, in Bordeaux there are the thirty or so premier producers. When you buy one of their bottles of wine, you are buying into a dream. It's like driving a Ferrari; it goes two hundred kilometres an hour but all the owner wants is for people to see him cruising down the Croisette with a blonde in the passenger seat. Drinking a Cheval Blanc or a Margaux is not for real people; it's for super-rich hosts to demonstrate the size of their bank balances.'

'But they are miles better wines than a Côte de Provence,' I challenged.

'Is a Rolex a better watch than a Swatch? Yes. But is it a hundred times better? No. With brands the price is rarely justified. Take Château d'Yquem. They have just started producing a limited edition, Nebuchadnezzar, costing three thousand euros. It's ludicrous – you'd need to be hosting a state banquet to drink that much sweet wine. But all the bottles have sold. Why? The name.'

Tanya gave an enormous sneeze, trying to cover her nose with a tissue that had dissolved into rags. 'How does a Saint-Emilion or a Pomerol compare to a Fronsac?' she asked.

'With Pomerol and Saint-Emilion you are paying for the name on the bottle when you drink it, so for the same money you're better drinking Fronsac.' Thierry went on to explain that after the top thirty or so producers in Bordeaux, there were maybe a hundred or so wannabes trying to build a brand and convince people that their wines were 'Aston Martins'. Unsurprisingly they charged prices to match their ambitions. But then there were also winemakers like Thierry, who were not interested in branding and just aspired to make a good bottle.

It all made sense. Perhaps my palate was seeing through the marketing when I preferred cheaper wines at tastings. If appreciating top wines was about purring over a bottle of Lafite like a woman entranced by a blue diamond, then I was an unmitigated failure, but if it was about searching for value, then I was probably OK. And if this vineyard visit was any guide, it was even beneficial once in a while to forget about taste and simply listen. At any rate that was my excuse, because my hand had developed an almost magnetic connection to the cough sweets in my pocket and in movements unconnected with any conscious thought I was continually popping them into my mouth. Thierry appeared to be unconcerned – at least it hadn't started hailing on his vines yet, and our questioning had clearly touched upon a subject he was passionate about.

Without any prompting he was off again: 'I read an article recently that said that French consumers drink the worst wine in the world.' Thierry reached over and turned the fire up to full blast. Our clothes were already singed by the heat, but as another hurtful gust of wind chucked a torrent of water at the window, we drew ourselves closer to the fire.

'The French consumer is only influenced by the name on a label,' continued Thierry. 'A buyer for a London restaurant will come and taste all the wines in the area, evaluate their merits and compare the prices, whereas a buyer for a Parisian restaurant will come and buy Pomerol whatever the price.'

Thierry argued that the French were so hung up on the notion of *tipicité* – the idea that a wine should demonstrate certain characteristics that are typical of the producing area – that they scarcely questioned their own tastes. In the process they'd forgotten that red wine was not just about the land, it was about the man who made the wine, what he believed in and how he took advantage of the soil.

'If the vigneron expresses himself and the wine loses some of its *tipicité*, does that make it a worse wine? In France, people need to throw the old rulebook out of the window. The best wine I have tasted recently was from Languedoc, not Bordeaux. *Voilà*.'

Thierry poured us some of the estate's lesser red wine. After half a glass a soothing alcoholic fuzz settled over my brain and the prickling feeling that assaulted me every time I swallowed vanished. For once it was a relief not to have to describe a wine to a vigneron.

'And now have a taste of our premier wine.'

So far I'd agreed with everything Thierry had said, but as I took a sip, confusion descended again. Even through the fog of my cold I could tell I far preferred the cheaper first wine. The premier wine was so dry it stripped all the moisture from the back of my already sensitive throat. 'I don't like that as much.' The statement came from my sleepy brain before I had time to consider whether Thierry would be offended.

It would have been easy for him to lose his temper at this point. After all, we were just two strangers who'd begged an hour of his time with only the promise of a possible order at the end of the meeting. We'd arrived trailing tissues across his court-yard and ploughed our way through a packet of cough sweets as he talked. By now it was obvious to everyone in the room that at the moment I wouldn't be able to tell champagne from cider and yet here I was challenging the virtues of the vineyard's best wine – a wine that had been made from the oldest vines, lov-ingly cared for and pruned before being hand-harvested. Thierry was within his rights to chuck us out.

'It could be the tannins,' he answered calmly. 'The wine will become softer and rounder with age, and above all it needs a meal to complement it. Take a bottle home and try it with food.'

Opening the door, he led us out to the car. The three of us ran across the courtyard, attempting to shelter under our jump-ers, but the rain ricocheted off the tarmac, soaking our trousers. Winding down the window of the car, we said goodbye to Thierry and promised to be in touch with an order. His glasses were steamed up and his hair was now a sodden mop but he was still happy to chat. 'A famous sommelier was once asked what his favourite red wine was. This was a man who'd been tasting wines for the whole of his life and who'd travelled the world in search of excellence – and do you know what he said?' It didn't seem to matter to Thierry that the rain had now turned to hail and that a fork of lightning had just nearly eliminated his *cave*. "'The last glass I had with a friend.'" Slapping our boot, he sent us on our way.

The next day, after an overnight stay in a hotel, we headed home. On the way, we stopped in the Côtes du Rhône in the village of Cairanne to pick up some red. It was a quick visit. The vigneron Marcel Richaud led us around his *cave*, extracting wine with the obligatory pipette, squirting some into our glasses and the rest accidentally over his pet poodle, who turned from snowy white to blotchy red during the course of the tour. The vineyard was wholly organic, and Marcel believed in interfering as little as possible in the winemaking process, explaining that he made his wine according to artisan principles. Each year it tasted different, but that was the natural expression of the climate. Despite the dousing the previous day, our colds had nearly vanished. Tanya and I both tasted. We already knew we liked the man and that it was probable we would love his red – it was a rich purple colour full of sumptuous blackcurrant flavours.

'We'll take a hundred,' said Tanya.

Gradually, just gradually we were beginning to understand the red-wine business. Our mantra was simple – like the man, like his principles, like the wine. Some people needed Ferraris; others, like us, were content with a borrowed and battered BMW. At least it had character.

The following day we drove to Cavaillon to hand over our newly arrived wedding certificate at the Chamber of Commerce. The same female civil servant with the peroxide hair and the overly short, tight skirt feigned ignorance of our case, deposited a copy in our file and told us the final documents would be sent to our local *mairie*. She started filing her nails. 'You'll have to wait a week, maybe two.'

I was delighted at finally having ticked all the administrative boxes but also annoyed at the new delay. Every week the markets were getting quieter and our chances of making any money before winter gripped the Luberon were now remote. When we'd first visited Lourmarin Market, in September, the main *place* had been full of stalls stretching from one side of the square to the other. It was a browser's paradise, with four separate rows of stands allowing people to weave in between. Even the steps leading down from the *place* to the shady tree-lined avenue below had been in use, and such was the demand for space to display goods that the exterior wall of the public toilet had been hung with art. Looking down from the top of the steps along the long avenue below, all that had been visible were the parasols of traders, striped like football kits, and a highway of bobbing heads. From our elevated vantage point we'd watched a succession of panama hats being ferried forwards like sticks in a stream, occasionally getting stuck at one stand or another before being swept out of sight.

Back then the market had been draped in vibrant colours to attract the magpie tourists. Vendors of Provençal linen dressed the corners of their pitches with rich quilts and intricate tablecloths, using wicker baskets full of lavender to entice shoppers inwards, so that the rest of the market quickly vanished amid a whirl of soft fabrics. A stand offering hats of every description from berets to Stetsons relied on a nautical theme, with a mirror set amid a lifebuoy and a sign proclaiming, 'Welcome aboard,' while the vendor of Balinese furniture had created a contemporary living room, with a dining table, chairs and a bookcase, all fashioned from smooth, shining wood. Only the jewellers sweated in the sun, having sensibly dispensed with parasols to lay out their creations in bright, glinting rows.

On that September day we'd noticed an opera of accents – guttural German, stanzas of Scandinavian, the odd lilting verse of Italian and the familiar chorus of the English. Almost hidden in this multicultural mix were the French. They squeezed through the crowds carrying shopping baskets full of vegetables, ignoring all the stalls except those selling essentials.

At the far end of the alley of trees, heading towards the château, we had discovered our competition – a wine merchant. His stall was an upturned wine barrel with a silver ice bucket resting on top that contained an array of wine. The merchant was a small man with receding hair, square-rimmed glasses and an anxious manner. He poured us a glass of velvety white from Châteauneuf-du-Pape and showed us his price list. The cheapest bottle was priced at €40 and we'd wandered back towards our car confident that we could undercut the competition.

At the time we'd expected to be trading within a couple of weeks and had hurriedly visited the other local markets. Some, like the farmers' market at Saint-Martin-de-la-Brasque, we immediately crossed off our list, realising that we'd struggle to sell any wine. Others we were delighted by at first sight.

Just ten minutes up the road from us was the village of Cucuron. Like Lourmarin, it sheltered in the shadows of the Luberon, but it was built on a hill in a conical shape, broad at the base and narrow at the tip. At the top, fringed by pine trees, were the ruins of an old castle, and at the bottom was a large water basin, or *étang*, encircled by plane trees. These trees had been planted unusually close together, and just a third of the way up, each of their trunks split into thin, elegant fingers, which climbed skywards in search of light. Just like the spire of a church or the dome of a cathedral, they sent the eyes of observers spiralling upwards with awe, and on breezy days when they swayed rhythmically together they reminded me of the uplifted arms of an entranced crowd.

It was under these trees that one of the prettiest markets in Provence took place. The stalls ran the length of one side of the *étang* before fanning out into the village. Images of the passing procession of people rippled across the calm water to the café on the far side of the basin. The tables were plastic and the chairs warped, but the dishevelled look was somehow appropriate – a fanfare of furniture and white umbrellas would have only distracted from the sleepy tranquillity that always pervaded in the dappled shade.

We'd also liked another nearby market in Ansouis. The village was rated as one of the most beautiful in France. Its fame was largely due to the Renaissance château that presided over the village and which had remained in the same family for generations. Even in a country that specialises in picturesque tree-lined drives leading up to majestic houses, the entrance to the château at Ansouis was remarkable. Starting outside the village, the drive began at an arched entrance and fed through ornamental gardens, before bridging the public highway and continuing its private progress in a grand sweep to the pinnacle of the village. Every Sunday there was a small market in the *place* located just in front of this bridge. There were only four stalls – a butcher, an artisan biscuit maker, a vegetable seller and a stand full of cured meats, but every time we'd passed they'd been busy and so we'd added the market to our list on the basis that people always needed a good bottle of wine to go with their lunch on Sunday.

Nearly two months later, however, all these markets had changed. In Lourmarin, rather than the four broad rows stretching across the *place*, there was now just one narrow alley. Most of the traders had dispensed with their sun shades, and all the trinkets for tourists had vanished. Instead there were stands full of fruit and vegetables – ripe, round pumpkins in place of the lush summer melons; carrots and turnips rather than asparagus and strawberries. There were still racks of clothing, but the flowery skirts had been replaced by thick bomber jackets and piles of assorted gloves. The steps were empty, but the tree-lined avenue was full of stalls concentrating on staples like honey, olive oil and soaps. We walked amid the sparse shoppers towards the château and discovered that the wine merchant had disappeared.

In September in Cucuron, there had been roughly fifty stalls, but when we visited a week after returning from Bordeaux, their number had dwindled to just twenty. The stream of shoppers that had meandered around the market had become a trickle. Small groups stopped and chatted, but nobody seemed to be buying much. We ordered a coffee in the café and looked on, desperate to be part of the market, even in its diminished form. Our eventual participation was only days away, but the constant useless waiting had finally worn us down. We were both a little pensive through enforced inactivity. The lengthy build-up to opening our market stall had given me plenty of time to question what we were doing, but this was a subject that was almost impossible to discuss with each other.

We'd both taken huge career risks to try to live the dream, and in many ways our life was idyllic – the shutters from our bedroom opened on to an olive grove, and the sky was nearly always a peerless blue. In this context any conversation about doubts over the choices we'd made seemed churlish. At the same time we'd been living in France for nearly a year and a half, and both of us missed our friends and family. We worried whether we would be able to make a go of our life in France, or whether economics or just the isolation of being foreign would eventually drive us back to England. And then what?

We were at an age when we desperately wanted to settle and build a home where we could have children, but everything around us was so uncertain. For us to admit this to each other was too sensitive a subject; we'd invested too much in creating this opportunity to start snipping away at the seams. To talk to friends was equally impossible – how could we expect people whose Sunday-night dreams were terrorised by bullying bosses to empathise?

And so instead we sipped on our coffees in silence and worried how we would survive the winter. As we paid the waitress – a matronly woman with plump cheeks and a prominent cleavage

– we explained that next week we'd have our own stall. She smiled and handed us back our money. I got the feeling that she would have ruffled our hair if she could as she said, '*Vous vivrez avec l'amour et l'eau fraîche.*' Seeing our quizzical faces, she clarified, 'It's a saying – you'll be living on love and cold water.'

We laughed the comment off, but in fact it was unnervingly prescient. Driving through Ansouis on the way home, we noticed a large sign pinned to a lamp-post in the *place*. Out of curiosity we stopped to read it. 'By order of the *mairie* the market is shut until 15 March.'

6

Saint-Martin

A week later Tanya and I were waiting outside a tiny café in the Corsican village of Patrimonio. We sat on red plastic chairs emblazoned with the logo of an ice-cream company and sipped on tar-black coffee. It was late afternoon. The weather was warm, and a light wind blew through the sheltering trees. The odd car passed on the nearby road, which wound its way towards the summit of the surrounding mountains.

Seated opposite us was the president of the winemaking region of Patrimonio, Jean-Laurent Bernardi. His glasses rested on the bridge of his nose, and he made little ticks on a notepad as he fielded a call on his mobile. At every opportunity he looked across and signalled that he would not be long.

Memories of the overnight crossing to Bastia were still fresh in our mind: the serenity of our arrival as the ferry nudged the harbour side and the sun rose over the traffic-free streets; a quick breakfast on the quay surrounded by crumbling pastel buildings; watching the silvery ripples of freshly caught fish; and then the journey through the mountains, and our wry smiles as we slalomed the car round a stray cow, seemingly intent on taking a morning stroll to Bastia. But now with the euphoria of arrival fading and Jean-Laurent anxiously organising tomorrow's event, we were left questioning why we'd decided to come.

Just a few days ago Tanya and I had stood on the steps of the *mairie* in Lourmarin. In our hands we'd held laminated passport-sized pieces of paper bearing our photos, and an official stamp entitling us to trade in any French market. Grins half-mooned across our faces, and not quite knowing what to do to celebrate, we toasted ourselves with several glasses of rosé in the Café l'Ormeau. Our first instinct had been to start trading as soon as possible, and our first market should have been that morning. Instead we were in Corsica savouring the last bitter taste of our coffee and hoping that our decision to honour a promise made two years ago would prove worthwhile.

Jean-Laurent clicked his mobile shut and ushered us ahead of him down a dusty track. He wore indistinct clothing – a pair of old jeans and a light-grey jumper – and he spoke so quietly that his words were often carried away by stray gusts of wind. His body was thin and taut, and his face was deeply tanned and creased around his eyes and mouth. When he smiled, it was only ever a quick expression before his face found repose again. As we walked, people called out to him, shouting updates or just racing past and clapping him on the back. After a couple of minutes we came to the village amphitheatre. A series of steps cut from rock fringed three sides of a grass square. There was a large stage, again fashioned from the local stone, and to our left, overlooking the activity below, was a prehistoric obelisk carved with human features.

High above us, dominating the scene, was the l'Eglise de Saint-Martin. It rested on a rocky pedestal in between the village and the sea. Apart from narrow slits, the nave was windowless, and with its stock sturdy buttresses it looked as if it had been built as much for defence as worship. In the tower, two heavy bells, mounted one above the other, hung suspended in front of the blue sky, and leading away from the church, a track curled round the rock down to the amphitheatre.

'You see we are nearly ready,' said Jean-Laurent, drawing our attention back and pointing to the tables that ringed the square and the barrels of wine that were being rolled into position. 'Over there will be the spit-roast veal and mutton, and this table's for the cakestand. Come on, I'll show you inside the church.'

We followed the uneven road, climbing steadily upwards. Even this late in the season the scent of wild herbs – marjoram, thyme, rosemary – hung in the air. To either side of us, the occasional track cut away into the dense undergrowth, and on the hillside we could make out the family tombs to which these spidery paths eventually led.

Jean-Laurent pointed up at the swirl of cloud that fringed the peaks of the mountain, 'Don't worry, the saint always protects us – it won't rain tomorrow.'

Back in Lourmarin, the forecast had been good for the week-end, and by now we would have been counting our takings from our first market and considering heading to Apt on Saturday. I'd been without a salary for nearly half a year now, and however well intentioned, our finances could ill sustain trips such as this one. In our time in France we'd attended plenty of festivals, including a *fête du vin* in Saint-Rémy-de-Provence, where a tipsy Bacchus had nearly fallen from his chariot, and the annual celebrations of Bastille Day, where whole villages ate together on long tables laid out in the square. We'd enjoyed them all, but typically we'd happened upon them rather than travelled hundreds of miles. What could possibly be distinct about tomor-row's occasion?

But somehow we'd once again been lured to Corsica. The French called the island 'savage'. There were peaks as high as the Alps, and the rugged scenery was awe-inspiring and unforgiving. For decades, though, it wasn't the landscape the French were describing; it was the people. The symbol of the island was a white flag with the black silhouette of a face wearing a bandana that trailed in the wind. To many Corsicans, it represented their fight for autonomy from the French government and the flag was flown from boats and hotels, even washing lines.

The secondary symbol was a knife with a wooden handle into which a 6-inch serrated blade folded. These weapons were on sale in great numbers, and the locals treated them like you or I a watch, only taking them off when they had a shower. Judging by the number of people we'd seen with deep slashes by their eyes, they were far from just accoutrements.

Fortunately the scars didn't seem so prevalent among the younger generation. In fact all we'd ever encountered in Corsica was kindness and a generosity that went well beyond anything we'd experienced anywhere else in France. The people's pride in their island was immense, as was their desire to show it off. Perhaps they were just grateful that the dark terrorist past was over and the nationalist fever was fading.

'The procession will follow this exact route,' said Jean-Laurent, unaware that it was still only with the goodwill of the wind that we were able to hear him. We passed beneath the walls of the church, which loomed some 20 metres above us, and through the soothing shadow of an ancient olive tree, with a trunk so thick that it made those in our grove look like mere saplings. The doors to the church were as outsized as the olive tree, making us feel Lilliputian as we passed into the interior.

The contrast was marked. While the exterior walls were crumbling away and apparently threatening to slide off the rocky precipice at any moment, the inside was freshly painted. The ceiling was a soothing sky blue, and a large fresco depicted a Roman soldier sitting astride his horse handing his cape to a naked beggar.

'I must leave you now,' said Jean-Laurent. 'Make sure you arrive in plenty of time tomorrow morning – the church will be full.'

In some churches the sheer grandeur can be overwhelming, and the mind strays to the days of unremitting labour necessary to construct such edifices and the awe with which worshippers must once have entered; in others, like l'Eglise de Saint-Martin in Patrimonio, there is peace in simplicity. In size – apart from the impressive doors – it is no bigger than the average parish church. There are about fifteen rows of pews and then an additional five rows consisting of mismatched wooden chairs. Gold is used sparingly and instead the overall feel and smell is of freshly varnished wood. The altar is only slightly raised and set just a few yards from the congregation.

Stepping back outside, dusk was falling. The courtyard fanned out in a semicircle towards the surrounding mountains, which had turned a dark shadowy blue in the half-light. High on the slopes we could see the village of Farinole. The lights in the symmetrically spaced windows made it look like a toy town, as if we could reach out and pluck a house between our fingers and set it down elsewhere. Between the small gap in the peaks we could see the sea and the bobbing glow of the final yachts making for harbour in Saint-Florent.

Unnoticed by us, a young girl had arrived. She was wearing a pretty floral dress and was accompanied by either her mother or a teacher. Standing on the low wall that surrounded the church, the girl began to read: '*Dieu a conclu avec Saint Martin une alliance de paix; il lui donna pour toujours le pouvoir et la dignité du sacredoce. Souviens-toi, Seigneur, de David, ton serviteur.*'

Again and again the girl repeated the passage, changing the inflection and projection of her voice as instructed. Finally, after twenty minutes of practice, the couple walked away into the darkness. We heard but did not see them part. '*A demain.*'

The following morning we arrived half an hour before the service was due to start. As predicted by Jean-Laurent, Saint Martin had ensured a blue sky presided over the day's events. Inside, the church was already three-quarters full, and we took a seat at the back and listened to the pleasant hubbub of expectant voices.

Within ten minutes all the free seats had disappeared and still a crowd pushed through the doors. Tanya gave me a nudge as a black-clad, cane-wielding lady appeared at the end of our row. On an island obsessed with flick knifes, it was wise to remember our manners and we shuffled out of our seats and joined the people standing at the rear.

At the innumerable weddings we'd attended back in England, I'd developed a handy rule of thumb for estimating the length of ecclesiastical events. While the rest of the congregation was launching into 'Jerusalem', I would be counting the pages of the order of service. It usually worked out at about 7.5 minutes a page, unless the service included 'Lord of the Dance' – just how many times do you need to repeat a chorus? In any event, according to my calculations the *messe de Saint Martin* was going to be at least an hour long.

The majority of the service was centred around the *confréries* sent from churches across the island. The members wore multi-coloured robes with short capes fastened round their shoulders, and the heads of each different church carried enormous crosses, the butt of which they wedged in a leather pouch on their thigh, allowing them to hold the crucifixion scene high above their heads.

Being able to sing seemed to be the only membership require-ment for a *confrérie*. The rich sound they produced was totally unfamiliar and seemed to echo down the centuries. The language was Latin, and the words were sung as a haunting chant, which managed to be simultaneously uplifting and yet sorrowful. To my shame, I began glancing at my watch, aware that the point of our trip was approaching.

Midway through a chant, which was making 'Lord of the Dance' seem short, there was a commotion behind us. Turning round, my eyeball was nearly impaled on the end of one of the large crucifixes. The crowd parted and a small woman dressed in the full regalia of one of the *confréries* scuttled forward. Trying to maintain her dignity, she slowed as she walked down the aisle before genuflecting to the altar. Then panic set in. There was nowhere for her to sit. The members of all the other *confréries* held fast in their place, and her head twitched nervously this way and that. The chanting continued, and in the absence of alternatives she dolefully made her way back towards us, like a child excluded from Sunday school.

It probably didn't help that her unfortunate intervention was immediately followed by the young girl we'd watched the previous evening.

'*Dieu a conclu avec Saint Martin une alliance de paix; il lui donna pour toujours le pouvoir et la dignité du sacredoce. Souviens-toi, Seigneur, de David, ton serviteur.*'

The recitation was perfect, with each inflection identical to the final version we'd heard last night. As she walked back down the aisle, the girl tried to keep a serious face but pride shone from her.

At the altar, the priest too was feeling the pressure. Earlier that morning Jean-Laurent had visited all the vignerons in the village – and there were over thirty – and collected a little wine from each in a clay urn. The wine from this urn was poured into the Communion cup. Unfortunately as he raised the precious liquid skywards to perform the blessing, the priest's hand slipped. A great clunk resounded around the church as he grappled to rescue the wine. The deep chanting began again, and the sweating priest refilled the cup and called the congregation to Mass, doing his best to ignore the puddle by his feet.

For us, such harmless mistakes softened the solemnity of the occasion, and as people pressed forward, we slipped to the side, making our way into the sunlight. In the courtyard, the atmosphere was more relaxed. Men wearing the deep-blue robes of the Ajaccio Church Confrérie sat on the wall smoking. They didn't seem to be the least bit interested in squeezing their way into the church and taking Mass; instead, they'd rolled up their sleeves in an attempt to get some autumn colour. The elderly leader was engaged in a schoolboy prank using his large cross to tap unsuspecting people on the back. Seeing us emerge, he spotted a new opportunity to relieve the boredom. Offering us a smoke, he proceeded to tell us how Ajaccio's *fête* was a lot more fun. 'The lead boat takes the saint on a trip around the harbour and hundreds of small boats follow. We all throw petals into the sea and then we get drunk,' he said with a toothless grin. 'You're welcome to come.'

At that moment the procession began to emerge from the church. Scrunching his smouldering cigarette underfoot, our companion hoisted his cross into the air and hid with the other members of the *confrérie* behind the far wall of the church. Their intention was clearly to join the column when nobody was looking, and our friend held his fingers to his lips to ensure our silence.

Tanya and I circled away from the church down to the amphi-theatre and watched as the procession came towards us. The moment we'd talked about for the two years since we'd first heard about the festival was approaching. At the head of the column, supported on wooden planks hoisted on to the shoulders of six men, was a life-sized figure of Saint Martin. Following behind came two robed men carrying the urn full of blessed wine and then the *confréries* sent from different churches across the island. Once again the air was filled with deep rhythmic chanting, although I noticed the *confrérie* from Ajaccio were miming the words. With bright sunshine glinting off the golden sceptre of the saint, the rhythmic march towards the square looked almost celestial.

We noticed a familiar diminutive figure was carrying the urn. We'd met Mark Giovanetti on our Extremely Pale Rosé trip. He measured millimetres over 5 foot, was almost completely bald and was seemingly eternally on the lookout for the love of his life. He was friends with everyone, a confidant of Jean-

Laurent's, a business partner of the mayor and had the enviable ability of lightening even the heaviest of hearts. What do you say to a man who enquires whether bees in England fly on the left? As he passed, a grin of recognition swept across his face and he gave Tanya an insouciant wink.

Hoisting the consecrated wine on to his shoulder, Mark poured the contents of the urn into a larger barrel of wine, which had been positioned in the centre of the arena. Two years ago Tanya and I had sat outside Jean-Laurent's house and heard him describe just this moment. He'd explained how according to legend a Roman soldier called Martin had taken off his cloak to clothe a beggar. The same soldier had journeyed to Corsica and climbed the mountains that separated Bastia from Patrimonio. As he'd crested the final peak, he'd looked down upon the village and declared, 'There is my home, Patrimonio.' The soldier had later been canonised and his name for ever associated with charity.

To honour him, the vignerons of Patrimonio filled a barrel with a little of the new season's rosé from each *domaine*. The wine was consecrated in the church and then given away to the villagers, who demonstrated their own charity by baking cakes for the occasion. At the time we were obsessed by rosé. We'd been travelling through France for months and this was the first time we'd heard of a festival around pink wine. We'd chattered excitedly away, trying to picture every detail, and at the end of the conversation Jean-Laurent had taken our hands and earnestly told us that we must attend. Looking him in the eye, we'd promised to return.

To our shame, we'd not been lured back by the idea of a two-hour church service or the image of a young girl practising her reading in the twilight. Instead it was the excitement of witnessing the great barrel of rosé being cracked open and the anticipation of the ensuing party. On our quest we ended up finding the palest rosé in Corsica, albeit a slightly oxidised bottle, and it had felt right to return, as if witnessing the Fête de Saint Martin was the proper conclusion to our first journey.

But when we'd heard Jean-Laurent's description, I don't think we'd ever imagined the size of the event. The church congregation had been swollen by an additional thousand people from across the island, and as well as the rosé, there were stands ready to serve red and white wine.

At a signal from Jean-Laurent, Mark produced a large hammer and drove a stake into the wood. For us, there couldn't have been a more appropriate person to start the festivities than this tiny vigneron, who'd once told us with an impish grin that he added rays of sunshine to his Muscat. As the hammer fell, bright-pink wine spurted out in a translucent torrent. A tap was quickly affixed and people surged forward with plastic cups to get a taste of the new season's rosé.

The food stands opened and queues formed to get slices of the juicy roast meat, the smell of which had been teasing our stomachs all morning. Musicians filtered on to the stage, and as the sun dipped in the sky, small glasses of wine became tumblers full. But still the free bottles flowed, and the seemingly inexhaustible spit-roasts turned over the glowing coals. Children chased each other around the cake tables. Jam was smeared across their mouths, and their fingers dripped with chocolate.

Late in the afternoon Jean-Laurent grabbed our arms and led us away through the village, stopping only to throw a football back over a fence to a group of clamouring boys. Our destination was a sprawling villa, set in heavy shade beside a babbling stream. To the side of the house was a wooden lean-to sheltering a long table. Seated round the table were the singers from the village *confrérie*. They'd changed into jeans and shirts, and were drinking red wine with ferocious speed, pitching whole glasses back into their throats. An old man at the head of the table began to count a beat, rapping his hand on the wooden table. As he raised individual fingers, one by one the surrounding people began to sing. The language was neither French nor the instantly recognisable lilt of Italian, so I assumed it must be Corsican. Unaccompanied, the men sang a love song, always waiting to be counted in or out by the patriarch at the head of the table. At the end of the song they tossed more wine back and then started again. Such was the concentration and intensity of the musical stories being told that our presence seemed barely to be noted. Apart, that is, from Mark, who'd found himself a stool and was sitting happily on high, winking at Tanya.

After a while a young woman came into the room. Her hair was curled in long ringlets down her back, and her eyes were caramel brown. Her face, however, was far from conventionally pretty – she had an angular nose and square jaw, which gave her a haughty appearance. The men laughed and joked and drank more wine, but the challenge of her presence was clear. At a signal from the patriarch, one of the younger men rose and began to sing to her. Immediately she set her plaintive song against his deep baritone and they edged closer together, eyes locked on each other, bodies – whether through the effort of singing or emotion – trembling. With each completed verse they paced around, circling like combatants looking for a weakness. As the notes faded, they came together in an embrace and then stepped apart, retreating step by step while keeping their eyes fixed on each other. The table erupted into applause. Then, as if drawing a curtain on a scene we'd been privileged to see, Jean-Laurent made a small gesture and escorted us back to the main party. 'They will sing well into the night.'

Back in the amphitheatre, human nature was beginning to exert an unpleasant force. The meat on the spit-roasts was running low and people were pushing and shoving to get to the front.

'Why isn't there more food?' somebody shouted.

'The barrel of wine is empty,' cried another.

Jean-Laurent's face remained impassive as he directed people to the wine stands where there was plenty more. As for the food, he shrugged his shoulders. Together with his fellow vignerons he'd paid for a whole spit-roast veal and mutton – what more did people want?

The sun finally fell behind the hills, leaving only shadows and the distant orange glow of the sea. A column of men formed and hoisted Saint Martin on to their shoulders and began the long walk back to the church. Tanya and I sat with Jean-Laurent on the steps of the amphitheatre watching the last of the revellers cavorting around the square. This year's festival had been twice as large as the last. If the event kept on doubling in size, how long could the vignerons afford to keep it going? According to Jean-Laurent, Saint Martin was rising in the Catholic hierarchy of saints and the Vatican was considering recognising a pilgrimage route with Patrimonio at its finish. We sipped on the last of the blessed rosé and reflected. We'd come to witness a rosé festival but instead we'd experienced something quite different.

'Perhaps you are the first of the pilgrims,' said Jean-Laurent with a kindly but tired smile.

7

Sébastian

The room was midnight black. I'd only just become accustomed to being awake and was trying to identify the vague anxiety I was feeling when my mobile began to vibrate. Could it really be morning? I had seconds before the full alarm went off and I wearily fumbled for the handset, succeeding only in knocking over a glass of water. Moments later the shrill ring reverberated around my head and woke my consciousness. Today was the day of our first proper market. I nudged Tanya awake. Full of nervous energy, I slipped quickly from the bed and opened the shutters. Outside, the colourless moonlit world awaited. Long shadows fell across the courtyard, and fragile fingers of mist swept underneath the cumulus swirls of the branches of the nearby olive trees.

I hurried from the house and began the unfamiliar process of loading the car. A long, wooden board clunked obligingly into place, but the detachable legs of our market table screeched a metallic protest, stirring the cockerel into protest at the impending dawn. Overhead, the heavy moon sank in the sky, levering the weak sun over the horizon. I glanced at my watch for the tenth time that morning. It was twenty to seven. Although the markets had been getting emptier and emptier, I still felt pressurised to arrive on time. We had no real idea about how to get our wine into the market and where we should leave our car once we'd done so. I was also concerned about our reception. French markets had always seemed friendly enough places, but we'd always been the customer. How would the locals react to two English people selling wine in their markets? Would they welcome us, or would they try to exclude us? All these thoughts combined to create a sense of unease.

We started the car and crunched our way slowly down the drive. To our right, two shadows danced amid the rows of vines, keeping a cantering pace with the car, and as we turned on to the main road, our favourite stray dogs, Scruffy and Gentle, howled a canine farewell.

In the village, the traders were already clicking their stalls together, but encouragingly there were plenty of spare spaces. The air was cold, and with the first rush of light, colours flooded into the day – the bright yellow of the flowers being manhandled from the rear of the van, the rows of parasols unfurling like peacocks' tails and the tumbling trays of bright, ripe fruit. New vans arrived, nudging and shunting their way into the tight unloading area. The air was full of the sickly sweet odour of diesel fumes, shouted greetings and the grating and scraping of goods. As the market assembled itself, we stood redundant at the foot of the stairs leading up to the modern *place*. The temptation to select a favourable spot and put up our table was strong.

'Shall we just set up?' I asked.

'The flower seller said to wait here for the *placier*, Sébastian.'

Losing patience, I walked back to the car, but halfway there I changed my mind and rejoined Tanya.

After five minutes a woman joined us. She nodded a curt hello, and in the following ten minutes another two dozen people arrived. Like us, they apparently had to wait before setting up. Most of them knew each other and there were plenty of good-morning kisses. With each new arrival I became more anxious. On our recent trips to the market, there had been plenty of space in the modern *place* and even the odd pitch on the tree-lined avenue, but with numbers swelling there was going to be competition. Our fair hair and foreign accents marked us as outsiders, and we sat and listened to the others.

'Have you seen Sébastian?'

'The bigger his ego gets, the later he gets out of bed.'

I wondered whether they were nervous too. Certainly they seemed a little jittery – they were clapping their hands together and moving from foot to foot in an exaggerated display of keeping warm. Presumably their relationship with the *placier*, Sébastian, determined where they could set up and therefore how much money they would make that morning. Perhaps the idle chatter helped to take their minds off the powerless situation they were in. Quite why some traders were allowed to set up while others waited was a mystery.

The crowd we were surrounded by was composed of people of all ages. Young girls with pierced noses and gangly walks, older women hidden in the depths of puffa jackets, men with worn trainers and belt-less jeans and others in smart chinos and shirts. For a while it amused me to guess what they sold – the young girls probably jewellery, the scruffier men fruit and vegetables, and the older traders perhaps the Provençal linen that was too expensive for us to afford.

Tanya put her arm round my shoulder. I suspected like me she was feeling a little worried. However much time we spent in France, we would never quite understand the culture, and in delicate situations like this when we had to deal with official-dom we felt our nationality keenly. The *placiers* we'd met at Apt Market had been as pedantic as solicitors – 'No papers no place' – but it seemed from listening to the conversations around us that even the French were unsure how to deal with the Lourmarin *placier*, Sébastian.

Tanya adjusted my collar as the idle chat continued.

'Saint-Rémy Market's getting worse – all the tourists have *oursins* in their pockets.'

'What's an *oursin*?' I whispered to Tanya, but her attention – like everybody else's – had shifted.

At the top of the steps, availing himself of a weekly opportunity to loom over everyone, was the village's *police municipale*, Sébastian. His head was bald and creased like a St Bernard's chin, and his legs were long and spindly. His torso was so skinny that it was completely swallowed by a puffy sleeveless body-warmer, and this ensemble teamed with his hairless scalp and his sinewy neck gave him the appearance of a turtle poking its head from its shell.

'There are no more places,' he announced. 'You can all go home,' he continued delightedly as he began to descend the steps, moving with the self-satisfied swagger of a movie star.

'I'm sure there's a space for me,' cried out one lady, as she obsequiously bowed her way up the steps. For a moment I thought that she was going to curtsy and kiss Sébastian on the hand, but instead she restricted herself to pecking him on both cheeks. In response he twitched a quick smile at her and nodded his head.

A man was next. Being careful not to reach the same level as Sébastian, he reached out and shook Sébastian's hand, while using his other arm to clap him on the back. 'Take the same place as last week,' said Sébastian with a superior wave.

One by one the people who'd been waiting with us approached the policeman. There seemed to be an accepted order and we were definitely at the bottom of this unwritten hierarchy. Soon there were just ten or so of us left.

'I told you, there are no more spaces,' he chortled down at us.

'Don't worry, it's just his sense of humour. There's plenty of space.' The speaker was a young man. He had dark, round, luminous eyes with which he'd already twitched two winks at Tanya this morning. His skin was a rich brown, and he wore his long, dark hair slicked back into a ponytail. If we'd met in a nightclub, I'd have gently guided Tanya away from his predatory smile, but despite a cloying whiff of aftershave, we were in need of friends. 'My name's Julien,' he continued jovially, 'and it's my first market too.'

Sébastian shuffled up the steps, and the remaining unplaced traders shadowed him as he paraded around the square. If Sébastian moved in one direction, then his trail of followers would whip out behind him as if attached by a cord, and since his progress across the square was haphazard and full of U-turns and sharp rights and lefts, his followers resembled a disorientated shoal of fish, anxiously twitching this way and that. Periodically somebody would find themselves face to face with the policeman and he would jab a small, skeletal finger towards a spare metre of gravel. In this ungracious manner one by one our companions were picked off and distributed across the square, but still Sébastian managed to completely ignore our existence. Whenever I tried to present myself in front of him, he wheeled away on his heels or snapped open his mobile. His thick, fleshy eyelids made it easy for him to shield his glance.

'You'll get a spot,' said Julien, as Sébastian gave him a place near the entrance to the square. 'Just be patient.'

By seven forty-five the market was assembled. A corridor of stalls led from the entrance to the *place* across to the stairs. The intention was to corral visitors down this passageway, making them pass every stall before they descended to the main part of the market. There was plenty of spare room outside this corridor, but we both knew that severed from the main limb of the market, we would look ridiculous.

Sébastian was still doing his best to deny our presence, directing a late-coming van into its parking spot, but we copied his every move – standing behind him like lapdogs and only occasionally losing patience and racing ahead in energetic circles to try to confront him. Finally Tanya trapped him, haring into his eyeline from an oblique angle. With me behind and traders to either side, he had to face us. Without saying a word, and without making eye contact, he flicked his hand out, rather like a diner lazily dismissing a waiter after a long lunch, and then sidestepped Tanya.

It was hard to know whether we'd been placed or not. On the one hand there was a spare space in the central column of stalls in the vague direction in which Sébastian had swished; on the other his gesture had been so tiny it could have just been a symbol of irritation that his path was blocked. We looked at each other, shrugged and decided to set up anyway. At the very least we could claim there had been a misunderstanding.

With the rest of the market already in place, we self-consciously erected our stand. Whatever could go wrong did go wrong. The metal legs to our table refused to snap open properly and I spent five minutes furiously shaking them, blushing red with a mixture of exasperation and embarrassment. In the rush to get out of the house in the morning we'd also left our tablecloth behind. All around us the other stalls were put together with meticulous attention to detail – skirts were fanned out invitingly to display their colours, pumpkins were cut into precise segments, and biscuits presented on neat little serving trays – and then there was our wine, jumbled together on a piece of old board. It was hard not to feel that we'd let the market down. At least it was only our first attempt, and with each successive market we could improve the overall look.

'Never mind,' I said to Tanya, who was doing her best with the aesthetics. 'It's only a crowd of strangers.'

Almost as the words left my mouth Rupert Birch, the maker of our Domaine de la Brillane red, bounded up brimming with his usual enthusiasm. His short, dark hair was a rumpled mess, suggesting he'd been in such a hurry to get out of bed and get on with the day ahead that he'd not even had time to look at himself in the mirror. We'd given Rupert a list of the markets we intended to do and he'd promised to visit us as soon as he could. Unaware of the bureaucratic delays we'd endured, he'd managed to pick our first outing.

'We're just setting up,' said Tanya defensively.

'Shall I get the rest of the stuff from the car?' I bluffed.

'Now, let's have a look at you two. Hmm. It's not quite there yet,' he said with a grin. 'You're going to need to double the size of the stall, and get yourself some stools – people will feel intimidated if you stand up. And have you thought of offering some tapenade? It will make customers want a drink.'

Despite the weeks we'd had to plan, Rupert had dissected our sales strategy in seconds, and given the inauspicious environment we'd created, I began to wonder whether he might change his mind about letting us sell his wine.

'Come on, come on, let's get the corks out. It's nearly nine.' Opening a bottle, Rupert poured a glass and gave the wine a little twirl before tossing the contents to the back of his throat. He then sucked the liquid forward and spat it on the ground like mouthwash. 'You're going to have to get used to tasting every morning, so not too many late nights,' he admonished.

As he was talking, a new idea occurred to him. 'The problem is, all the bottles are on the same level. You need some height.' Leaving us with this cryptic thought, he disappeared to his car.

On the one hand I was grateful to see Rupert. Alone as we were in the market, it was nice to have a friend. But I also wished that we'd had more time to work things out for ourselves, to discover that a taste of tapenade was a good idea rather than be told. Even though our small business had only just started, I felt strangely protective. Fail or succeed, I wanted it to be through our own endeavours. However, it was impossible to harbour any ill-feeling towards Rupert, such was the engaging warmth of his personality. Striding back over towards us, he balanced takeaway coffees on top of two wooden wine boxes. 'If you mount the wine on these, you can create a staircase effect. Oh, and I should bring you some magnums.'

For an hour there was little to do. Although the market was ready, the villagers were still munching their cereal and leafing through the paper. We chatted idly to Rupert and observed the other traders. Three stands to our right was Julien, whom we'd met on the steps in the half-light. He was selling leather goods and was busy circling his stall as he made final adjustments, hanging belts, puffing out handbags and opening wallets. Occasionally I caught him glancing over at our open bottles of wine, and although I may have imagined it, I think he even licked his lips.

On the left, a lady was busy cutting tiles. Her stall was filled with rows of ceramics imprinted with letters and mock street names – 'Place des Boules', 'Place de Pastis'. Directly opposite us was one of the more curious stands in the market. Two old gentlemen in suits, one of them wearing a matching trilby, sat behind a low desk. In front of them were various pamphlets weighted down with stones. I smiled over at them and they nodded courteously back. Looking around the rest of the market, the other traders stood chatting to each other, examining new merchandise and begging cigarettes of each other, but everybody avoided these gentlemen.

The only stand that had any customers was the vegetable stall. Every couple of minutes a different old lady would arrive with a wicker basket, fill it with produce and then hobble away. The rest of us waited.

The town clock chimed ten, and Rupert wished us luck and headed off to another meeting. Gradually the market was becoming busier. Now, rather than make straight for the vegetable stand, people stopped and examined the other stalls, touching a bag or picking up a piece of jewellery. Nobody was buying anything, but at least they were looking. One or two potential customers slowed near our stall. Keeping a safe distance away, they strained to read the labels on the wine bottles.

'*Vous voulez goûter du vin?*' I asked optimistically, but they shook their heads and moved on.

After half an hour I thought we had our first customer – a short man with square-rimmed spectacles who looked familiar. He studied our labels for five minutes and accepted a sip of each of our wines, professionally sucking the liquid around his mouth before spitting it to the ground.

'What prices are you paying for these?' he said in heavily accented Provençal French.

I pointed to our list.

'No, I mean *you* – what's your profit?'

Avoiding the question, I stuttered that we were selling at the same prices available at the vineyard.

'Well, good luck. I'm off to make a delivery. You'll not find any clients in the market at this time of year.'

I looked blank as he walked off and Tanya nudged me. 'Don't you remember – he was the wine merchant we saw when we first came to the market.'

All around, the other traders were busy, but for us it was beginning to appear as if the wine merchant's prediction was right. Tanya left to stroll around the market, and I stood alone, feeling that everyone – the other traders and their customers – had the same question on their lips: 'What's he doing here?' Occasionally out of the corner of my eye I caught sight of Sébastian. I was still worried that he'd not officially allocated us the place and I was anxious for him to see the stand and register our presence, but even when he walked along the corridor of stalls, he appeared to make a point of passing with his back to me.

The stall opposite was as quiet as ours. I smiled again at the two smartly dressed gentlemen, and the man wearing the trilby stood up and came across. He took off his hat, revealing a full head of grey hair. 'I would very much like to buy a bottle of wine,' he said in excessively formal French.

I offered him a taste but he declined, saying that he would take whichever wine I recommended.

'I worked in England once.' He changed to hesitant English. 'I was a cameraman at White City for the BBC. I even met Charlie Chaplin.'

There were no other customers, so we talked about silent movies and London in the old days, and after ten minutes I handed over a bottle of wine.

'Thank you very much. I hope we can become friends,' he said, shaking my hand.

I jingled the coins in the money belt I wore round my waist. If he liked the wine, he would probably come back next week and buy more, and if we could develop a clientele of good repeat customers, then we would prosper. For now the one sale made me feel part of the market and I stood smiling in the sunshine.

'We're in business,' I said excitedly to Tanya on her return.

'Well done.' She patted me on the cheek and reached down to pick up a discarded book that had appeared on the corner of our table. 'And look, he even left his Bible behind for you to read.' She grinned.

The rest of the morning passed slowly. We rearranged the wine, cleaned the tasting glasses and tried not to scare off the occasional person who took an interest in the stand. The atmosphere was different from my expectations. Nobody cried out their prices or prodded their products under prospective purchasers' noses. Instead there was a serenity to proceedings. People almost seemed to whisper as they purchased their goods, as if the crumbling bricks and weathered stones of the architecture imposed a good-mannered restraint. It was rare to see a shopper alone; instead people met friends, interlinked arms and explored the stalls together. It was a pleasant pageant to watch. Although we weren't managing to sell anything, the gentle pace of affairs and the soothing murmur of voices made it hard for me to think of a more relaxing place to spend the morning. It was almost like sitting on the bank of a babbling brook waiting for a fish to bite.

Unfortunately for us, the bait wasn't working. The experience brought back memories of our attempt to run a rosé bar that summer. The French, it seemed, were just not interested in drinking. They would pause suspiciously in front of us, eye up the bottles of wine and then walk away. Disconcertingly a number of people left shaking their heads.

The leather trader, Julien, came over to chat. '*On peut goûter le vin?*' he asked.

I poured a large glass and he made a flamboyant show of sticking his nose almost into the liquid.

'Summer fruits,' he announced, before taking the first in a series of large gulps.

Before long I had to top him up, but at least we were learning as he was drinking.

'Don't worry, it's like this for everybody. It's the wrong time of year for the markets. You might sell some wine around Christmastime, but other than that it's supposed to be dead until March. January and February are the worst months – there's nobody here. I'll probably just travel to the tanning houses, buy leather and make some handbags and wallets.'

'And what about the other markets?' asked Tanya.

'*Il faut essayer*,' encouraged Julien, letting loose another flirtatious wink. 'It's worth trying them all. L'Isle-sur-la-Sorgue attracts tourists all year round and so you might do OK there, and Apt is usually busy. Find some other wine merchants, look at their stalls and learn how they sell wine. Remember, *petit à petit l'oiseau fait son nid.*' We looked quizzically at him and Julien explained in halting English, 'A little by a little the bird makes his nest.' Switching back to French, he continued, 'It's what my dad said to me – he was a trader too. And remember, when you do make some money, don't tell anybody. The markets are strange places – the minute you start to do well, people become jealous and then the problems start: the taxman visits; your car keeps getting a flat tyre. You have to be careful. If people ask, just say, "*Ça va.*" if they see you sell something, say it's your first sale of the morning. Watch your backs.'

Keen to keep the conversation going, I asked, 'Have you sold anything this morning?'

Julien grinned. His smile stretched right across his face. '*Ça va.*'

'And how do we get a permanent place?'

'Ah, that's almost impossible. You can write to the *mairie* but you won't get anywhere. I've a friend who has written every year for the last fifteen years and received the same letter of rejection. You just have to show up every week and get your face known. Even then you might not secure a place for the summer.' He looked over my shoulder. 'I've got a customer,' he apologised, drained his glass and practically skipped – his customer was a pretty girl – back to his stall.

It was just after twelve o'clock and I could see Sébastian making his way down the rows of stalls. He seemed cheerier than first thing this morning, pausing to chat and make jokes with the traders as they handed over the money for their stalls. The favoured women gave him a kiss farewell; others smiled winsomely, judging a kiss too uncertain, but knowing that if they wanted to prosper in this market, it was a boundary that they would have to cross. The skill was all in the timing.

Sébastian paused to have a cigarette at a stall four down from us and then hurriedly took the money from the next two traders. Already I was beginning to appreciate that it was important to analyse his every gesture. The traders who'd confidently strolled up to him at 7 a.m. were those within his trusted clique. Others who hoped to join this group had been placed quickly, and those who refused to play the game had been placed last. How we were treated by Sébastian when we handed over our money would have a direct bearing on how confident we could be in asking for a place next week.

At the very least he had to ask to see our market passes. We'd spent months trying to get them and were proud of our laminated official documents. At home, I kept them in the drawer with our passports, and in the market, in a tightly zipped pouch. I was paranoid that if we lost them, the whole official process would have to start again.

As we waited, Tanya and I discussed offering Sébastian a glass of wine. In an English market we would definitely have done so, but in France we had to be careful. In a country so reliant on public officials, bribery was an ever-present problem and such a gesture of friendship could easily be misconstrued. In the end it wasn't a problem. Standing at the leather-goods stall next to us, Sébastian engaged the trader in conversation, keeping his back turned to us. As he talked, he ripped a ticket from a little book, reversed his palm and held it out behind his back. Not knowing what else to do, I took the ticket. It read, 'Droit de Place No. 00123, Lourmarin, €1.50.'

Counting out the money, I placed it in Sébastian's hand, which had remained palm upturned behind his back. The whole transaction was completed without him speaking or looking at us, and with his back still turned, he edged past to the other stalls. Our market passes were still tucked redundantly in my pouch.

'Well, I guess we know where we stand,' said Tanya, as we replaced the bottles in their boxes.

We'd opened three wines for tasting and sold one, and including the cost of our place, we'd made a loss of €20 on our first day. All around us the other traders were packing up, edging their vans as close as possible to their stalls. Although it appeared to be a haphazard operation, everyone assisted each other in shifting their stalls crucial centimetres to allow the vans to back into the market. On the road, a jam had developed as the traders waited to squeeze into the *place*. Unwilling to disrupt the organised chaos, I began carrying our wine, box by box, to the car.

As we drove away from our first market, we both felt a sense of exhilaration. We were traders at last. It was now up to us to learn the tricks of the trade and make a success of our nascent little business. At least we already had one customer, even if he was a Jehovah's Witness.

8

'Il Faut Essayer'

Julien had advised us to try as many markets as possible, but working in a new market was a convoluted process. Determined not to contradict local practices, we started by approaching the mayors' offices and discovered that nearly every market was organised in a different way. In some, like Lourmarin, the *placier* was in charge of everything; in others there was apparently an additional layer of bureaucracy to tackle before we could start. Officious secretaries told us there was no point in turning up until we'd written to the mayor applying for a place, and even more officious secretaries told us not to bother coming at all – the market was full and had been for years.

A week after our first market in Lourmarin we'd visited all the surrounding villages and written the various letters required of us. The responses began to trickle in. All of them contained the same disheartening answer – 'There are no free pitches. Apply again next year.' Yet whenever we visited a market, there were plenty of spare spaces and so, ignoring the letters we'd written, we just showed up.

Each different market was an exhilarating new experience. Some, like L'Isle-sur-la-Sorgue, were fraught with logistical headaches, and the charm of the place – the gently turning water-wheels, the fast-running stream filled with trout and bordered by cafés – quickly became lost on us. Instead we queued and cursed with the five hundred other traders trying to negotiate the maze of medieval streets for one of the most popular markets in France – the Sunday *brocante*. Prangs were inevitable. Vans shunted against other vans or grazed the cornerstones of buildings, leaving trails of paint. In this market the stakes were much higher than elsewhere. Nudge the car in front too hard and if we were unlucky, rather than bruise a few oranges, we'd shatter thousands of euros worth of antiques. And since road signs apparently lost their meaning at this time in the morning, head-on collisions up one-way streets were a worrying possibility.

Other markets were unexpectedly gentle. We'd been to Roussillon on a number of occasions and observed how the plunging blood-red cliffs that surrounded it acted as a Mecca for the region's tourists. Buses clogged the narrow roads, and the nearest available car parking space was often twenty minutes' walk from the narrow cobbled streets of the village. The congestion was so bad that I was surprised that the *mairie* could even contemplate a market. But on the morning we turned up – out of season, admittedly – we slipped into the car park at the base of the village and set up our stall. As well as us there were three other traders – a woman selling cheese, ham and pasta from Italy, a vegetable stall and a *poissonnerie*. Apart from the drive through the Combe de Lourmarin, a winding mountainous viper of a road, it was the easiest market to date.

Nearer home, the adjoining village to Lourmarin – Cadenet – proved a disappointment. Viewed from the outside, it was among the prettiest villages in the region, built on a hill guarding the road south across the Durance river. There was an attractive main square dominated by the statue of a drummer boy born in the village, whose personal heroism helped drive back the Austrians at Arcole in 1796, but somehow the village lacked vitality. Its tough, no-nonsense feel was reflected in the market every Monday. Gone were the stands selling delicacies; instead there were rows of low tables offering doorknobs, corkscrews, keys, knives and curtain rails. Our stand full of wine felt out of place.

The next nearest market to our house was underneath the shady plane trees in Cucuron. We were placed within minutes of arrival (despite the letter from the *mairie* that declared the market was full) and we passed a pleasant morning selling a little wine and watching as the stallholder next to us created a massive paella. First he simmered three bags of rice, scattering a little saffron over the gently bubbling liquid. Then he gradually added chicken, pork, prawns and mussels, standing back like a painter regarding a masterpiece as he moved from ingredient to ingredient. By mid-morning there was a symmetrically perfect scattering of ingredients over the canvas of rice.

With each successive market our stall changed a little. We marked the prices of the wine on corks, which we hung round the necks of the bottles. We brought along a spittoon and, as advised by Rupert, doubled the length of our stall and started offering people tapenade. It took less and less time to set up and pack away our equipment, but even so, doing a market swallowed a whole day. Up at six to reach our destination before seven, there were a dead couple of hours while we waited for the customers to arrive. We then traded until one. If we were lucky, we managed to slip away before the rest of the stallholders, but more often than not we became trapped in narrow streets and had to wait for half an hour in a line of vans seeking the open road. Usually we were home by three, but then we had a late lunch and unloaded the car, meaning that a day that started at dawn came to an end in the late afternoon.

Perhaps it was because we were selling wine, but the response of the other traders to us, the English interlopers, could not have been more friendly. By mid-morning they trickled across, professionally proffering their comments on our selected vineyards in a good-humoured attempt to disguise the fact that they fancied a free glass. While they chatted away, Tanya and I learnt words in the local patois, countless recipes and all sorts of useful facts about where we lived. For us, the markets acted as an indispensable Provençal crammer.

One morning in Apt we were positioned on the very fringe of the market next to a man with a long goatee, drainpipe jeans and white winkle-pickers, who was unloading boxes of vinyl LPs from the back of his van. With his sunglasses on he resembled a hip villain from a Tarantino film. His wife – heavy black boots, purple make-up and a skull and crossbones nose stud – arranged the records in alphabetical order. She started, rather incongruously, with Abba.

Our pitch was so isolated we might as well have cultivated a clientele of stray wild boar, so instead mid-morning I passed the wine around. Our goth neighbour produced a round goat's cheese wrapped in dried leaves and a serrated penknife. '*Profitez bien,*' she said, explaining that it was the last fresh cheese of the season, because the goats were about to have their babies. '*Ils sont mignons,*' she cooed, somehow ignoring the fact that her dress sense suggested a vampiresque penchant for other people's blood, rather than a love of cute baby goats.

We cut the cheese into Trivial Pursuit-shaped portions, nibbled, sipped and chatted. Other lonely customer-free traders gradually joined our cheese and wine party. The conversation moved from LP prices – €3,000 for one with a sleeve depicting the Beatles eating a sandwich outside a Parisian brasserie – to the location of illegal raves in the Luberon valley, which were organised by text message by the youth of Marseille. Apparently it wasn't the police the young ravers had to be wary of; it was the arrival of the *chasseurs*, or hunters, in the morning. They tended to be a lot freer with their firearms than the gendarmerie.

Accepting another glass of wine, a foie-gras salesman began to volunteer all sorts of useful information. 'Have you registered for the Christmas markets yet? What do you mean you haven't? Second-best time of the year. Tell you what, give me your phone number and I'll phone through a list. Better hurry, though – they fill up quickly.' His conversation came out in scattergun bursts, and as he talked, he twitched his way around our stall examining every item.

'If you want, I can do you a great deal on foie gras and Sauternes. It'll sell like tea to the English.' With each new bite and sip he generated another money-making idea, spliced with some more market patter. With swept-back greased hair and a battered brown leather jacket, he wouldn't have been out of place on a pitch in the East End of London.

As people passed without buying, he muttered, '*Il y a degain*' – we'd already learnt this was patois for an empty market. '*Il faut attendre le gibier d'été.*' Tanya and I looked confused. 'You know, summer's prey – the tourists.'

In other markets we learnt yet more vocabulary. In the village of Rognes, on the south bank of the Durance, we encountered an ancient vegetable fair. There were tables full of pumpkins of every shape, size and variety – some that went with spaghetti; others that were perfect for soup; some had skins flecked with colour and were warped out of shape; others were grey like giant mushrooms or coiled like serpents. The stallholder we set up next to explained that they were all ancient varieties that had been discarded because the strains weren't productive enough for modern agriculture.

'Try some of these tomatoes,' he said, proffering a punnet with fifteen varieties in it. 'Each one has a different taste.'

I selected a yellow one that looked like one of those long, thin balloons that always refuse to blow up. With a snout like a dolphin and a body as long as a chipolata, it would have failed any supermarket conformity test, but its taste was like sweet wine. Within an hour our neighbour had sold out. We were having no such luck, and seeing yet another customer move on, our neighbour muttered, '*Oursins dans les poches.*'

This was the same phrase that we'd heard in Lourmarin.

Seeing our confused expression, the stallholder dragged us off to the nearest *poissonnerie*. There, lying on a bed of ice, was a tray full of *oursins*, or sea urchins – little round balls of salty anger covered in barbs like miniature World War II mines. 'There. If you had one of those in your pocket, you wouldn't spend any money either,' he advised triumphantly.

In the village of Lauris, our education continued when we were introduced to the harsh realities of country life. A pair of Provençal farmers arrived in a battered van and laid out various misshapen vegetables, bruised cucumbers, withered salad leaves and mouldy carrots. After setting up, they sat together in their van. I could only assume that they were offering thieves the opportunity to make off with their rotten stock.

The older of the two was bald with scraggy stubble. He had a hearing problem that materialised with his limited customers, enabling him to short-change them efficiently – no matter how loud the protest, he hobbled back to the van and shut the door. The other man, who I guessed was his son, chain-smoked roll-ups, puffing his way through whole cigarettes without removing them from his mouth. He had short, dark hair, a lean face, gaunt cheeks and grunted to himself as he rocked back and forth in the passenger seat.

After an hour of trading the police arrived and a crowd of people gathered at the rear of the van. Some of the more affluent local residents walked away shaking their heads in disgust, and we pushed our way through to see what the fuss was about. On the floor was a basket full of floppy-eared, doe-eyed, speckled puppies, mewling away as they searched for their mother and milk. They can only have been a week old.

As far as I could understand from the rapid French being spoken by the police, the vegetable traders and the multiple onlookers, the problem was not separating such young animals from their mother – although in the UK this would have been reason enough to call in the RSPCA – but the fact that the dogs were being sold. As we knew, every trader had a set of papers specifying what they could sell, and day-old dogs were not on the list. An agreement was eventually reached and the farmers put the basket of dogs at the front of the stall and gave the puppies away for free.

'I guess it's better than drowning them in the Durance,' said Tanya.

The other shock we had to get used to in our first weeks in the markets was our lack of clients. Our daily sales figures remained stubbornly in single figures and almost entirely dependent on good-humoured wine lovers with a soft spot for the English. Unfortunately for us, such customers were as scarce as a Provençal plumber in August. And so, instead of selling wine, I spent empty hours watching church clocks tick round, rearranging our stall, flicking through *La Provence* and studying the shopping habits of our prospective clientele. I ended up identifying three types of people to whom there was absolutely no point trying to sell wine.

Firstly the magpies, who swooped on anything pretty or new. They were easy to spot from a long way off: male or female, they glinted with jewellery – bracelets, chains and watches – which flashed in the sunlight as they examined merchandise. Usually magpies shopped in pairs, sharing their munificence with each other, twirling gaily to display some new frivolity, before diving off in another direction, emitting high-pitched shrieks at the next sparkling discovery. It was practically impossible for a magpie to pass a stall without buying something; in fact the only goods in which they showed little or no interest were essential items like vegetables and, unfortunately for us, semi-essentials such as wine.

Next was a more dangerous breed of shopper and the bane of every trader's life. A hybrid of the magpie, they too whooped through the market expressing interest in everything, but their behaviour was subtly different. They tended to tarry much longer at stalls, and whereas proper magpies showed no interest in wine, the hybrid was only too happy to taste everything we had on offer. Their conversation was always totally irrelevant to the matter at hand and they could talk seemingly inexhaustibly on any range of subjects – the weather, the new roundabout outside the village or their nephew in Paris who'd just moved to London. They arrived at the market first thing in the morning and worked their way in slow motion around the stalls, eating people's time before they emerged at the other end of town with not a single purchase to show for their efforts, no doubt congratulating themselves on a pleasant morning and their parsimony.

Finally there were the mice, timid little animals who started at the slightest noise. They tended to walk in the middle of the road, keeping a buffer of at least a metre from any stall. It was almost tragic to watch them take an interest in something and struggle closer, as if oxygen was short and every millimetre required an immense effort. Just as they were on the verge of reaching out and touching an item, the stallholder would break the silence. To the mice, the voice of another person, however quiet and polite, sounded like a shotgun, ripping into their solitude. They invariably scurried off, bowing their heads as if to apologise for their very presence.

After an intense three weeks trying as many local markets as possible, it was time to decide in which villages to concentrate our efforts. Not, however, before Tanya persuaded me to try one more different location – Saint-Tropez. The market was held every Saturday morning in the pine-filled Place des Lices. High on the hill, away from the celebrity-fuelled parade ground of the port, this shady square was an oasis of sanity and a reminder of why Saint-Tropez had become popular in the first place.

'It's not far away and think of all the yachts and villas. There's so much money there people won't even look at our prices.

And it's the right time of year to go,' continued Tanya, sensing that the argument had yet to be won. 'The traffic will have disappeared. It will just be us and the residents.' She should have been right.

We left home in darkness on a cold, clear morning in late November, and after two hours turned on to the single road that led up the Saint-Tropez peninsula. In the height of summer, travelling the 5 kilometres or so up this narrow finger of land could take an entire morning. At 7.30 a.m. we expected the road to be totally clear, but rounding a bend, we came across a slow snaking queue of tail lights. For the next half-hour we chugged into town, bemused by what could possibly be going on. Nearer the centre, traffic policemen with luminous batons waved us on to a one-way circuit, which fortuitously led to the Place des Lices.

There, as the sun rose graciously over the bay, we witnessed mayhem. Our car was directed into a dead-end street, and before we could turn off the ignition, another car shunted up behind us. We walked slowly back towards the square, still hoping to find a place to set up our stall. A gaggle of girls raced past, struggling for balance in their high heels as they excitedly whirred their handbags over their heads like helicopter blades. One of them wore a pair of leather trousers with a hole cut in the rear, revealing a G-string and a heart-shaped tattoo. In the season I wouldn't have been surprised by this type of avant-garde dress sense – when we'd first visited two years ago I'd watched a woman walk through town naked beneath a transparent dress, obviously too proud of her surgically enhanced breasts to consider covering them up – or perhaps they were just so new that she'd yet to buy a bra that fitted – but that was August and this was November.

More surprises were to follow – the normally mild-mannered Place des Lices had been cannibalised by hundreds of stands. It was as if the surrounding shops had swallowed the square.

Rails of clothes extended out like incisors, scissoring between the pines in a fashion-filled maelstrom. Even this early in the morning there was the smell of the fairground with crêpes frying on greasy pans and nuts roasting on hot braziers. Outside the boutiques – Chanel, Gucci, Fendi, Pucci – queues were already forming. Old women sat on stools guarding the doors and whipping the shoppers into delirious anticipation: '*Soldes! Demain le prix, c'est normal. C'est Armani. C'est Versace. Le prix normal, c'est trois milles euros – maintenant c'est un mille euros.*'

Preposterously small shoes were squeezed on to flabby feet, and girls wedged themselves into slip dresses that would have been indecent in a brothel. The attitude of the shop assistants was aggressively dismissive, as if each shopper were fortunate to even touch the clothes at the quoted prices. Breasts were poked, asses tugged and intimate areas invaded, all in an effort to smooth the lines of clothes only ever designed for models.

Once we'd recovered from the shock and found a shop assistant with the grace to spare a second, we asked what had happened to the market. Regarding us with disdain, she shook her head. '*Il n y a pas un marché. Aujourd hui c'est la Braderie de Saint-Tropez.*' Panicking that a sales opportunity had been squandered, she raced away, no doubt thinking that she'd given a perfectly adequate explanation.

Since there was clearly no chance of doing the market and no way we could get our car from the cul de sac, we walked down the hill towards the port, pushing our way through the thickening crowd. Clothes from every shop in town stretched into the street, and contented people balanced armfuls of carrier bags, the slightest push sending them skittling sideways under the weight of their purchases.

Seeking peace, we headed towards the *plage*. In the summer, beach clubs sprawled across the golden sand and paparazzi picketed the entrances, but now the clubs were boarded up and just a single old Tropezien meandered along the water's edge.

'*Attention – il y a toujours les méduses,*' he warned as we passed. Looking into the clear water, we spotted bulbous jellyfish being swept towards shore.

We found the only restaurant that was still open and sat on the sand looking at the blue sea, rejoicing in the warmth and the fact that we were eating on the beach in November. Trails of smoke rose skywards from across the bay, and the smell of burning autumnal leaves was the only reminder of the time of year. When the waiter came to take our order, we asked him to explain the *braderie*.

A look of disbelief washed across his face and then receded with the latest wave. 'The *braderie* is the fashion event of the year. People fly in from Paris just to be here. Nice and Marseille will be empty today because everybody is in Saint-Tropez. It's the busiest day of the year.'

With each course we elicited a little more information. The *braderie* was in fact the biggest clearance sale in the south of France. All the boutiques put last summer's stock on to rails, slashed the prices and wheeled the garments into the street. If you arrived first thing in the morning, as we had, it was common to find €1,000 coats slashed to €100. 'Some of the girls go a little mad,' shrugged our waiter as we paid the bill.

Walking back to the car, the streets were full of people flaunting their new purchases. A black man sat outside a bar in a shady corner twirling a new designer umbrella over his head with a big toothy grin on his face, while next to him women rummaged amid multicoloured bags, pulling out clothes to show to friends. We reached the car, performed a twenty-point turn to squeeze ourselves back on to the road and rejoined the hideous traffic.

'*Il faut essayer,*' said Tanya, slightly apologetically, as we finally pulled clear of the Saint-Tropez peninsula and pointed the car north towards the sleepy hills of the Luberon.

Behind us, the view of the coast was blocked by an array of

shopping piled high on the back seat. Each item, I was faithfully
assured by Tanya, was a bargain.

9

Le But

During the three weeks we'd been working in different markets, we puzzled over the apparent inequalities between the traders. Why were some people able to set up straight away? Why were some traders given good pitches where the public were likely to tarry — under broad-leaved plane trees or next to cooling fountains — while others were shunted to the fringes where the crowds were inevitably thin?

Gradually we came to understand the complex relationships involved. Every market was supposed to be governed by the *mairie*, but in the majority of cases the mayor's office, despite still claiming to be in charge, had handed over real responsibility to the municipal policeman, and because there was no uniform set of regulations guiding who could trade where, everything depended on his attitude.

Some policemen chalked all the available pitches on to the tarmac, marking each with a number; others kept a mental map in their head. Some tried to cluster together people selling the same items, so that the corners of some markets were dominated by neatly stacked triangles of colourful fruit and vegetables, while others separated similar traders to try to allow them a chance to build up their own clientele. All tried to exercise their discretion to uphold an unwritten hierarchy.

At the bottom of the pile were traders such as ourselves – new faces who'd never been seen in the region before and who had no family connections. To prosper, we needed to be related to a butcher or a baker in one of Luberon's villages, or a minor functionary in a *mairie*. Perhaps we should have let it be known in the various *boulangeries*, the accredited village-gossip centres, that my grandfather flew Spitfires over France in the war. It can't have hurt.

In any event, with no recognisable regional credentials, the accepted practice was that all the regulars, the not-so regulars and even the downright irregulars should be found a place before us. The more we showed up, the higher we would climb in the policeman's estimation and the earlier he would find us a place. For now we had to expect to wait for at least an hour before our requirements were even considered. Eventually if we were loyal enough to individual markets, we might be considered for a semi-permanent place and then we would start again at the bottom of a new pecking order.

Semi-permanent places were awarded by the policeman when you'd reached a certain degree of familiarity with him – you knew his name, shook his hand in the morning and had a six-month history of being cooperative. Once you'd reached this stage, then eventually you would get the nod to set up in the same place each week and gradually you would gain some rights to the metres you'd been allocated.

There was broad agreement that if the same pitch had been in someone's possession for a season, then they had a right to it. If the trader failed to turn up for a couple of markets and someone else started trading in his place, they were viewed as squatters, to be kicked out the moment the rightful owner returned. In such situations there were rarely disputes. But what happened, for example, if a trader became ill and didn't turn up for a month, or two months? Should he forfeit his rights? The situation was unclear.

Complicating matters further there was another class of traders, whom we'd never met. They'd disappeared at the end of September and would return with summer's first warm breath. They'd had the same pitches (officially awarded by the *mairie*, not the police) in their families for generations and felt no need to guard them over the cold, customerless winter. But already we'd heard stories of discontent from the other traders: 'Why should I stand here all winter and try and build a business only to be kicked out by someone who has been warming his toes by the fireside?'

In these kinds of disagreements it was the role of the *police municipale* to intervene and settle matters. If they made an incorrect decision, one that contradicted the other traders' sense of justice, then the matter would not be forgotten. We'd already encountered a number of vendors who, so it was said, had gained possession of their pitches through improper means.

To me, it was no surprise. The judgements the policemen had to make were fine, and inevitably personalities became involved. The traders with enough swagger and bluster to intimidate or ingratiate themselves with the police gradually ensured themselves better and better pitches and, because there was constant pressure to grow, larger and larger ones. The cost of a metre of space in a market was usually less than €1, and everyone believed that the larger the stalls, the higher the sales. And so there was an ongoing battle to absorb spare space, or to move to another pitch that was larger. People were ingenious in their quest to claim extra metres, learning how to construct stalls round corners and using adjustable-height legs so that their stalls could climb stairs.

This constant jostling for position created friction. The female traders grumbled about the chauvinist nature of the *placiers* and how they were always overlooked when a good pitch became free, and the men griped about how the *placiers* had an eye for pretty women and showed a preference towards them when deciding disputes. The allegations of sexism and bullying were redolent of a London office, except there was no industrial tribunal to complain to.

There was also corruption. Some years ago in one of the region's towns there had been a major scandal when the locals began to notice the *placier*'s standard of living creeping upwards. Eschewing the dusty boules pitch where he had once been a regular, he began to strut around town in shiny brogues and a pressed shirt. He even disappeared for a couple of weeks, fuelling rumours that he might have taken, horror of all horrors, a foreign holiday. As a civil servant, his salary would have been minimal and nowhere near adequate to support such new extravagances. People presumed he was dodging tax, but in a country where the culture of denunciation (reporting your neighbours to the authorities) was widespread, such behaviour was perilous.

The fraud office investigated and found all the *placier*'s tax returns to be in order but they also discovered a garage full of expensive motorcars and a house brimming with flat-screen televisions, reclining leather sofas and the obligatory accessory of the newly wealthy, a Jacuzzi. The *placier* was plucked from his whirlpool, where he was nibbling strawberries and being served champagne by two leggy blondes (I made this last bit up), and confessed to taking bribes from the local market traders to improve their position. For an extra €20 each a week he'd guaranteed a prime spot to a cartel of twenty traders, earning him an illicit income of over €1,600 a month. Not bad work if you can get it.

The motivating factor behind such dishonesty and all the jockeying for position in the markets was the amount of money to be made in the summer. In the half-empty markets that we'd been attending, the other vendors had talked about the months of July and August with a wide-eyed longing. They described how there wasn't a spare pitch in any of the Provençal markets and how the crowds swelled between the stalls. A tradesman with the right product and a good location could make enough money to support himself for the year. Apparently if vendors of the brightly coloured Provençal linen worked seven markets a week, they could clear €30,000 a month in the peak season.

In this respect the nickname which we'd heard bandied around for tourists – *'gibier d'été'*, or summer's prey – became even more meaningful. Without this annual migration of money the traders would never survive. They waited through the lean winter months, becoming hungrier and hungrier, and then for a brief interval when there were almost too many customers to serve, they prospered.

It all reminded me of a nature documentary I'd seen, and if my French had been up to it, I would have attempted to explain the parallels between the traders and African crocodiles – every year as drought hits the savannah the crocodiles search for the last remaining mudpools. Then, after six lean months, there is the patter of rainfall, and the sound of floodwaters, and eventually the distant drumming of hoofs on the ground. The crocodiles wait as an inexorable urge drives the wildebeest hundreds of miles to the edge of the river, until one by one they plunge into the water, which fast becomes a frothing pool of blood as the crocodiles feast. Then within days there is nothing but a still river, the hot sun and the fear of another drought. On reflection it was fortunate that my French wasn't up to scratch. Comparing my workmates with crocodiles was unlikely to win me many friends.

The reality of our situation, however, was perilous. To make our business work, we had to secure a prime pitch in a number of summer markets, markets that everybody said were already full. Our hope, like a number of other fledgling traders, was to battle through the winter and form some sort of relationship with the *placiers*. At the very least we wanted to be the first people in line for a place if one of the regular traders failed to show up, but the ultimate goal was to stand before the various *placiers* in spring, shake their hands and receive the nod that meant we could set up in the same place for the rest of the season.

In pursuing this goal, Tanya and I were at a distinct disadvantage to the other novices – we were English, and whether or not there was any prejudice against us, we were unequipped with the cultural knowledge that would enable us to play the system to our advantage – would a bottle of wine at Christmas be considered a bribe or just a nice gesture? Should we offer to buy the *placier* a cup of coffee first thing in the morning? From the conversations we'd already had, such behaviour was viewed with suspicion. Markets where the *placier* was susceptible to having a *saucisson* slipped into his pocket were talked about disparagingly.

In any event, our charm offensive had to succeed. I'd calculated that if we averaged five markets a week over the course of the year (working in slightly fewer markets in the winter and slightly more in the summer), then we would need to sell thirty-five to forty bottles of wine in each market to make a living. In July and August I hoped that we might get lucky and secure a couple of big contracts to supply villas and that these spikes would help to cover our lacklustre winter sales. In total we would need to sell 8,000 bottles a year. Neither Tanya nor I expected to make a fortune, just enough to survive and to enjoy the better quality of life on offer in Provence.

After nearly a month's trading I was already dubious about our future. In our best market we'd managed to sell fifteen bottles of wine, still some way short of the target, but not bad. The problem was that this was our best market: average sales were currently languishing at about five or six bottles a morning, which was barely a bottle an hour and meant we were doing a lot of clock-watching.

On the positive side, our fellow traders had advised us that it took a long time to build up a relationship with the local shoppers. In order to spend money with you, they had to have seen you on a number of occasions – the tongue-in-cheek consensus was at least a year of markets – and inspected your prices and products. Only once they'd concluded that your business was '*correct*' – in other words that we were committed to providing wine at a reasonable price and not just present to rip off the tourists – would they begin a slow courtship, speaking to us for the first time, enquiring about our background and eventually, if they liked us, purchasing.

There had certainly been enough interest in our stall to suggest that in the long term we might reasonably expect to pick up custom. The locals spent inordinate amounts of time studying the labels on our bottles. They would invariably refuse a taste of any of the wines and then depart with a comment such as '*Je connais cette domaine*' – 'I know this vineyard' – implying that they would be checking the prices that week. If our mark-up was considered '*pas correct*' we would be exposed to the whole village. Since we weren't in the business of overcharging, I had to believe our trade would increase, although in my more pessimistic moments the jokes of the other traders seemed uncannily accurate – it would take us a year before we sold anything to a Provençal.

I'd planned for the parsimony of the locals, but another threat to my average sales figures came as a surprise – the weather. Markets were social occasions, where people came out on to the street, gathered in groups with their shopping bags and discussed the week's news – the scandalous cost of a new village roundabout or the trial of a tax-dodging politician. Under clear autumnal skies with the auburn leaves slowly floating to earth, there could be few more pleasant ways to spend a morning than debating with considerable indignation two-faced politicians who underdeclared the worth of their Côte d'Azur boltholes to avoid the new wealth tax. Unfortunately just a drop of rain could spoil the day. People retreated into their houses, closed their shutters and forgot all about gossip.

Showers were in fact unusual, because when it rained in the Luberon, it really rained. Cascades flooded from the tiles of our house, and the hills were obscured by a curtain of water. Driveways turned into muddy rivers, and the locals shored up their doors with sandbags. In such conditions no traders even thought of doing a market.

Worse than the rain was the wind. Since we'd started trading, only one market had been wiped out by a heavy thunderstorm, but the mistral was a much more frequent visitor. Every night before a market I would check the weather forecast, paying particular attention to the wind speed. If I woke in the night, I would listen to the branches of the trees as the gusts played inconsistently between their leaves. Then first thing in the morning I would poke my head out of our bedroom window and watch the tops of the tall, thin cypresses. If they were bent over at more than a right angle, I'd flop back into bed, believing that a market was impossible that day.

The real problem with the mistral was its fickle nature. At 7 a.m. it could slam the front door back in my face and slap our shutters so hard against the wall it sounded as if it was applauding its own might. Then moments later the wind could disappear. There was no gradual tailing off, no final apologetic whimpering whine down the valley. In an instant the trees were ramrod straight and the only memory of the mistral was the scattered garden furniture and the washing from the line that had been chased into the vines. If the wind disappeared early enough, there was still time to collect our things and rush to market, but if it waited until nine or ten, we were left sitting at home regretting that we'd not ventured out.

Then there were the mornings when the wind arrived after we'd set up. Usually the weather forecast would have predicted it, but in the still dawn air a fierce wind sometimes seemed inconceivable, so we would drive an hour in the darkness to one of our markets and mount all the wine on our stall. Another trader would shrug as he left and say that the mistral was coming, but we'd ignore him and assume that the innate French hypochondria extended to the weather as well.

The remaining few would then start tying bricks to the bases of parasols, but after previous markets in the wind, we knew such efforts were futile. If the mistral came, there would be a few warning puffs and then cold air, which sweeps down the Rhône valley from the Alps, would rush across the market square. Parasols would be lifted into the air, upending stalls, before landing with heavy crashes against distant walls. The pretty tablecloths that covered the stands would be whipped away as if by a magician, who for his next trick would choreograph them into performing airborne waltzes across the square. Dust would blow into eyes, produce would be swept on to the floor, and we would hurriedly have to deposit our wine back in its box.

Being a successful market trader at times depended on an ability to second-guess the weather. Invariably we seemed to get things wrong. When we stayed in bed because the wind was battering the house or rain was rattling against the skylight, two hours later the sun would be out and shoppers in the markets would be basking in a perfect Provençal day. The next morning, when we were still berating ourselves for our idleness, we would take a cavalier approach to the storm warnings and head off to work as dark clouds gathered over the hills. The promised rain would then arrive and we'd be left huddling under our parasol, without a hope of a customer. Week by week we became more professional in our approach. We learnt that if the mistral was blowing, we should search out a market further to the east, because the further away we were from the mouth of the Rhône, the lesser the effect of the mistral. Often when there was a gale in Lourmarin, just twenty minutes away in Pertuis the trees were perfectly still.

Although the weather in November was generally good, with clear blue skies and a hot sun melting red leaves from the vines, just one day of bad weather every week and one day when we got the weather wrong meant that sales fell even further below my expectations. Our only consolation was the discovery that the cost of living for market traders was unexpectedly cheap. Once the other vendors began to recognise our faces, the prices they charged started to fall. By the time they'd seen us five or six times at different markets, we were able to buy produce at cost. French beans that were €5 a kilo to the public were €1 a kilo to us; a free-range chicken that usually cost €15 was reduced to €5. In return we sold on all our wine at the price at which we'd purchased. Since the produce available in the markets was some of the best in France, we were able to indulge expensive tastes on a minimal budget. Even clothes shopping was cheaper for Tanya. Cashmere shawls were sold for a third of the marked price, plus 'a bottle of your best red'.

Despite the worrying lack of sales, November and the winter months to follow were really just a training camp. What was going to determine our ability to survive as traders was our performance during the summer. Thankfully there were already some markets in which we felt confident of getting a permanent place. We'd been told that Ansouis, the market that was shut for the winter, was a possibility, as was Cadenet. As well as these markets we had to ensure we had a presence in the big tourist markets, because if we didn't, we'd never sell enough wine to survive. The largest two locally were Lourmarin and Cucuron.

Lourmarin Market was one of the wealthiest in the surrounding area, and as residents we might have hoped to be treated more favourably than, say, a trader who'd driven from Marseille. So far the reverse had occurred. We'd now completed three successive Fridays in the market and each morning had been a test on the nerves, as we waited to see whether we would be awarded a place. Sébastian appeared later and later at the top of the stairs, presumably enjoying the experience of keeping everyone waiting. I'd hoped that after our tough initiation he would gradually become more friendly. Unfortunately the opposite seemed to be true. Whenever we finally managed to slip into his field of vision, he appeared genuinely distressed and not a little perplexed to see us again.

It was as if he couldn't understand why we kept coming back for more punishment – hadn't he done enough to put us off yet? For three weeks we'd been the last people in the market to be offered a place and on each occasion it had been next to the Jehovah's Witnesses. Not only had we traded in the least favourable pitch in the market, we'd also had to manage an hour of polite conversation about our eternal damnation.

Throughout all our encounters Sébastian had managed not to utter a single word to us. We paid for our place by putting €1.50 into the palm of his hand, and even if there was nobody around to provide the alibi of a conversation, he managed to take an intense interest in something going on elsewhere in the market. Julien, the leather-goods salesman, who seemed to be flirtatious and thirsty in equal measure, still encouraged us not to worry and predicted that Sébastian's attitude would eventually change.

'The important thing is to get him to like you by next April.' He nodded his head in approval as he sipped on the large glass of wine we'd poured him. 'One Friday before Easter Sébastian settles the placings for the whole of the summer. Whatever you do, don't miss that date. If you're not there, you're dead.'

'How do we find out?' I'd asked.

'He tells a select group and they tell other people and so on. You need to have enough friends in the market to find out the date. He'll confirm the position of all the people who have been here for years and then he'll work his way through everybody else. If you are last on his list, you won't stand a chance.' Julien drained his glass. 'This is a good new wine,' he said approvingly. I didn't have the heart to tell him he'd tasted it for the last two weeks in succession.

It was already evident that we had competition. Rather than disappear for the winter and reclaim their pitches in the spring, plenty of people were staking a claim to a few metres of dirt every Friday, in the hope that their continued presence would carry some sway in April. And all this despite the fact that the market in the summer was officially full.

In Cucuron we faced a similar problem. The *placier*, Olivier, was a young man with a gentle manner and a desire to help. On each of our visits so far he'd swiftly placed us next to the paella vendor, but it was the end of November and there was no pressure on space. Come summer things would be different. The village had recently been popularised in a Hollywood film and the *étang* around which the market was set was used in one of the signature scenes. Busloads of tourists were expected to descend, and somehow Tanya and I had to cling to our place.

As Julien explained, the only point of us being here now was to try to guarantee the summer. We might sell the odd bottle of wine, but certainly not enough to live. By January, February and March we'd be down to the last of our savings, but we had to look upon it as an investment in the future. Come spring if we were lucky and persuasive, and if we'd been persistently faithful to the markets even on bitterly cold days, then we might be awarded a place for the summer in Lourmarin and Cucuron.

'If you are,' said Julien, 'you will sell so much wine. Enough to keep you alive for the rest of the year, and *ça, ça c'est le but.*'

As Julien said, that may have been the goal, but I couldn't help but wonder what would happen if we didn't get the place.

Little did I know that we would find out sooner rather than later just how difficult it was to get a place in popular markets. A run of special Christmas markets was approaching, and these seasonal events were rumoured to be the second-most profitable time of the year for traders – if, that is, you could get a place.

10

The Cucuron Christmas Market

On 1 December I opened the shutters to come face to face with our landlord, Monsieur Bernardi. His ladder rested against the top of the nearest olive tree and he stood high amid the leaves with his feet wedged against a sturdy branch. He took off his cap and wiped his forehead. '*Salut. On récolte.*' I noticed that he'd spread a broad green net on the ground beneath the trees to catch the falling olives, and amid the lower branches Madame Bernardi was busy stripping away the small green fruit.

On the rare occasions that I'd managed a conversation with Monsieur, the most popular topic had been his olive trees. Nearly every day he could be found in the middle of the grove sitting high on his tractor and spraying or ploughing the field to prevent weeds growing between the trees. He'd informed me at least twice that he didn't expect to harvest until early January, so why was he now halfway up a tree?

Since we had no market that day, we pulled on some clothes and went to help. It seemed like a good opportunity to develop our relationship. Apart from friendly waves as we passed each other, the language barrier and the fact that we only really talked when there was a problem with the house – the gas had stopped working, a tile was loose or the door to the kitchen cupboard had fallen off – meant that a distance had developed between us. Inevitably the problems were seen as our fault. One day the mistral had blown the front door open and then slammed it back shut. When I showed Monsieur the damage, I could read the unspoken thought: Careless English. The olive harvest was a chance to show that we could be helpful too.

Descending from the tree, Monsieur showed me the olives they were picking. Each of them was covered in miniscule black dots. 'The marks are tiny insects. We can't eat the olives this year, and if we don't harvest now, we will lose the entire oil crop.'

Madame showed us how to strip the olives by running our hands firmly down the branches, allowing them to fall into the netting below. In the local garage I'd seen a handheld picking machine for hire that could have been used to speed up the process, but apparently our landlords wanted to do things the traditional way. They even avoided the batons that other farmers used to beat loose olives from branches. And so for the rest of the morning Tanya and I circled the olive trees harvesting away, clambering between the branches and sticking our feet into precarious footholds to reach the most elusive spots. Our necks were forever craned upwards, looking through the pale-green leaves to the clear blue sky.

As they harvested, our landlords joked away with each other: 'No olives for eating this year, boss'; 'We'll do that tree next'; 'Whatever you say, boss'. It was a pleasant way to spend the morning, and given the urgency of the harvest, our help was appreciated. The action of picking was repetitive and conducive to small talk. Madame happily divulged her marinating recipes – 'Keep the green olives in water for eight days, changing the water every day, then add salt, garlic, aromatic herbs and some oil, and leave the flavours to infuse.'

After we finished each tree Monsieur unclasped the net – which was shaped like a barber's cape with a circular hole in the middle, allowing it to fit round the trunk of the tree – and tipped the olives into a container. From each tree our landlords obtained about 18 kilos of olives and it took approximately 6 kilos to make a litre of oil. By mid-morning we'd received a master class in olive farming. Thanks to Monsieur, we could recognise trees that dated back to the severe 1956 frost – most olive trees have one trunk, but the surviving older trees had three or four slim trunks that grew close together to form a circle. This was because over half a century ago the deepest roots of some of the frost-ravaged olive trees managed to push their way back to the surface, clearing away the dead debris and sprouting anew.

We'd also noticed that the trees in front of the house had been neatly cut into shape, whereas the ones behind the *mas* had been allowed to grow wild. I'd assumed that this was for aesthetic reasons, but as we were picking, it became clear that the topiaried trees produced less.

'Next year we will leave these ones to grow and trim the other trees,' said Monsieur. 'Cutting them back is a way of encouraging them to sprout quicker and increase the overall yield.'

On the stroke of twelve Monsieur looked at his watch. '*C'est midi, chef.*'

Madame emerged from the centre of one of the trees, and Monsieur climbed down from the higher branches. The net was left half full on the ground as they rushed off to the table. Even a marauding plague of olive-eating insects wasn't sufficient to interrupt the French lunch.

At 2 p.m. precisely we joined them back in the fields. My fingers were aching from the morning's labour, but our landlords kept up the pace, efficiently stripping branch after branch. Wanting to be as useful as possible, we kept going without complaint.

'Last year we harvested in the snow in January. The olives were covered in ice, and each time we grabbed a new branch a mini blizzard engulfed us,' said Monsieur as we started on yet another tree.

In the afternoon Madame's culinary focus turned to Christmas. There was the local *chocolatier*, whom we must visit, the artisan salmon smoker and the *glacier* (ice-cream maker) outside Ansouis. As I lost myself in the conversation, the pain in my fingers receded. Christmas, I came to appreciate, was Madame's favourite time of year. Her voice was never more expressive than when she talked about the seasonal delicacies – the truffles, the foie gras and of course the thirteen desserts. Tanya and I paused mid-branch. Madame had mentioned the thirteen desserts with such authority we felt we should have known about them. Thankfully we didn't need to encourage her to keep talking – with each olive she picked, she listed one of the desserts that formed the traditional end to the Christmas Eve meal: '*nougat noir, nougat blanc, amandes, raisins secs, fougasse, dattes, oranges, poires, pommes, abricots secs, noisettes, manadarins et figues.*' The desserts represent Jesus and his twelve disciples, and are served with jams, honeys and the local speciality *gibassier* – nicknamed the 'oil pump' because of the amount of olive oil used to bake it.

As Monsieur loaded the final crate full of olives on to the back of his tractor, he encouraged us to go to midnight Mass in one of the local villages. 'The congregation bring the thirteen desserts with them, and then after the service they give the desserts away for free to the poor who have gathered outside.'

'Many thanks for your help,' said Madame Bernardi as she waved goodbye. 'I'll bring you some oil when it's ready.'

Then, almost as an afterthought, Monsieur turned and said, '*Ce n'est pas Madame et Monsieur Bernardi – c'est Rose et Antoine.*'

Christmas felt a long way off, but in Provence, just as in England, it appeared that the preparations began early. 'Jingle Bells' was being piped into supermarkets, and the *poulet rôti* stands had begun advertising specialties such as *pintade*, or guinea fowl, stuffed with truffles. In the first week in December the Christmas lights were strung between the trees in Lourmarin. Silver waves rippled along the avenue of trees, and in the main street each of the shops placed a small tree outside their door. On the windowsills of houses small pots containing a trinity of wheat seedlings appeared. Santa Claus figures scaled the outside of the houses, and even the bell tower was illuminated, with its glittering spire visible for miles around.

The other sign of the season was the lack of people. The roads became ever emptier, and the Parisians deserted their *maisons secondaires*, choosing to remain in the north. Bars stacked away their outside tables and chairs, and slid their glass doors shut, leaving huddled card schools visible through steamy windows. In the countryside, the vines finally surrendered their leaves to the cold, leaving row upon row of skeletal stumps. The comforting smell of burning wood filled the air, a constant reminder to those who had ventured outside to seek shelter. Withered almonds clung to the bare branches of trees, and every night as darkness clasped the hills, the temperature plummeted. Outside, the cockerel lost his voice. Perhaps it was just too cold in the morning for him to crow.

Signs on the lamp-posts began to advertise each village's Christmas market. During December there was one every weekend, and some of the towns, such as Apt, even hosted all-week events. The idea of having a stall for seven days appealed and so we drove to Apt and applied for a place. It was still a week before the market was due to start and so we didn't expect any difficulties. The *police municipale* surprisingly had no responsibility for the event, and we were sent to register at the tourist office. When I asked for a place, the girl behind the desk looked at me as if I were insisting Santa Claus was real. I got the impression that it was all she could do not to laugh.

'The market's been full since October,' she replied, choking on a giggle, 'but I can register you for next year if you want.'

And so began a depressing series of days driving around the villages of the Luberon seeking pitches.. The Christmas markets were organised by committees from the village and so we met the chairmen and -women in their place of work – the SPA supermarket, teashops and bars. Whether it was over a cup of Darjeeling or a *demie pression*, however, the answer was always the same – we were far too late.

In desperation we drove to the bigger cities. Along the Cours Mirabeau in Aix, a series of small wooden huts had been erected with pretty Nordic trellising and a draping of fairy lights. The huts sheltered under a cascade of sparkling decorations, which looped between the plane trees and stretched from Santa's grotto at the top of the Cours Mirabeau to the dancing fountain of water at the base. Trading in these cabins had started at the beginning of December and lasted all month. A number were still boarded up, so we presumed there must be space and enquired about the cost. Romantic notions of spending a cosy month in a log cabin selling warming red wine vanished in a second. The price was €10,000 for twenty-four days. Although the Mirabeau was busy, I just couldn't see how people could recoup their costs. The traders were selling items such as children's toys carved from wood, essential oils and glinting jewellery. Either their sales volume was huge or their profit margin on each item extraordinary.

Most popular of all were the stalls selling *santons*. These small painted figures had come into fashion after the French Revolution, when the government had cracked down on human performances of the nativity story, and so rather than placing a real baby in a crib and leading the village donkey to church, people built up small displays that they could keep in their own home. It must have all begun on a very simple level – donkeys, sheep, wise men and of course the baby Jesus – but at some stage rampant commercialism had taken over. On sale in Aix we could buy painters, miners, vagabonds, fishermen and shepherds.

More incongruously Bethlehem, according to the *santon* makers, was a hotbed of card schools and boules players. I'd also never read about fields of lavender in the Bible, but following closely on the heels of the wise men were women clasping bundles of the stuff. For €100 I could have bought a stable complete with a glowing fireplace – a bit risky with all the hay around – and a flowing stream and turning waterwheel just outside. A couple of Duracell batteries do wonders for the nativity story.

Even if we'd ordered some wine-swilling *santons* to sell, Aix's Christmas market was just too expensive for us. We returned home and continued doing our regular markets. Every Friday morning in Lourmarin we waited for Sébastian at the bottom of the steps, enjoying the illuminations, which had been left on overnight, and hoping that some festive cheer would creep into the policeman's demeanour, but still he refused to speak to us, placing us each week next to the Jehovah's Witnesses, who with the arrival of December had gone into conversion overdrive, barely leaving us alone for a second. Meanwhile every week-end we visited the Christmas markets we were excluded from. We supped on mulled wine and listened to the seasonal music, but they brought us no real pleasure, because we could see the crowds thronging around the stalls, and we knew we'd missed out on our last real chance to make any money until the tourist season began the following year.

Fortunately my gloomy disposition didn't last long. On a Saturday evening in mid-December there was a message waiting for us on the answer machine. It was the organiser of Cucuron's Christmas market. One of the stallholders had pulled out – would we like to stand in tomorrow as last-minute replacements?

The day of the market dawned crisp and clear. It was the type of weather eulogised by the locals – during the course of the morning the sky would take on a rich blue hue, as if every hour an additional lustrous coating of colour had been added. People would breathe the clear air, look up in wonder and make comments like 'Nowhere else in the world' or, 'It's a little corner of paradise.'

We packed up the wine and arrived at Cucuron at 10.30 a.m. – Christmas markets were all-day affairs, lasting from mid-morning till early evening. Instead of a *placier*, the manager of the local supermarket greeted us. As with most markets, however, he was too busy to place us. Around him was a circle of other traders, all trying to cajole their way into a better pitch. It was a fruitless exercise because the market was full, but I'd come to see this sort of behaviour as a kind of ritualistic preening, an almost animalistic protection of territory. If a trader was known for continually causing a fuss about his position, nobody would dare trying to steal even an inch of his pitch.

Eventually the organiser sorted out the disputes and was able to place us. Handing us a welcome croissant and a Santa hat each, he led us along the side of the *étang*, underneath the now bare branches of the plane trees to a small pitch marked with chalk. We were delighted. It was right in the centre of the market, where the flow of people was likely to be at its highest. We were going to be selling red wine under a clear winter sky, instead of rosé under a beating sun, but the experience of being in such a good position was going to provide the best guide yet to our possible fortunes in the summer.

As we set up, it became apparent that the atmosphere was more like a fairground than a market. At the far end of the *étang*, the covers were being taken off a bumper car ride, and just two stalls down from us was an enormous van selling crêpes, *frites* and cuddly toys. Amid these new stalls we could still make out familiar faces: people offering high-quality food – cured hams and foie gras – and others selling artisan gifts – leather hand-bags and wallets. A *ferronnier* had arrived from a neighbouring town and created a small boutique of iron lamps and statues, and there was the usual mixture of jewellery and lavender-scented products, but thankfully not a sign of the Jehovah's Witnesses.

As the morning progressed, people filtered into the market. A steady stream of onlookers passed between the stalls, picking up objects, examining them and replacing them. For some reason people felt freer to approach stalls, tarry and talk to the traders without feeling any pressure to buy. Kids distracted their parents with high-paced escapades next to stalls full of pottery, or pulled them away to look at some trinket or other. People tasted our wine, but during the course of the morning it became clear that most were treating the Christmas market as a day out rather than a shopping trip. I'd thought that the higher price of the stall – €50 rather than the normal €1.50 – implied that the locals would be stocking up for Christmas. Apparently not. I glanced at the other market traders, who shrugged their shoulders at the lack of business. 'It'll pick up in the afternoon,' commented one as he passed.

Tanya and I were alone among the traders in having given little thought to lunch. We'd assumed that the market would continue as normal between twelve and two, but just after midday the crowds began to thin. Our colleagues produced picnic tables and chairs, and began to lay out their spreads: salads in Tupperware bowls, plastic plates full of cold meats and the odd treat bargained for with the other traders – perhaps a small pot of foie gras and some accompanying Sauternes. Completely outclassed by the dining arrangements around us, I sauntered away to get a portion of chips each, and so Tanya and I sat in the sunshine, wearing just light jumpers and our Santa hats, popping greasy ketchup-covered chips into our mouths, while the French around us enjoyed long, and obviously long-thought-out, lunches. There was, however, one distinct advantage to our snack lunch. Most of the traders had assumed they'd be able to get some wine, either from a café or the local cooperative, but we were closer and word soon spread that our wine was very good. Bottle after bottle was purchased and for one hour we were the busiest stand in the market. As Tanya commented, 'We didn't really have time to eat anyway.'

By three the market was reaching its busiest point. The temperature was also dropping rapidly. We put on woolly hats and extra jumpers, clapping our hands together and jiggling from foot to foot to try to keep warm. As darkness fell, my toes started to ache with the cold. In the centre of the *étang*, there was a flicker of light and then a round of applause as a 12-foot Christmas tree was lit in gold. Those traders with the foresight to bring fairy lights, including, surprisingly, us, plugged them into the municipal supply and the alley between the stalls was roped with silver.

A pair of violin-playing clowns performed their way towards us, moving their bodies elegantly in slow motion in time to the music, miming alternatively sadness and happiness as customers rejected or purchased items from stalls. Stranger still were a couple of stilt-walkers, who dressed in red and, wearing insect masks, hissed their way around the market, trapping shoppers in a cage made from their elongated legs. The bumper cars whirred away in the distance, children munched on candyfloss, and as the crowd swelled gradually, we began to work.

Despite the fact that the temperature of the wine was practically Arctic, the French shoppers still performed the familiar rigmarole of sticking their noses deep into the proffered glass and swilling the liquid round before eventually tasting. Whether it was because of the length of the day or the time of year – or that it was practically impossible to say anything about a wine when your fingers threatened to freeze to the glass – we ended up having a number of strange conversations.

If your French is just passable – such as mine – here is a list of concepts never to try to explain. Firstly the difference between English and French law, a discussion that started when I confessed to a university lecturer from Marseille that I used to be a lawyer. As I tried to wrap my limited vocabulary around the distinction between the French Napoleonic code and the English precedent-led jurisprudence, I realised that there was nothing I wouldn't do to sell a bottle of wine. My next customer asked for a restaurant recommendation in the area – somewhere with a spacious inside – and before I knew it I'd used 'Tardis' as a descriptive word, expecting the doctor to have transcended national boundaries in a similar fashion to Coke. I was wrong and my only consolation as I started talking about police boxes with larger-than-average insides was that Tanya was having similar difficulties. Someone had spotted the book she was reading on the market stand – *Salmon Fishing in the Yemen* – and asked what the story was about. Although her French is much better than mine, her exasperation as she attempted to explain the tale of a sheikh who'd dreamed of setting up a salmon fishery in a Yemeni wadi was evident.

Despite the tongue-twisting conversations, for the first time since we'd started trading we began to sell wine in sizeable quantities. Plenty of the early-evening customers had enjoyed long liquid lunches – perhaps another reason for the spate of ridiculous conversations – and were in the mood to stock their cellars for the festive season. Most bought one or two bottles, but some customers took cases. All the activity around the stall temporarily allowed us to forget the biting cold.

By seven the last stragglers were leaving the market and we were packing our remaining stock back into boxes. We'd sold just over fifty bottles of wine in a day, which made me think that with the right pitch in the summer markets we could probably hit my targets. As I was counting the €50 notes in my money belt, the organiser of the event walked by. Without even considering my actions, I whipped one of the remaining bottles of wine from the stall and proffered it to him. '*Joyeux Noël*,' I called.

Rather than look grateful, he took a couple of steps backwards, glanced around and held both hands up to ward off the bottle. '*C'est pas necessaire,*' he stumbled.

'*Mais c'est un cadeau de Noël,*' I pressed.

He shook his head and kept his hands raised. 'I'm also in charge of the night markets in the summer and I've already had two wine sellers apply today. The others will think you're trying to bribe your way in.'

He shuffled virtuously away, as Tanya and I quickly came to terms with two conflicting thoughts – the opportunity to sell wine in the night markets, and the fact that they were already full of vignerons.

11

Les Truffes and the Christmas Capon

All December Tanya and I had been taking an unusual interest in mushrooms and in particular the black diamonds of Provence – truffles. The reason? A special guest was coming to stay for the Christmas period and we didn't want to disappoint him with our lack of knowledge or recipe ideas.

Earlier in the month we'd found ourselves in L'Isle-sur-la-Sorgue trading next to a mushroom seller, Paul. Whereas most of the vendors go to extraordinary lengths to make their stall look pretty, Paul had covered his tables with some rough sacking and stacked it with wooden boxes. Digging out some plastic punnets, he put a handful of different mushrooms in each. It was all done in a seemingly haphazard manner, but the lack of attention to detail was actually quite deliberate. Paul wanted his customers to know that he'd arrived at the market fresh from the hills. He had no time for the fripperies and frills of the other traders; in fact he didn't even have time to wipe the mud from his crop.

While we'd stood scarcely selling a bottle of wine, the French had formed a crowd around his stall. They stuck their noses into the mushrooms and took great sniffs. They broke chunks from the cap and rubbed them between their fingers as they questioned Paul about his hunting grounds. Selling just a single punnet of mushrooms required more explanation as to provenance and taste than a bottle of wine.

In fact it was surprising he sold any at all. One woman was carefully sniffing a punnet when Paul interrupted her. 'You've got to be careful with those. They've got a poisonous relative. A year ago an old woman went missing. Her friends didn't know what had happened: they called her family, they went to the police, and eventually a couple of months later one of them found her in the anti-poison unit of the hospital. She'd been picking mushrooms all her life, but she'd made just one mistake.'

Perhaps such tales were meant to discourage amateur hunters and engender confidence in Paul. He was certainly full of stories about the dangers of mushroom picking, explaining to another customer how light and temperature changed the colour of the top of poisonous and non-poisonous mushrooms in the same way. Mushrooms growing side by side were subject to the same atmospheric conditions and often looked the same as a result. The secret was to always look at the underside of the cap; if you forgot just once, it could be the end of a career, and possibly a life. Then there were some immutable laws such as never pick *girolles*, or chanterelles, near an olive tree – they might appear identical, even under the cap, but in fact any mushrooms looking like *girolles* and growing close to olive trees are a poisonous relative of the friendly mushroom that people happily scattered on their steaks.

Had I been a customer, the effect of all this idle chat would have scared me back to the supermarket, but it had the opposite effect on the crowd in the market. The throng around the stall barely let up all morning. Paul was offering an opportunity to dance with death and the Provençaux were seemingly all eager for a waltz. As a sales technique, it was surprisingly effective: the stories created a sense of awe and separated the mushrooms from just an ordinary foodstuff. 'Look what I've brought home from the market, dear. We'll mix up a nice omelette, have a lie down after lunch and then see what happens. If we're still alive this evening, perhaps we will go for a nice walk before a risotto supper.'

During the few pauses in Paul's trade we quizzed him on the various varieties he was selling: *trompettes-de-la-mort*, black but not as deadly as the name suggested; *pieds bleus*, which when fresh had an almost translucent colour, like a passing cloud caught by sunshine; *grisets*, which were orange, earthy and unremarkable; and *lactaires délicieux*, which were large and ugly with blue and red veins crisscrossing the surface, the OAP of the mushroom world. Mid-morning Paul picked up one of these *lactaires* and cut the stem, showing us how they bled. Wiping the juice on his arm, it suddenly looked like he'd been in a knife fight. 'They're really not very nice, but the locals like them. They boil them in water with a little vinegar, soak them in olive oil and eat them with an aperitif.' We'd nodded and crossed this particular mushroom off the list for our Christmas visitor.

'It's a pity the season will be largely over when your friend arrives.' Paul advised, 'Mushrooms depend on rain, the moon and a minimum temperature of twelve degrees. This year has been excellent, but with the colder weather it's now time for truffles. They're not poisonous, but they can be equally as dangerous,' he'd finished enigmatically as he began to stack away his empty crates.

We served some customers a little wine and by the time we'd turned round to find out more, he'd disappeared.

Over the next few weeks the newspapers were full of stories about truffles. Diagrams explained how they grew at the base of oak or ash trees and were connected by a thread as fine as a strand of silk to the roots of the trees. Cut the thread and the truffle would die. Wild truffles were the most prized, but local landowners planted fields of suitable oaks to increase their chances of a find. Even so, the eventual crop was wildly unpredictable and dependent on the weather and myriad other factors, allowing the truffle to retain its mystique and of course its outrageous pricetag.

Newspaper article after article speculated on the possible price per kilo. There were also stories of cross-border wars, as mayors near Italy banned cars with foreign number plates from their villages. Restaurateurs from across the border were apparently sending midnight scavenging parties into France, ripping up the land in their desperation to find truffles.

Meanwhile all our local restaurants began posting truffle-inspired offerings. The price for a seven-course *dégustation*, or tasting, menu started at around €70, but in the more expensive restaurants this rose to nearly €200. It seemed that each of the local chefs was trying to outdo the others with a new and ingenious use of this ingredient, which was somehow supposed to imbue food with semi-magical qualities. Truffles could be used in dishes as commonplace as omelettes and as strange as sorbets. In fact there seemed no limit to their virtues, particularly since the price of every dish could automatically be trebled.

In the village, not being able to converse about the predicted volume of the truffle harvest was a badge of dishonour akin to being ignorant of Arsenal's fortunes if you lived in Highbury. No longer did people pray for clear skies and sunny days; instead they scanned the paper for signs of rain, hoping that the weather would deliver a bumper crop and bring this luxury foodstuff within range of more modest purses. Interestingly no one could quite agree on exactly what weather was needed. Some said the average temperature for the first few weeks in December was important, while others talked about humidity and the variation between daytime and night-time temperatures, others still claimed the crop was dependent on the amount of rainfall the previous spring.

Everyone, it seemed, was catching the bug – adverts for courses designed to teach dogs how to hunt for truffles were posted in local *tabacs* and within days they were oversubscribed. Fat, faithful Labradors, which had lolled in the shade all summer, were suddenly being pressed into action, and poodles used to being preened in the *coiffure chien* had to compete with malodorous pigs in the race to find these black diamonds. Perhaps the quiet state of the pre-Christmas roads could be ascribed to the fact that everybody was in the hills truffle-hunting. There was certainly a lot less dog *merde* on the pavements.

Eventually curiosity overcame Tanya and myself. We'd never even seen a truffle, let alone tasted one, and so we took ourselves off to the biggest truffle market in the area – Carpentras. We arrived mid-morning in the centre of a sprawling market. The stands were full of €1 Christmas toys and cheap clothes, but we convinced ourselves we'd yet to reach the centre. I was expecting a square full of vendors selling truffles, piled high on top of each other and perhaps an auctioneer to keep the buyers from the Parisian restaurants in check. Given their notorious odour, it was surprising that we couldn't smell the truffles. In Uzès during the previous summer, the whole town had whiffed of garlic during the Fête d'Ail, so Carpentras should have been giving off an earthy aroma.

Finally we gave up and asked directions. The truffle market, we were told, took place outside the Café de l'Univers on the outskirts of town. Hadn't we seen the opening ceremony at the end of November? The mayor had cut a ribbon and the first truffles had been priced at €300 a kilo. Despite its notoriety, when we reached the café, there were just the normal rows of seats and an empty pavement. The waiter shrugged his shoulders. 'Some days they come, some days they don't. It depends whether they've anything to sell. They call the best buyers on their mobiles to let them know.'

We ordered a drink and waited. By the third espresso we'd worked ourselves into a frenzy of anticipation. When the vendors arrived, we'd negotiate hard and leave with a bargain. But how would we recognise them before the other customers? It was a €1 million business, so would the truffle kings purr into town in sleek Mercedes? Then again the location of the market – on a large ring road – suggested speedy getaways from prying eyes were a priority, so perhaps we wouldn't even recognise a vendor if we saw one. As the caffeine buzz faded and the pavement remained empty, the truth became obvious – there were going to be no truffles today.

Our disappointment was short-lived. Back in Lourmarin, an enormous banner had been unfurled. The market on the final Friday before Christmas was dedicated to truffles. It was an appropriate day for our Christmas guests to be arriving – Peter Tate and his wife, Jenny. The idea was to spend a couple of nights at our house before heading over to Tanya's sister's flat in Montpellier for Christmas lunch. But as Peter was fond of saying, 'all firm plans need a little latitude', and with Peter around they usually did.

We weren't even sure whether we would be able to afford to buy a truffle in a more touristy market such as Lourmarin, but we spent the next few days researching recipes. The traditional dish on Christmas Day in France is a large rooster called a capon and our idea was to use some truffle to enhance the flavour of the bird. One friendly local chef suggested stuffing shavings of truffle under the skin before roasting, but another disagreed, claiming this was an extravagant waste of a truffle, and said our best option was to treat the truffle like a piece of Parmesan cheese and grate it over the meat once roasted. By now we were hooked: the constant press references, the debates in the village and the truffle menus at restaurants had all convinced us that this was a foodstuff we couldn't miss out on.

The morning of the truffle market was a bright, clear December day. Tanya and I were awarded our usual pitch opposite the Jehovah's Witnesses, but we noticed that several other traders were turned away. They'd demanded spaces three or four times as big as ours, but it was at least a sign that we were slowly moving up the pecking order. For the first time in months Lourmarin Market was full. Many of the summer vendors had returned for just this one market, and there were various squabbles with the traders who'd quietly expanded to fill space that didn't belong to them. There were also one-off traders trying their hand at roasting chestnuts or selling satsumas from Corsica, which were so fresh they came in bunches still clustered on a branch.

Sébastian scurried around trying to resolve the disputes and, in another sign that our relationship was improving, even managed to speak to us. 'Your stall is twice the price today – it's a truffle market; everything is expensive.' I was so stunned at being addressed I didn't realise that he was joking.

The truffle vendors set up outside the hotel of Lourmarin's Michelin-starred chef, Edouard Loubet. But one crucial thing was missing – the black diamonds. Instead there were truffle-infused oils and truffle-based spirits and even ready-made truffle omelettes. But come mid-morning a couple of battered vans parked up. The occupants set up small tables by the rear doors, marked a price per kilo on a piece of cardboard and placed what looked like a jar of muddy golf balls in front of them. Interestingly truffle vendors could seemingly arrive whenever they wanted. Perhaps no one dared to gainsay them, not even the fearsome Sébastian. There would presumably have been a near riot had the Lourmarinois been denied their favourite seasonal delicacy.

These new vendors had taken great care to look as downtrodden as possible. Despite the price of their merchandise, their clothes were soiled and their vans falling apart. They were apparently too poor even to afford watches. Of course it was a charade – if they managed to sell all their truffles, they would return home with thousands of euros. It was just best the taxman didn't realise.

We recognised one of the local vignerons stacking his wine

into the back of one of the truffle trader's vans. Box after box was shunted to the depths of the van. Once the vigneron had finished loading, he accepted a small plastic bag containing two truffles. He winked at us. 'They're too expensive to buy, but one can always barter,' he commented. '*Elles sont magnifiques.*'

Tanya sent me across to check out the prices. The cheapest truffles on offer were €400 a kilo, which worked out at roughly €75 a truffle. Even though we'd decided to purchase one, I faced an additional problem. One truffle on each stand was cut in half, displaying a dark interior crisscrossed with white veins. From examining the truffles, an experienced purchaser could tell whether they were local or not. The danger for the inexperienced purchaser – such as myself – was that a disreputable vendor could sell me a Chinese truffle. These impostors looked almost identical to the native Provençal truffle, but there was one crucial difference: when cooked, they were almost flavourless. The advice from all the locals I'd spoken to about our prospective purchase was to buy from some of the higher-priced dealers, thus lessening the chance of being ripped off, and so I moved along to a dealer selling at €500 a kilo.

I held one of the truffles to my nose and sniffed. The effect was explosive. A rich, overpowering odour swept through my nostrils and across my brain, making me feel almost dizzy. The smell of this gastronomic marvel, this ingredient prized above all others, can only be described as revolting. Quite what possessed the first human being to take a chance and have a nibble on a truffle is beyond me. Presumably he was amply rewarded for his heroism and died a very rich man. I quickly replaced the truffle and began to count out some notes, reassuring myself that the little black diamond would reveal its true value when sprinkled on our food.

Just as I was on the verge of paying, I heard a cry from across the market – 'Marvellous, absolutely marvellous.' Turning back to our stall, I saw that Tanya had disappeared into the mass of arms and shopping bags that was Peter Tate, fresh from the airport.

I am not sure which took precedence – Peter's love of food or his love of France. For two summers we'd travelled with him and explored the far reaches of what I considered palatable food – *foie gras de tête de veau* was my personal nadir – but to Peter every restaurant promised the joy of a new discovery. I often wondered whether he would be the same in another country. Would bowls of pasta, creamy risottos and sautéed veal bring quite the level of excitement? I doubted it – there was something about France and Provence in particular that fitted Peter's personality. His incessant curiosity about food and wine matched that of the French, and his love of and pride in the countryside were enough to make him an honorary Provençal. Even the little French he did speak was pronounced with the local accent – '*vent*' sounded like '*ving*'.

Behind Peter, I could see his pretty wife, Jenny. She wore her hair long like a schoolgirl and had a peaceful, almost hippy air to her that perfectly set off Peter's at times overenthusiastic nature. While Peter was known for his boisterousness at dinner parties, Jenny had the unfortunate habit of falling asleep. It could happen mid-sentence. She'd be chatting about her latest hobby, beekeeping, and – clunk – her head would hit the table. On holiday she would often disappear for whole afternoons, find herself a shady spot, roll out a mat and become so involved in studying the flora and fauna that she missed meals. With their divergent natures Peter and Jenny had developed the perfect way of living together, spending plenty of time apart and then taking an indulgent interest in each other when they were together.

After several minutes of hugs and kisses, many shouts of 'Marvellous' and plenty of kind comments about how the Provençal lifestyle was suiting Tanya and myself, Peter took us on a tour of the impressive array of shopping bags he'd collected since stepping off the plane barely two hours before. Nothing had been left to chance. An eclectic range of pastes and pestos were tied together by a dainty red ribbon, the muddy green hair of a bunch of carrots poked from a plastic bag full of vegetables, and a box of twenty-four chocolates ranging in flavour from curry to a more commonplace praline was clamped under one arm, but the true excitement lay in a large brown bag full of 'smellies'.

'Look at this, and this,' Peter giggled as he piled an assortment of cheeses on to the kerb. 'Stick your finger in that and have a taste,' he said to Tanya, proffering a liquid goat's cheese. 'And look at this Brie – it's got shavings of truffles in it.' He slapped my hand as I tried to break off the nose.

Just as we thought we'd reached the bottom of the bag, Peter produced a small Tupperware pot. Snapping off the lid, he began unwrapping the contents from a wet cloth. 'There we are, Provence's finest truffle.' He passed the dirty ball of mud under all our noses, sending the pungent swoon-inducing odour straight to our heads. 'Isn't she marvellous?'

I nodded enthusiastically and then signalled apologetically to the trader I'd been on the point of purchasing a truffle from.

For the next couple of days we showed Peter and Jenny our region, visiting the ancient château of the Marquis de Sade in Lacoste, the old Roman bridge – the Pont Julien – on the plains below Bonnieux, enjoying a drink and a dose of vertigo on the terrace of the Hôtel la Bastide in Gordes and soaking up the season – the cold plumes of breath and the still mists lying over bare vines first thing in the morning, the clarity of the sky framed in the branches of leafless plane trees, twilight in a café with a pastis and then the plunging cold and ensuing starlit night.

Ever present in our conversations was the truffle and the growing sense of anticipation as to just how it would taste. It was as if all cooking up to this point hadn't existed, as if everything we had ever tasted was in black and white and our palates were about to switch to colour. Peter watched over the truffle like a military secret, checking its position every couple of hours and moving its location within the kitchen several times a day. The care it received was of a level rarely afforded to a newborn child. Even though removing the wet cloth from around the truffle was as malodorous an experience as changing a nappy, Peter, as instructed by the vendor, tenderly performed the ritual every morning and night. By the time Christmas Day arrived and we had to travel to Tanya sister's, Claire's, for lunch, I was surprised the truffle was not afforded the luxury of a seatbelt.

Claire's children couldn't have been less interested in the culinary miracle about to be performed in their kitchen. They'd received an old rocking horse for Christmas and by the time lunch was ready they'd already covered thousands of imaginary furlongs. Tristan, Claire's little two-year-old boy, chose this moment to begin capering around naked wearing only a pirate hat. Rosie, his elder sister, tried to calm him, and then, deciding the game looked like too much fun, pretended to be a princess imprisoned by aforesaid gallivanting naked pirate.

The food was passed around the table – slices of succulent capon, stuffing, gravy, Brussels sprouts and parsnips (procured with great difficulty because the French insisted that they were fit only for feeding to cows) and roast potatoes – but all efforts were focused on getting the children to calm down. Eventually crackers were pulled and we began to eat.

Nearly half my plate had disappeared by the time Peter remembered. 'Christ,' he shouted, taking a great glug of wine and disappearing to the kitchen. With all the distractions we'd forgotten the key ingredient. Moments later Peter reappeared with a chef's hat on his head, a cheese grater and the precious truffle. With great ceremony he circled the table shaving thin black slices over everyone's plate. It seemed rude to start before Peter sat back down and so we all waited, looking at our plates with reverence, wondering just what alchemy this ingredient, which cost €500 a kilo, could be working. Already there was the familiar earthy smell, but somehow it wove itself into the aroma of the food, creating a sense of depth and luxury.

'Right, here goes,' said Peter, tucking into a piece of meat, liberally scattered with the curled shavings of the grated truffle. A big smile spread across his face. 'Fantastic.'

For me, the experience was nowhere near as good. To begin with I imagined that all the flavours in my food had been mysteriously uplifted, as if the capon tasted like the best I'd ever eaten and the gravy was the richest sauce ever prepared, but the more I ate, the more I began to doubt. In fact the only effect the truffle seemed to have had on my food was to make it taste gritty. Pieces of the black diamond grated on my gums and stuck between my teeth. Yet all around the table people were making positive noises about the truffle.

We cleared away the plates, topped up our glasses with red wine, laid out some cheeses for dessert and just gradually the truth began to emerge.

'It wasn't quite how I imagined it.'

'The smell was there, and the food richer.'

'Yes, but not that much richer.'

Perhaps Peter had fallen prey to a local conman and bought a Chinese truffle, I reflected.

'Did anyone else find it gritty?'

'Yes. At times it reminded me of eating earth.'

At this point a smile started in Peter's eyes and spread across his face, until the whole table was silent, watching him chuckling quietly to himself. 'Damn it,' he said, cutting himself a slice of truffle-infused Brie. 'I did everything they told me – wrapped it in a wet cloth, allowed it to breathe for a couple of minutes each day, put up with the stench – and I had to go and forget just one thing.'

'What?'

Silence. Peter was always one for the dramatic pause. Looking around the table, he finally confessed with a laugh that made the china tremor, 'To wash it.'

It took a moment for the truth to become apparent. I visualised the dirty great golf balls I'd seen in the market and the diagrams of the truffles buried deep underground, attached by their fine cords to the oaks.

'So we've all just been eating Christmas lunch dressed with grated mud?'

Peter nodded, still laughing. 'But it was still marvellous, absolutely marvellous.'

Thankfully the Tates were not due back in England until New Year and we had the time before Peter's departure to wash the truffle and appreciate its delights. In the days following Christmas we enjoyed a cabaret of extravagantly rich cooking that would have made Rose, our landlady, proud – omelettes, risottos and foie gras all infused with truffle.

A day before Peter's departure we met Paul, the mushroom seller, again in a small market in Cheval Blanc, just outside Cavaillon. Instead of mushrooms he stood behind a diminishing pile of truffles. Peter picked one up and, his sense of smell having been suitably acclimatised by his close relationship with the Christmas truffle, took a deep sniff. A look of pleasure crossed his face as he imagined the feast that he could conjure. 'Do you think we could get one past customs?' he asked Jenny plaintively.

As the Tates debated how much more they could squeeze into their suitcase and how they would ever get the smell out of their clothes, we asked Paul about his pre-Christmas warning – that truffles were as dangerous as other mushrooms.

'It's about time somebody told you. The locals here are a bit crazy. They do silly things. They are jealous of the money that foreigners – not just the English, but anyone who wasn't born in their village – bring to the region. Five years ago I bought a puppy, and when it was still suckling I rubbed truffles on the teat of its mother.' He paused to check that we were understanding his French.

We nodded – wondering what this could possibly have to do with the mindset of the locals.

'This is the best way to train a truffle dog,' Paul continued. 'When they grow up, they associate the smell with their mother and they become champion trufflers. And this is what happened with my dog. We hunted for wild truffles and we became very successful, too successful. One morning a year ago I woke up and found that my dog was dead. Poisoned by a piece of con-taminated meat thrown over the fence.'

'That's dreadful,' said Tanya.

'That's the locals. They resent outsiders – you should be care-ful.'

The following morning as Jenny was busy backing the hire car out of the driveway, Peter removed his glasses case from his breast pocket. Winking conspiratorially at Tanya and myself, he snapped the lid open. Inside, neatly sliced in half, was a truffle. 'It's airproof,' he said, proudly tapping the container. 'Just don't tell Jenny.'

As we waved farewell and the Tates bounced off down the track, Tanya turned to me. 'If I can smell it from here, I'm sure the sniffer dogs won't have any trouble.'

For a while we forgot about Paul's warning. Since moving into our apartment, we'd been welcomed by everyone locally. Admittedly Sébastian, the Lourmarin *placier*, was cold towards us and once or twice some of the other traders had made life difficult – refusing to move their van, or taking an exaggerated length of time to load away, so that we were blocked in the market – but nothing had happened that made us feel on edge or suspect that there was any real antipathy towards foreigners in the Luberon.

12

Life in the Luberon

With the departure of Peter and Jenny we began planning for the year ahead. Whenever we talked about the months to come, the adjective that occurred most in conversation was 'interesting'. We knew that the rest of the winter was going to be tough, the weather was likely to be bitter and the markets deserted. As the waitress in the café had memorably put it a few months ago, we would 'be living on love and cold water'. Spring would bring the first trickle of tourists and the start of the competition for places in the markets. If we didn't manage to secure good pitches in the major tourist markets by May, then our first year in business would most likely be our last. If we did, then the excitement would begin – was it possible to make a living selling rosé in the markets?

We were both desperate to succeed. We loved our life in Provence, and the longer we were abroad, the more distant life in London seemed. It was strange to think that we'd once accepted as norms the crush of the commute and the sterility of office life. Although it had taken a while, we'd finally adjusted to the calm pace of country living, the empty roads, the quiet supermarkets and leisurely early-evening drinks. We'd slowed down and the prospect of returning to a hectic life of salaried servitude was increasingly unappealing, and yet with the tenuous nature of our business the possibility always hung over us.

One other worry dominated our conversations in January – over the last two years we'd delayed having a family, always preferring to wait until we were finally settled. Was now the right time? We felt at home in Lourmarin. There was wide-spread incredulity that we hadn't fled back to England with all the other tourists, and there was a welcome acceptance at local events such as the reopening of the Café l'Ormeau. The exterior remained the same – beige chairs with a green awning – but the inside had been completely revamped. To celebrate, the owner, Martine, held a Brazilian evening, and as we searched for a table, it surprised me how many people stopped to talk to us – French clients we'd sold wine to in the market, shop owners, staff from the other bars, even people we'd met walking out in the country-side. With half the summertime population of the village in Paris and half of the remaining permanent residents skiing, we were members of a small and privileged club.

Despite this sense of belonging, finally deciding to try to have a baby wasn't a simple decision. While one of us could easily man the stand at the moment, in the summer this wouldn't be the case. There was no such thing as maternity leave for traders and Tanya would have to move from market to market in the sweltering sun. In order to make enough money to keep us in France, we would need to do as many as six markets a week. Hard work for anyone, let alone if you're pregnant. On the other hand it could easily take us more than six months to conceive, so why delay?

'What else is there to do in the Luberon in winter?' joked Tanya.

The answer, rather surprisingly, was plenty. The remaining inhabitants wanted to celebrate the fact that while others had fled they'd remained steadfast to see out the dark January days.

One of our best clients from the market, Claude – an elderly gentleman from Cucuron, who was rarely seen without a jacket

and tie, and a copy of *Le Figaro* under his arm – started inviting us out for lunch. Since he'd spent most of his working life
in Paris, he was less reserved with strangers than most of the
population of the village. He'd approached us before Christmas,
tasted our various wines and purchased a half-bottle of Rupert
Birch's Brillane. Once he'd ascertained that we sold good wines
at a reasonable price, he began to talk to us about his vinous
experiences. Then, perhaps because he was a little lonely, he
took us to local restaurants, together with other young people
he felt we might be interested in meeting – from sommeliers
to estate agents. It was almost as if he'd taken a philanthropic
interest in seeing us properly assimilated into French life. Most
of the meals were pleasant occasions and a good opportunity to
practise our French, but one evening went particularly badly
– when we dined together with some friends of Claude's from
Aix-en-Provence.

In the Luberon hierarchy of disdain for foreigners the Aixois,
always pronounced with a globule of phlegm in the back of the
throat, came a close second to the Parisians. In fact, as one market
trader pointed out, the Aixois devoted their lives to being more
Parisian than the Parisians, so this assessment was probably rather
unfair on the Parisians. Take clothing, for example – despite
being one of the fashion capitals of the world, Parisians remain
extremely conservative dressers, as if the last thing they want is
to be noticed. Among the Aixois, this dismissal of individualism
has reached its apogee. Major fashion trends completely bypass
the city – instead the Aixois devote their wardrobes to classic
cuts. To have a lapel askew or a tie poorly knotted is social
suicide and invites a year in a dinner-party-free wilderness, a
fearsome punishment for an Aixois, because theirs is a community that thrives on pseudo-intellectual conversations over
late-night coffees.

The Aixois were already at our table when we arrived. They
were a tight-lipped husband and wife team who I guessed were

in their early forties. They rose, displayed their immaculately pressed clothes and lightly shook our hands. Claude explained, in his charming way, that we were experts on wine and we began talking about the region's rosés. At this stage there was still the hope of an enjoyable evening lingering around the table. Perhaps the Aixois would liven up once they had a drink. I should really have known better – a glass of red and a glass of white is considered a boozy evening in Aix.

Dining with the Aixois was a tiring experience. Just as their dress had to be immaculate, so did the food. When my *steak tartare* arrived – finely minced pieces of filet steak with onions, gherkins and chopped anchovies around the outside of the plate and half a raw egg sitting proudly atop the meat – there was a chorus of tutting. '*Ce n'est pas correct.*'

I happily began to mix the various ingredients, but the Aixois shook their heads.

The husband explained, 'In a proper restaurant it would be prepared in front of you. The steak should be chopped by hand, never minced. The waiter should then mix the onions, capers, gherkins and the yolk of the egg, together with two whole anchovies.'

His wife took over. At least discussing the ingredients had provoked an outbreak of bonhomie between them. 'The anchovies should be crushed with a fork. Then add two spoons of French mustard, two spoons of Worcester sauce and two spoons of ketchup.'

The husband continued, getting more excited about the perfect *tartare* than any subject we'd discussed so far. 'Then a dash of Tabasco, a shot of Cognac, eighteen twists of the pepper grinder and fifteen of salt. Add the steak and beat together. Serve with a green salad or toast. And *voilà*.'

I nodded as the lesson continued, fighting the urge to say that I quite enjoyed the do-it-yourself approach. Throughout supper both Tanya and I had tried hard with our French, but the Aixois reduced us to performing clowns, smiling patronisingly when our grammar was correct and shaking their heads vigorously at our errors. At times they whispered between themselves, trying to work out the provenance of our strange accents – obviously English but with a strange in-built patois. After the main course was finished, Claude enlightened them by explaining we were working in the local markets.

It was as if he'd suddenly laced their food with poison. 'You really work in the markets?' It was an accusation rather than a question.

Plates were pushed away, the mineral water – of which they drank plenty – froze into jagged icicles of horror around their lips, and the occasional spiked word broke free and speared towards us. During the following uncomfortable hour I tried to rationalise the psyche behind such behaviour. It seemed to me that the Aixois saw themselves at the pinnacle of French society. They were the evolutionary winners, the French super-breed, entitled to treat even a Parisian with haughty disregard. Aix had everything that Paris had – a thriving intelligentsia, beautiful streets, a café society – and it also had sunshine. Any Parisian with half a brain, they thought, should quit the capital and join their self-appointed elite in the south. Of course what the Aixois didn't realise was that such arrogance was as unbearable to the outside world as sitting round a table with a couple of rosé vendors was to them.

Ironically it was our job as market traders – not a profession that would open many doors in London – which smoothed our path into expat society. Countless clubs and organisations existed for the British to meet other British people abroad. But to admit firstly that you wanted to meet other English speakers – after all, wasn't the point of buying a house in France to change lifestyles and integrate with the locals? – and secondly that you needed a club to help make friends was just not done. Instead, through a complex web of connections an English dinner-party circuit had emerged in the Luberon. People three or four times removed from the host found themselves invited because their friends were the right type of people. Of course this network was excellent if you were on the inside, but terribly frustrating for those on the outside.

The solution was our market stall. After our first couple of months most of the English in the local villages had visited us and at times on a market morning our stand became an unofficial meeting place. We offered a free half-glass of wine and the opportunity to bump into other people who spoke the same language. And as our clients were discussing how many hectares they'd bought and the relative merits of an infinity pool versus an 'authentic' basin, they began inviting each other to supper. To avoid being rude, we were generally asked along as well.

These suppers were often quite parochial affairs. Tanya and I were always the youngest by at least twenty years and the only people to be working, as opposed to enjoying a wine-flushed retirement. Conversation centred around which Michelin chef had moved where, makes of garden furniture and the tyranny of France's new wealth tax, which was always chipping away at their retirement funds. Since our budget for eating out extended to the *plat du jour* at the local café, our garden furniture was plastic and borrowed from the landlord, and paying the wealth tax was a dream – we would have to have the most successful rosé business in France for our profits to reach such stratospheric levels – we had little to add to the conversation.

Nevertheless, observing our countrymen abroad was an interesting social study. Dinner parties in England usually consist of three courses – starter, main course and dessert – with the hostess bashfully admitting afterwards that two out of the three had come from M&S. In France things were different. The expats apparently felt an undeniable urge to out-French the French. And in a country in love with gastronomy this required some serious culinary feats. Usually there were six courses, sometimes

seven. Almost inevitably, as if they formed part of the ten com-
mandments of polite entertaining, a kind of ever-present Holy
Trinity, we were offered an *amuse-bouche*, a chilled soup and
a seasonal risotto. Hosts were allowed to freestyle a little after
this, but the rule seemed to be that the main course must have
Provençal roots. *Daube*, or stew, *légumes farcies*, or stuffed vegetables, and aioli were all acceptable – as if by showing skill in
cooking the local food the hosts could demonstrate how long
they had lived in the region and how well integrated they were.
In this respect inviting a token French couple was also a good
ploy. The host or hostess could then parade them like a birthday
badge – except in place of '60 today' the intended message was
'I'm so good at French I have French friends.'

The main course would always be followed by a simple green
salad and then cheese and a dessert. At about the time the Brie
was doing the rounds things usually got interesting. Up until this
point all the people round the table would have been involved
in a complex game of charades. Since they barely knew each
other, and because admitting to doing nothing in the sun might
be considered lazy, they would all have claimed some sort of
occupation – the more Provençal and artistic, the better. During
the various dinner parties we attended we met potters, painters
and jewellery makers, who for nearly two hours managed to
continue the pretence that they made a living from their craft.

Then, and it took just one guest, somebody would suffer a
crisis of confidence. Perhaps an unpleasant comment set them
off, perhaps glazing pots didn't do it for their ego after all; in
any event once the mask slipped, the rest of the table followed
like dominoes.

'Of course, when I was global head of securities at DPT, I
used to deal with millions on a daily basis.'

'Oh, you were at DPT. Did you know Bob Zakowski?'

'Used to be Bob's boss. Where were you?'

And in that one second of emotional frailty, the dream of

eking a living making bracelets vanished and the one-upmanship of the City of London came flooding into the room. At moments like this, sitting round a table with various fifty-year-olds who'd made millions and yet still couldn't let go, I was glad that I'd left the law when I was relatively young. Following an espresso – and some exquisite accompanying chocolates – Tanya and I usually made our excuses and left. After all, in true French fashion, once the coffee had cleansed the palate, no wine was served.

In January it was perfectly possible to attend one such dinner party a week and I found myself dreading spring, when apparently the social season really got into full swing. In the busy buzz of metropolitan London it was always easy to find reasons to avoid events – theatre tickets, family birthdays, football matches – the list was comfortingly long, but in the quiet of the Luberon we often found ourselves fumbling for excuses as the host-to-be looked plaintively at us. If only I could have been honest and explained that I was looking forward to having a meal with my wife after working in a market, but for some reason such truths are considered rude.

There was also another problem. However social our lives became, we realised that we would always be outsiders. Our age separated us from the expat community and our nationality from possible contemporaries. Some random occurrences did at least provide encouragement that we would eventually find a group of friends. By accident we met a forest ranger when we were out walking and he invited us for a cup of tea – a rare idea for the French, who are much more reticent about letting people into their houses than the English. He turned out to be the same age as us, lived no more than fifteen minutes' walk away and after our first meeting was always asking us to hear local bands perform. Tanya's upbeat attitude towards socialising also somewhat mitigated my reclusive tendencies, and we continued to attend the expat dinners and gradually the excessive formality and overt Frenchness began to seem less strange.

Then, late in January, with the debate about whether to have a baby still ongoing, there was an unsettling outbreak of the local madness that Paul, the mushroom seller, had warned us about. Arriving home after a market, our landlords, Rose and Antoine, waved our car to a stop.

'Did you hear anything last night?'

Tanya and I shook our heads. 'Why?'

'Thieves came and stole fifteen olive trees. They dug them up as we slept and loaded them on to the back of a van. The police have been, but what can they do?'

I could see that Antoine was struggling with his emotions. He spent day after day tending to his trees, clipping their branches, weeding the soil around them and spraying them against blight. It's often said that good vignerons know each individual vine, a claim that I'd never believed, considering that the number of vines in a small vineyard runs into the thousands, but I am sure that Antoine knew each of his hundred or so olive trees. Many were about the same age as him and he'd watched them grow and tended them over the years. And his reward? Some idiots looking for a quick profit had dug them up.

The difficult truth was that we lived in an agricultural area that had once been among the poorest in the country. Its beauty lured people from throughout France and across the world, and as property prices rose, locals found it impossible to afford houses. Every ramshackle old *mas* nestling in the *maquis* had been dusted off and sold for an enormous price and was now occupied for a fraction of the year. The majority of people benefited from the tourism boom, but a tiny minority resented change and now perpetuated petty crime against those perceived to be responsible – not just foreigners, but anyone who wasn't born in the local villages.

Our own experience of this madness came a week later, when we woke up one morning in late January to find rubbish strewn across our driveway. Our bin had been overturned and newspapers, old vegetables, cereal cartons and wine bottles were scattered in an ugly pastiche outside the front door. My first thought was that a wild dog or even a wild boar had got at the bins, but then I looked at Peter's car.

Ugly green paint was sprayed across the bonnet and the graffiti artist had even found time to write us a message: 'Anglish you our filthee.' Picking up the black bag that had contained our rubbish, I saw that it had been slit open by a knife, rather than raked apart by claws. As we were clearing up, we both calmly accepted what had happened. It was as if we were looking at events on a TV screen and that the drama depicted couldn't really hurt us.

Over the next hours and days, however, we were overcome by a sense of sick numbness and then anger. What had we done to deserve this? Yes, we were English, but we were working in the local community, paying our taxes, doing our best to get on with everyone, so why should we be singled out? And then there was the worry – what if this was only the beginning? Would they target us again? Of course, rationally the revelation of the dark underbelly of the Luberon should have had no effect on our decision to start a family, but we talked about the idea less, letting it slip away for a while, until we once more felt at home.

13

The Flagstone

In early February the peak of Mont Ventoux lay under a permanent blanket of snow and the olive grove outside our house glistened with frost. The thud and splinter of Antoine incessantly chopping logs echoed in our apartment. Smoke trailed from chimneys across the Luberon, and everywhere we went the countryside smelt like a homely kitchen. The vines stood moribund in the fields, offering the hares no camouflage from the hunter's gun. Withered autumnal leaves clung forlornly to bony branches, and flocks of birds scattered with the morning reports.

Day after day the sky was a bright, vivid void. In the villages, the fountains froze, glaciers of ice crept down walls, and commerce hibernated. Shops and bars were boarded up, and the opening hours of the essential stores – the *tabac* and the little supermarkets – became ever more haphazard. On market days stray dogs ceased their bickering and lounged in packs around the *poulet rôti* van, warming their bellies next to the rotating fire. The traders stuffed newspapers in their shoes, pawed the ground and clapped their muffled hands, but still the numbing cold seeped under nails. Shoppers shrouded in coats as thick as duvets purchased root vegetables before scuttling away to tend their fires.

I found myself pitying the editor of *La Provence*, who had to fill a daily newspaper from such a vacuum of activity. Amid a plethora of births, deaths and near deaths were stories such as 'Dry Weather Spells Disaster for Next December's Truffles', but my personal favourite was when news of Pertuis's new potato *confrérie* made the front cover. Apparently the farmers of Pertuis had formed a protest group to ensure that local restaurants used the Pertuis potato. According to the article, the local spud was an Olympic decathlete of an all-rounder – roast it, mash it, slice it, fry it, the Pertuis potato wouldn't disappoint. I presume the reserve story was 'Old Lady Crosses the Road'. Luckily for the editor, and all the readers of *La Provence*, Cucuron Market was about to generate a veritable bonanza of stories. Well, two in fact, but it was winter and these things are relative.

February's most eventful market began with the usual gaggle of old men gathered around the entrance to the Cucuron basin. I recognised them as much by their clothes as their faces. Every week each of them wore the same mismatched, ill-fitting combination. I still wasn't sure whether they saved their best or worst clothes for market day; if it was the former, I'd hate to have seen them when they were dressing down – jeans with rope for belts, tracksuit bottoms and torn cords, fleeces and tailored jackets, trainers and mud-clogged hiking boots formed a melange of fashions.

Tanya and I named people by their hats: the Skipper, with his sailor's peak emblazoned with a wheel and anchor; the Yank, with a faded 49ers baseball cap; the Native, with his beret; and the Ski-Instructor, with a balaclava rolled up and perched over his ears. Defying their age, the crowd of men exuded good health. Their skin was dark and leathery, and their hair full, snow white and erupting from every orifice. Plastic bags full of shopping hung tightly about their wrists as they stood for hours, almost like a bung at the end of the market, preventing people from exiting, so that by the minute their numbers swelled. Their conversations were as bright and cheery as their eyes.

Over the course of winter we'd gradually begun to know a couple of them. There was the curator of the local museum, who was a close friend of Picasso and used to paint with him. There was the aptly named Monsieur Le Foret, a great trunk of a man who reminded me of a cross between Rudyard Kipling's Mr Happy and Mr Strong. 'Regardez,' he would say to us, pointing at the sky, 'c'est magnifique.' He'd been born just down the road and couldn't think of ever moving from this 'coin de paradis'. In fact, his roots were so strongly planted in the region that he claimed to be part of the 'terroir'. With his name and heavy, creaking limbs, it seemed to be at least half true.

Despite these strengthening relationships, it still proved almost impossible to interest any of the locals in buying wine. It was hardly surprising, given their prudent attitude towards money. 'Look, a ten-centime piece,' one of them joked, stooping to pick up the coin and ignoring the catcalls that greeted his parsimony. 'If I find one a day, I'll soon have a euro,' he said, beaming.

One or two men would occasionally break from the group and come over. They would nod courteously at us and then spend the next ten minutes studying the labels of our wine bottles with forensic interest. I couldn't believe that it could take so long to read the twenty or so words, but there they would stand, bent over, bum angled to the sky, eyes pressed right up close to the bottle. In the end I had to conclude that sourcing wine labels was a hobby akin to stamp-collecting and that they were all on the lookout for the equivalent of the penny black.

On the Tuesday in question, there was the usual bonhomie amid this group of men, but also a little excitement. Overnight a branch from one of the village plane trees had crashed down on a house. Nobody had been hurt – in fact just the odd tile had been dislodged – but since nothing else had happened for a week, and nothing else was likely to happen for a month or so, the falling branch was going to be front-page news. The editor of *La Provence* had thanked the Lord that at last he had a proper story and dispatched his lead journalist together with an expert to offer informed comment.

The issue was a serious one – across France plane trees were being ravaged by a fungus that was rotting their branches, and much to everyone's despair, it had reached Cucuron. The usual solution to the problem was to cut down the infected trees, but in Cucuron the plane trees were the symbol of the village. A procession of artists painted the lapping idyll of the basin beneath their branches, and then of course there was the market, whose summer popularity depended on the romantic shade.

As the press got ready to interview the expert, the locals discussed who was to blame. I feel sorry for Americans. Their image in France is probably at an all-time low, and the behaviour of a small number of tourists who apparently have brains too small to memorise words such as '*bonjour*' and '*merci*' create problems for the polite majority. In any event, while George Bush and America were doubtless partly responsible for countless problems besetting the world – global warming, turmoil in the Middle East – I couldn't see how they could possibly be responsible for the threat to the village plane trees. But the whisper started, and it was quickly taken up around the *étang* that the fungal disease had originated from America. The journalists switched on their tape recorders and the market emptied as people gathered around the expert to discover whether the trees would have to be cut down.

We were too far away to hear and so we began chatting to our neighbour – a honey saleswoman called Martine, who looked as sweet as the product she sold. Her cheeks were round with a flush of warm red unusual in a southerner, and her hair a short cropped chocolate brown, which accentuated the chubbiness of her face. Our first meeting several months before, at seven o'clock on a November morning, had been far from cordial.

Martine had been coming to Cucuron Market for the last fifteen years and her mother-in-law for the fifteen years before that, and I'd had the temerity to unwittingly start unloading in her spot. It was dark and cold and she'd scowled at us as we shifted our table out of the way.

Since that moment our relationship had improved and improved. Tanya had bought some honey from her later that first morning – she had over twenty-five producing hives located in diverse environments, such as lavender fields, woods and prairies. The beam of a smile we were now so familiar with had arrived, never to depart. Each week she passed us a different gift – the dried pollen of flowers which when scattered over breakfast cereal acted as a natural pick-me-up, sachets full of lavender petals and of course honey, ranging from light and runny to a solid dark brown. In quiet moments in the markets we'd exchanged tongue-twisters. Martine had ably recited, 'Round the rugged rock the ragged rascal ran,' in English, while Tanya and I struggled with the story of a hunter without his shoes, '*un chasseur sans chaussures*'.

Now, as we sat on the stone wall of the *étang*, letting the sunlight bathe our faces and ignoring the crush that had developed around the journalists, she asked about our plans for the summer months. Which markets were we going to do?

To me, it appeared a strange question – we'd been standing in Cucuron throughout the winter months to guarantee ourselves a place for the summer. Like Martine, we'd traded by the *étang* through ugly squalls of rain and watched as the wind uplifted umbrellas and scattered produce. We'd returned home after bitter mornings and spent up to half an hour under hot showers to try and coax feelings of warmth back into our bodies. And we'd done all this because when we'd first started in the markets, everybody said that this was the way to get a place.

Martine shook her head. 'But the potter's returning and the

clothes lady. *Attendez un moment.*' She bustled away from us to find the *placier*.

Olivier was busy considering whether to give out a parking ticket. He'd already allowed ten minutes of leeway. Flipping away his pad and hunching back into his coat, he followed Martine over to us.

'*Olivier, vous avez deux metres en été pour les anglais?*' she asked.

I was surprised this moment had come so soon. We were only in mid-February and already our future for the rest of the year was being decided. Would we have the opportunity to sell to the summer tourists? We'd once been one of them, spending our two-week holiday lounging in the sun and pottering around the markets, but now they seemed a distant breed. The other traders regarded them as almost mythical creatures to whom money held no value. They would arrive with a flurry of €50 notes and distribute their largesse almost whimsically on whatever trinket caught their eye.

Standing between us and them was Olivier. We only needed 2 metres of space. Surely he could shift a few of the other stalls along a little and create a position for us. This, after all, was a man who found it almost impossible to give a parking ticket. He would stand, book in hand, next to the offending vehicle for up to fifteen minutes before starting to write. I'd watched him fill out the tickets with a methodical slowness that must have been calculated to allow the offending motorists to return. When they finally did, he gratefully tore up the ticket.

Olivier couldn't catch our eyes. '*Le marché, c'est plein,*' he answered. '*Plein, plein, plein.*'

'But they've been here all winter,' argued Martine.

The *placier* shrugged to indicate there was nothing he could do. Regardless of the recent unfortunate incident with our rubbish, I was convinced that Olivier's decision had nothing to do with xenophobia. He was just stating a fact.

'And what about your other markets?' Martine asked us, still ignoring the ongoing hubbub next to the café about the fate of the village plane trees.

As I was about to answer the journalists flicked off their recorders and the crowd around them dispersed. People appeared content with the outcome. Eavesdropping, we learnt that the expert had recommended securing the branches of the trees with ropes to prevent any more falling on to roofs. He had then advocated a watching brief for a couple of years, before, if necessary, felling some of the plane trees. America had also escaped blame; instead the fungus that had caused the disease was identified as indigenous to Bordeaux, which was a satisfactory outcome for the locals. The Bordelais and their aggressive wine industry were not well liked in the area, and since the Americans and the Parisians couldn't be blamed, the Bordelais made a more than adequate scapegoat.

Perhaps it was the crowd of people moving away at once that made one of the locals lose her bearings. In any event, as everybody bustled back towards the market, a cry went up as an old lady tripped over a large flagstone that divided the market from the road. It had been there for years, solid and unmoveable, about twice the size of a crate of wine. Small children had sat on it, munching sweets while their mothers shopped, people rested bags on it and tied their shoelaces against it, but apart from these minor roles, no one even noticed it. The flagstone was an insignificant detail in the pretty pastiche of the market. Until now.

The old lady who tripped over was quickly back on her feet, smoothing down the rumpled creases in her dress. She appeared more shocked and embarrassed than hurt. Her hair was dyed the indistinguishable colour of someone who visits the hairdresser too much – there were shades of purple and touches of pink. Her gold glasses, which had fallen off, swung loosely round her neck. For a couple of minutes she proudly turned away help, assuring everyone that she was OK, but as the group of well-wishers swelled, she played to the gallery, allowing herself to be escorted to a seat in the nearby café. There, various gallant old men prodded and poked at her wrist, convincing her that there had been some considerable damage. A whisky was ordered to calm her beating heart, and the municipal policeman, Olivier, was called over. What followed was extraordinary.

Despite the fact that the offending stone had harmed no one and fulfilled its purpose for the past half-century, and despite the fact that it was in plain sight and impossible to miss other than through carelessness, the whole incident was blamed on the *placier*.

Various locals gathered around, gesturing furiously at first the policeman and then the injured wrist of the woman. Doing his best to mollify the baying crowd, Olivier summoned the doctor on his mobile phone. In England heart-attack victims can wait over half an hour for the arrival of an ambulance, but in the tiny Provençal village of Cucuron, a sprained wrist was attended to in minutes. The doctor prescribed another whisky and tenderly wrapped a bandage round the woman's forearm. Meanwhile the argument continued about Olivier's culpability. He was in charge of the market – how could he possibly have let such a serious health and safety risk exist for so long?

We stood and watched, marvelling at how such a minor incident had provoked so much drama. The editor of *La Provence* would be rubbing his hands with glee, happily tearing up the story of the restaurateurs' reaction to the Pertuis potato *confrérie*. Not only was there an exclusive on the Bordelais threat to the plane trees of Provence, but his journalists were present to record a major health and safety crisis in the markets. Lenses were already being trained on the offending flagstone and microphones shoved towards obliging witnesses.

Unfortunately now we knew that a summer place was out of reach, it all seemed less relevant. A thin layer of ice had formed at the corner of the *étang* and a reflection of the long-fingered bare branches gleamed in the sunshine. Shoppers blew plumes of cold air and fumbled with their gloves as they tried to extricate some money from the folds of their clothes. But the scene had lost some of its allure. I knew that when the first buds appeared on the plane trees and the rich green canopy began to grow, the other traders would return and we would be kicked out of our place.

A further commotion around the flagstone drew me from my reverie. Olivier had organised a team of volunteers to try and make the area safe. Judging from their equipment, you'd have thought they'd arrived to deal with a major road traffic incident. The village's entire supply of traffic cones – five – had been produced, together with a roll of tape of the type that the police usually use to seal off crime scenes. The cones were placed at strategic angles round the flagstone and linked by the tape, until an area several metres square had been cordoned off. All that was missing was a van with a large flashing arrow on the side, to direct pedestrian traffic around the major threat to life and limb which was the Cucuron village flagstone.

As it turned out, these measures were only temporary. Once *La Provence* had filled a week of papers with cross-sections of plane trees, pictures of the amoeba-like fungi at work and some computer-generated images of some of the south's most famous squares *sans* plane trees, the editor turned his attention back to health and safety in the market. To read the paper, one would think that potentially lethal hazards awaited shoppers – the kerbs in Cavaillon were too high, the railings by the side of the Sorgue too low, and the insurance cover carried by the traders insufficient. In every article the incident in Cucuron was cited. The sprained wrist was listed as broken; the story of the doctor walking down from his nearby surgery was told and retold until the established truth became that an air ambulance had been called from Marseille. In any event, in the glare of publicity the already excessive five traffic cones, police tape and hazard sign were seen as insufficient and the *mairie* made even grander plans to make the area safe.

Luckily there were going to be some unexpected beneficiaries.

14

Le Concours Mondial du Vin Rosé

Apart from the cold, and the dark, and the fact that customers were as elusive as the local wild boar (despite the daily
firefights, only one hunter had returned with a carcass in the
last four months), the winter markets could not have been more
enjoyable. With no pressure on space, it was possible to turn
up whenever we wanted. Even arriving at ten in the morning,
there was still a plentiful supply of pitches for us to choose from.
As well as serving the odd – and I mean very odd – customer
and making our presence known to the *placier*, we spent most
of the morning gossiping with the other traders. It was a relaxed
and easy way to meet people, away from the sales pressure that
everybody would be feeling in the summer. And since our position in the various markets changed every week, by the end of
February we felt we knew nearly all the traders in the Luberon.

Among our favourites was Lambert, whose stall was full of
every conceivable type of sock, from 100 per cent anti-allergy
cotton to polyester knee-length numbers with 'God save the
Queen' imprinted on them. To begin with, I wondered how
it was possible to make a living from selling socks, but Lambert
grinned, ran his hand perhaps a little ruefully over his bald head
and asked, 'How many other people have you met selling socks?'
When I confessed none, he laughed loudly. 'There's your answer.

Poulet rôti – plenty; vegetables – hundreds; but socks – just me.'
And of course he was right.

While we stood scouring the market for prospective tasters, a steady number of customers purchased from the perennially jolly Lambert. We spent one morning discussing his upcoming holiday to London. 'It's not cheap,' we warned, but Lambert shrugged off the costs as unimportant. He wanted to show England to his children and he apparently sold enough socks to enable him to do so.

Other popular traders included Didier, the vegetable man. While the majority of the vegetable vendors bought their produce from a wholesaler and then doubled the price, Didier grew everything at home and still managed to do two markets a week. He was so little his waist was barely higher than the wheel arch on his van, and he was permanently out of breath from vaulting in and out of the rear, searching for the last remaining boxes of various vegetables. Even in mid-winter there was a queue, thanks to the local conviction that Didier's mud-covered produce was three times as tasty as anything on offer. Since we were fellow traders, he kept a selection back for us at the end of each morning, including parsnips, which he grew especially for the English.

Finally there was Julien, the trader who'd helped us out on our first visit to Lourmarin Market. His sales technique seemed impeccable, praising prospective purchasers without fawning and underpinning his shameless patter with a wry smile. Whenever Julien got thirsty, and this was fairly frequently, he paid a trip to our stall to taste our latest wine. He would rather diffidently ask for a *dégustation* and we would always pour him a full glass. Very occasionally, after what he professed were rare good days, he bought a bottle. Almost invariably he flirted with Tanya, but the winks and the compliments were so intrinsic to his personality I am not sure he could stop himself.

Our friends in the market formed an impartial circle of

advisers as we tried to figure out how to approach the upcoming summer months. In Cucuron, we could cling on and hope that a space opened up, or we could accept the inevitable and look elsewhere. In Lourmarin, we faced a similar choice. Since it was the middle of winter, we no longer had to wait to be placed every morning. Instead we could just turn up a little later than usual and find a spare spot. For a couple of weeks we'd been doing just this, tagging ourselves on to the end of the market. We'd abandoned the *place* and instead set up in the more popular tree-lined avenue below. In summer spaces here were impossible to find, and we could see why – since changing, our trade had increased threefold.

The only problem was that the *placier*, Sébastian, now refused to acknowledge our existence. He would smoke cigarettes with the other traders and laugh and joke as he took their money, but the moment he came near our stall, he would swivel on his heels and make off in the opposite direction. The upside of this strange behaviour was that we no longer had to pay for our market stall. The downside was that we had no official record of attendance at the winter markets. Our loyalty would not be remembered when the other traders returned.

Apart from Cucuron and Lourmarin, we wanted to get a permanent place in Ansouis and Cadenet, and then we planned to take our chances at one other big market a week – perhaps Apt or L'Isle-sur-la-Sorgue – and just hope we could find a place as a result of one of the permanent traders not turning up. With night markets that would make an exhausting six markets a week in the summer months. But it all depended on finding pitches, and looking at the other traders' serious faces, our chances weren't high.

'Cadenet and Ansouis shouldn't be a problem,' advised Julien, sipping on our wine, 'but if Sébastian continues with his current attitude, your prospects aren't good in Lourmarin.'

It was nearly March and very soon some of the summer traders would be returning to claim their pitches. If we could find more receptive *placiers* in other markets and establish a presence before this influx, then we could still prosper in the summer. We listened as the traders talked about our options: Folcaquier – excellent, but 'the *placier* is not *difficult*'; Vaison – also very good and run by two women who 'are scrupulously fair'. The only problem with the new suggestions was the amount of driving involved – usually over an hour. Transporting our wine on a daily basis in the boiling sun wouldn't be good for it, but what choice did we have?

While we considered our strategy, we also slowly began to change our wine list, selling our remaining red wine and gradually replacing it with rosé. Crucial to our success in the coming months, and almost as important as good pitches, was choosing the right wines. The temptation was to go for the show-stopping names of the rosé world – wines such as Domaine Ott, which had sommeliers from Paris to Bandol hailing it as the first ever gastronomic rosé. But at over €20 a bottle, it was far from cheap and buying in large quantities to try to keep the price down was a considerable financial risk. What if the clientele in the market were unwilling to pay that much for a rosé? Kate Moss might casually strut along the beach in Saint-Tropez with a bottle peeking from her handbag, but would the average holidaymaker even recognise the brand?

Another wine that we wanted to have on our stall was Tavel. This small *appellation* across the Rhône from Châteauneuf-du-Pape made rosé from the same flinty soil as its more illustrious neighbour's red. The result was a wonderfully peppery wine, almost ruby in colour and ideal for drinking with spicy foods. Yet again the area had a good reputation, which drove prices up. Outside the village of Tavel, an enormous sign overshadowed the vineyards proclaiming that the area made '*le premier vin rosé de France*'. Plenty of tourists misunderstood the French and presumed that one day the vignerons, suffering from a collective bout of egotism, had anointed themselves as the best producers in the country. In fact the sign merely acknowledged historical fact. Tavel was the second area in France, after Châteauneuf, to be granted *appellation* status and the first to make rosé, hence the sign 'the first rosé in France'.

In the end we concluded that to make good margins we had to avoid the established names and source our own wines. We had plenty of contacts from our previous two years in France. Some wines like Nicolas Reverdy's Sancerre from Maimbray – a village surrounded by steeply sloping hillsides full of vines, where every homeowner was a vigneron – were so good that we would have no difficulty selling them. Other producers like the ever jovial Serge Chasson from Roussillon were prepared to be so generous with their prices that I couldn't understand how they made a profit.

We still needed an excellent local rosé and we decided to opt for an award-winning wine. In supermarkets across France it is easy to find plenty of wines with gold, silver and bronze medals. The retailing giants know that in the absence of any knowledge of the vineyard these shiny stickers reassure purchasers.

What the consumer doesn't realise is that every year there are hundreds of *concours*. Some, like the famous Paris and Mâcon Concours, are real badges of quality, but others offer more dubious accolades. The gold stickers look the same and only the discerning eye notices that instead of a panel of distinguished judges, the award was made by the agricultural board of a tiny village. In some cases the tasters are even related to the winemakers, and in extreme examples there might only be one vineyard in the village and one judge – the winemaker himself.

Rather than opt for one of the lesser *concours*, we wanted one of our wines to have been judged by the best rosé tasters in the land. Every year in Cannes the Concours Mondial du Vin Rosé takes place. Over 1,400 wines are entered into a three-day competition to select the best pink wines in the world. For the vignerons, it's a gamble. They ship six bottles of wine to the judges and then cross their fingers. A measly 30 per cent of the wines end up with a prize and under 10 per cent with a gold medal – the ultimate accolade for any rosé.

But once a wine has won a prize, it immediately becomes harder to bargain with the vigneron. The major supermarkets would be clamouring to take thousands of bottles, and the pleas of small market traders like us would fall on deaf ears. Which is why Tanya and I resolved to become the world's first rosé spies. Our plan was to travel to the *concours* in Cannes, observe the judging and somehow discover the winners before the information was officially released. We'd then rush to a gold-medal vineyard and strike a deal at a bargain price. At least, that was the rather far-fetched plan we made late one night. I even remember helping myself to another large glass of wine and quite seriously discussing the possibility of bugging the venue.

Arriving in Cannes was a culture shock. On days off from the market it was quite possible for Tanya and me to see no one. Often the closest we came to other people was the distant rumble of a car engine or the rustle of a hunter in the bushes. Even the villages were practically deserted. The doors of bars and shops were shut, and we could stroll down the high street in Lourmarin – a thoroughfare that bubbles with life in the summer – and not bump into anybody. Cannes apparently did not suffer from the same seasonal anaemia.

Porsches replaced tractors in our rear-view mirror as the traffic snaked slowly round the coastal road. The mimosa bloomed bright yellow, and the vain were already stripped off and baking – well, shallow frying – on the beach, working on their tans for the approaching summer. In the centre of the city we queued for twenty minutes for a space in an underground car park, an alien experience for country bumpkins like ourselves, used to leaving the car riding on a village kerb.

Emerging into the bright sunlight, we were immediately

assaulted by the number of people. Streams of them passed on either side of us, their multicoloured shopping bags fanning out in the light wind. Sunglasses looked like they'd had an optical version of Baby Bio sprinkled all over them, as triffid frames sprawled across faces, barely affording the wearer an opportunity to breathe. Men draped themselves in white linen suits like modern-day Don Johnsons; ageing women ignored the effect of gravity on their cleavage and wore plunging tops teamed with heavy jewellery, which counted time as they tottered along. There were sofas on beaches, cocktails sprouting tropical fruits and queues outside restaurants. It may only have been the beginning of March but we saw more *marcha* in the first hour on the Côte d'Azur than the whole winter in the Luberon.

In my head I'd imagined the *concours* taking place at a glamorous venue. Perhaps even the Palais des Festivals, where Hollywood stars swept down the red carpet wearing their smiles and little else as the crowd swooned. Unfortunately the address we'd been given was at the less salubrious end of the port. We passed the bus station, and the Saint-Antoine bar, where the previous summer we'd held a rosé festival, and headed round the bay, admiring the sleek lines of the yachts and envying the freedom they offered their owners. We strolled quickly by an Irish bar where an experimental, or just bored, French chef had dreamt up the culinary delight of *moules* poached in Guinness, and finally we arrived at our destination, the Novotel.

Our first task was to gain the organiser's confidence. Fabrice was a small, serious man who had the unenviable task of collating all the results. At first I thought he wasn't going to let us into the room, but as we explained the story of our life over the past couple of years, he relaxed. Finally when we discovered that we were mutual acquaintances of Gilles Masson, the boss of the Centre de Recherche et d'Expérimentation sur le Vin Rosé, Fabrice agreed to give us a tour. We began behind the scenes in a small basement room with a low ceiling and neon strip lighting. On the floor, hundreds of bottles had been wrapped in little black plastic body bags and marshalled in orderly rows. They resembled an army of toy soldiers waiting to be thrown into action. A great sheet of plastic tarpaulin had been spread across the floor to prevent any spillages staining the carpet. Fabrice then took us over to the most interesting object in the room – at least for us – the mainframe computer.

'All the judges' notes are uploaded here and set against the relevant wine. Then when the tasting is over tomorrow night, the results will be automatically put on to the *concours* website.'

I squinted at the screen to see if I could pick out any scores next to familiar names, but Fabrice led us quickly away. Sweeping open a curtain, he revealed the main event – the Concours Mondial du Vin Rosé – the biggest tasting of pink wine in the world and an event both Tanya and I had dreamt of attending since we first heard about it two years ago.

I'd expected a large hall with rows of tables sagging under the weight of wine and elegant servers swinging their long, blonde hair away from their faces as they served yet another glass to a tipsy judge. Being a taster at the *concours* should have been one of the great jobs in the world, attracting bons viveurs, humorists and all lovers of a good time. The plan had been to pull up a chair, get chatting with an indiscreet taster and elicit some trade secrets as we spent a pleasant afternoon looking out to sea and drinking the finest rosé in the world. Instead, Tanya described the scene that confronted us as 'like a conference of civil engineers'. There were ten round tables with about six judges per table. Rather than a pleasing hubbub of inebriated voices, everybody sat silently hunched over a small handheld personal computer marking scores with a digital pen. Fabrice explained in the hushed voice of a snooker commentator that the results were instantaneously transferred to the main computer. Nobody seemed to be taking any sneaky sips to relieve the monotony; instead the spittoons next to each judge were awash with discarded liquid. We edged closer to one of the tables, peering over the shoulder of a taster to try to catch his comments. From the scowl that was immediately directed at us, you would have thought that we'd interrupted life-saving surgery.

Fabrice ushered us away, sensing that our presence was disturbing the array of prima-donna palates he'd so meticulously assembled. I experienced a brief surge of excitement when we were invited to lunch, imagining that finally tongues would wag, but the meal that followed – an austere cold buffet – was as dry as the Sahara, with the judges opting to preserve their palates for the afternoon of data input ahead. Tanya disappeared to the loo, and I said goodbye to Fabrice and thanked him for his hospitality. It had been a fruitless trip.

Walking back towards the car, Tanya couldn't stop grinning. To begin with, I thought it was just joy at having escaped the tedium of the tasting hall.

'Does Château de Roquefort mean anything to you?'

'Didn't we nearly visit on the Extremely Pale Rosé trip?'

'I thought I recognised the name,' said Tanya, clasping my hand. 'I sneaked a quick look at the computer. The rosé scored ninety-five per cent – it's top of the class at the moment.'

We trotted back to the car, aware that we only had three hours before Fabrice's super computer uploaded the final results to the Web. At 5 p.m. the buyers from Géant, Super U and Leclerc would be on the phone to all the winning vignerons, including Château de Roquefort, but for the rest of the afternoon we had the price advantage.

Château de Roquefort was located in the hills above the pretty port of Cassis. A long, ruinously bumpy track led up to the vineyard. On our travels Tanya and I had noticed that an increasing number of *domaines* had started calling themselves 'châteaux' – perhaps because the vigneron wanted to attract American tourists, or perhaps he or she just had an inflated idea of their own importance. In any event, it was always rather deflating to arrive at a small farmhouse rather than a castle.

Thankfully Château de Roquefort more than lived up to our expectations. It had walls that looked solid enough to withstand cannon shot and two imposing towers built on either end of the structure. All that were missing were a drawbridge and moat. The oval-shaped front door was large enough for a team of horses to pass through, and the shadowy inside appeared cavernous.

Outside the entrance, a large lorry had pulled up. One side of the trailer was open, revealing a mini production line. Two women fed a conveyor belt with empty bottles. They rattled the length of the truck and, as they turned for home, were filled with wine and stamped with a label, rolling off the far end into a waiting box.

Shouting above the din, we asked to see the vigneron and one of the workers headed off to fetch him. Twenty minutes later we were still waiting. We'd learnt every nuance of the bottling process, stroked the appreciative nose of the resident donkey and gazed over every row of leafless vines. Having run out of options to entertain ourselves, and anxious to conclude the deal before the results of the *concours* came through, we asked again.

'Have you met Raimond before?' the foreman asked.

We shook our heads.

'*Ah, il est toujours comme ça.*' He shrugged his shoulders and returned to supervising the bottling.

'It seems Raimond is not famed for his timekeeping,' I said to Tanya, as we strolled back over to pet the donkey.

At that very moment a handsome, dark-haired, dark-eyed man appeared at the top of the flight of stairs that ran up the exterior of the château. He wore an old fleece, a scruffy T-shirt and boots covered in mud. 'Welcome,' he cried, as he leapt on to the banister and slid down with the panache of a movie star. I felt we should have thrown him a sword and a cape as he arrived at the bottom and gave a florid bow. 'Raimond de Villeneuve de Flayosc at your service,' he said with a cheeky grin.

We'd learnt that people with a 'de' before their surname were minor members of the nobility before the revolution, but we'd never met a double 'de' before. Double 'de's were the real aristocrats, usually related to the former royal family.

'So you are here to taste the wine?'

We nodded and Raimond led us into the cool of the *cave*. Grabbing a bottle of rosé, he filled three enormous glasses, 'Let us drink, not taste. Tasting is for wimps,' he said, laughing somewhat manically. 'Come, let me show you the winemaking facilities.'

It was impossible to say no. I'd hoped to make the visit as quick as possible and conclude a deal in the half-hour or so we had before the *concours* results were due to go live, but with Raimond dominating the conversation, it was difficult for either of us to complete a sentence.

'Luberon whites are dreadful – they use the wrong grape. How can you make a wine with Chardonnay when it is so hot? Chardonnay is at its best five hundred kilometres to the north in Chablis. It's not – how do you say? – rocket science.'

We sipped on his rosé and he showed us how the wine was being pumped to the bottling trucks.

'Today is a very special day,' he said. 'I have been waiting for this day for weeks.'

Tanya looked quizzically at him. Bottling was an important but surely fairly commonplace thing to be doing at this time of year.

'Today Jupiter is in the ascendancy over Taurus,' continued Raimond, oblivious to the ever more puzzled looks spreading over our faces. 'The signs are good for fruit and so Raimond bottles,' he said, slapping his chest and taking a great gulp from his wine. 'It's impossible to get a hangover on a day like today, so I can drink like a monster.' He giggled at his own good humour. 'In fact I can drink like your Loch Ness Monster.'

As I listened, I realised I'd read about vignerons like Raimond who insisted on doing all the work in their vineyard according to the astrological charts. They studied the stars as assiduously as forlorn lovers, but instead of the promise of a future partner in an ambiguously worded paragraph, they were looking for the ideal celestial patterns for fruit. The article had concluded that the vignerons who subscribed to these theories were slightly crazy. Having met Raimond, I could see why.

He'd now finished his glass of rosé and was reaching for a top-up. 'In a blind tasting you could easily confuse it with a Loire white, perhaps a Sancerre,' he said with pride, 'and look at the colour – it almost glows. It means the grapes were perfect when they were picked.'

Whatever my thoughts about astrologically influenced vignerons, I had to admit Raimond made fantastic wine. The judges at the *concours* were right, I thought – it was one of the most finely balanced rosés I'd ever tasted. It was time to close the deal before Raimond's mobile started ringing with offers from the supermarkets.

'We'd like to take five hundred bottles,' I said. 'Can you give us a good price?'

'All in good time,' beamed Raimond. 'First you have to meet my donkey and see where I live.'

'Actually, we've already met the donkey,' I spluttered.

'Ah, but you haven't seen his trick.'

A conspiracy theory began to grow in my head. What if Raimond was deliberately delaying until the results came out? There were now only ten minutes left and we were still no closer to purchasing. To be polite and because Raimond was infinitely entertaining, we followed. We climbed the stairs on the outside of the house and entered a small apartment. It was very comfortable, with an open-plan kitchen-diner and a balcony that provided a view of the vines and a wedge of distant sea, but it did beg an important question.

'Who lives in the château?'

'Come and see,' said Raimond, pouring us all another glass.

We passed the bottling lorry and entered through the large front door. The sight that greeted us would have appalled interior decorators, Raimond's ancestors and any future potential wife. Tanya and I thought it was one of the funniest things we'd ever seen. Amid tapestries, great heavy curtains, antique chaises longues and mahogany sideboards were piled crate upon crate of wine. The boxes rose as high as the heavy chandeliers and completely blocked the doors to most of the rooms. A flashing orange light and a beeping sound warned us of the approach of a fork-lift truck, which was coming towards us down a long corridor, hung with expensive-looking paintings.

'It's too big for one person,' explained Raimond, 'and the walls are so thick that's it's the perfect temperature to store wine.'

Tanya and I exchanged glances. We were standing in one of potentially the most beautiful and valuable houses on this stretch of the coast. Cassis, often described as a mini Saint-Tropez, was only a ten-minute drive away, the property was surrounded by sticky pines, olive trees and of course vines, and from the outside would have estate agents from across the region salivating like starved Rottweilers thrown a piece of prime steak. Inside, there was a grand sweeping staircase, a former ballroom and triple-height ceilings galore. Yet Raimond had ignored all this and, in his infinite wisdom, converted his ancestral home into a *cave* for wine. We both adored him for it.

I looked at my watch. There were five minutes left before Château de Roquefort rosé would became the hottest buy of the summer, but still the madcap tour of the vineyard continued, with our reintroduction to the donkey, Céleste. Even with one eye on the time I had to admit that she was an endearing animal, with the tiny hooves, bulging eyes and oversized ears of a cartoon character. Raimond stepped into the enclosure and patted Céleste on the nose. The donkey gave a joyous bray and opened her mouth wide like a yawning hippo. Raimond proffered his glass of rosé and Céleste's tongue shot out, scooping the pink liquid down her throat.

'There you have it,' said Raimond, struggling to be heard over a chorus of heehaws, 'the world's first rosé-drinking donkey. Interesting thing is, she won't touch red or white.'

Just as we turned to head back to the *cave*, I heard the sound I'd been dreading – the phone. Raimond chatted happily away on his mobile and I did my best to eavesdrop the order he was taking. It sounded like 10,000 bottles. Looking around at the vineyard, I estimated that the total production of rosé couldn't have been much more than 15,000. I raised my eyebrows at Tanya – we'd tried to beat the supermarkets, but in the end it hadn't worked. Raimond had just lost any incentive he had to give us a low price.

Nevertheless, just twenty minutes later we bumped back down the drive with our car sagging under the weight of wine. We'd got the full 500 bottles at a fantastically low price. And with the story of the donkey, the star charts and the stately home converted into a wine cellar, we knew we'd have no difficulty selling out. We'd also discovered that neither of us had a future in the espionage business. The order for 10,000 bottles had been for red wine, not rosé, hence the favourable price, and when we asked Raimond about his success at the *concours*, he'd looked completely confused. 'I decided not to enter this year.'

15

Spring

E very evening in March we watched the sun set from the terrace of our house. Wrapped in thick coats, we timed its fall from the sky, noting with excitement the final luminous glow of the hills, before we were chased inside by the ensuing darkness. We counted the progress of the seasons in the five minutes of light we gained each night, encouraging each other with the thought that in just two weeks we'd be able to share an evening aperitif outside.

Both of us were eagerly anticipating spring, a season we'd never experienced in the south of France. Everyone we spoke to said it was their favourite time of year, enjoying the clear blue skies without the bitter chill of the winter or the vicious heat of the summer. The villages would come to life, the terraces of restaurants and bars would be pleasantly filled with people eating lunch in the warm sunshine without the need for a parasol. April and May were the prize that awaited those who'd endured the long hard winter, a pleasant pause before the hordes of tourists arrived, throttling the roads and choking the community.

Like us, nature was carefully counting the days. First came the occasional butterfly in haphazard white-winged flight, then a bright flowering of wild rocket. But as the night-time temperatures plunged again, the trees remained resolutely leafless, and the fresh yellow fields of rape faded with the continued frosts. The seasons played a visible tug of war, and dogged step by dogged step winter lost ground to spring. First to bloom were the almond trees. In the fields with the warmest aspects a small bud of white appeared on the tips of branches. More and more butterflies circled, bumping into each other in mid-flight, and then one morning when the sun felt as hot as high summer, there was a race of growth. Snow showers of white blossom coated the landscape, drifting in the wind and confirming in a celebratory flurry of confetti that April was almost upon us.

For two further weeks the Luberon continued to straddle the seasons. Although the almond trees sprouted fresh green leaves and bright-purple thistles, and enormous daisies provided a riot of warm colour, the cherry trees stayed bare and the fields of vines so moribund and lifeless that it was hard to imagine them producing fruit. Then, finally caving in to the longer days and the warmer air, bright-pink blossom covered the cherry orchards and in a relay of furious activity first one field of vines and then those adjacent awoke to the new season, sprouting fresh growth so vigorously that their skeletal silhouettes were forgotten in days.

One variety of tree still held out. The plane trees, the ultimate symbol of Provence, stood unmoved by the new colours painted on a daily basis in the fields. Despite the fields of bright poppies, which were erupting below in a festival of red, the pruned patchy branches cast only a spidery shadow on the ground. Perhaps it was only coincidence, but one evening in early April Tanya and I rushed to the window, excitedly quietening each other, our ears keening for a forgotten sound. At first it was hesitant and faint, but within seconds the song became more confident. The deep beat of the cicadas – or, if we are honest, a smaller relative of theirs – had returned to the Luberon and in response, as if answering a direct request, the plane trees bloomed. Within a week they'd created the lush green canopy overhead that was going to be so vital to comfortable life in the coming months. Winter was finally over.

With the arrival of spring our fortunes in the markets changed. Gradually a trickle of sightseers returned. They carried rucksacks and walking sticks, stayed in campsites and rarely bought more than one bottle of wine, but the additional trade was welcome. Our winter sales were lower than I'd pessimistically predicted and we desperately needed a good six months. We'd thought hard about whether to desert our winter pitch in Lourmarin and try our luck elsewhere, but in the end we'd decided to gamble on being placed.

It was a risky decision but potentially worth it. One of the traders had told us that up to 50 per cent of his summer profits came from Lourmarin. According to market talk, the cobbled streets ran with gold. The wealthy from all over the world rented secluded villas in the hills and did their entire weekly shop in the market. They strolled among the stalls distributing their largesse without regard for prices.

Already Friday mornings were much busier, with more and more of the multicoloured parasols blooming like new-season flowers. Small ripe strawberries from Cavaillon arrived on the fruit and vegetable stalls. Slightly woody to the taste, they were the vanguard of their bigger brethren. There were even melons, outrageously expensive and flown in from the French colonies, but designed to fool the careless tourist into thinking they were local. Itinerant farmers set up small tables laden with freshly picked raspberries or mud-covered new potatoes. People paused and chatted and enjoyed the sun on their faces. Everything was fresh and exciting. Forgotten flavours lingered on the tongue, tantalising customers to purchase, even though the locals knew in their hearts that another week of sun was needed for full ripeness.

Having traded for a short time on the shady tree-lined avenue, we'd returned to the less sought-after *place*. In the height of summer it became a furnace, but even so pitches were still at a premium. Thanks to our winter service, we knew the majority of the other traders, and rather than wait for Sébastian to place us every morning, we asked around to find out who was going to be turning up. Without fail someone would be missing and I would unload into the free space.

I still had to be careful. In Lourmarin Market, presumptuous actions were rarely tolerated. We'd assumed that because our faces were now known, Sébastian would not take objection to such behaviour, but we'd heard stories of other traders doing similar things and of Sébastian screaming at them. In any event we never set up our stand until Sébastian had walked past our equipment lying scattered on the gravel. There was no conversation, but the subtext to his passage was that we'd been observed, that we hadn't overstepped the mark and that we were free to set up, arranging our newly arrived rosés in descending order of paleness – the violet clairets from Bordeaux, a ruby Marsannay from Burgundy, Raimond de Villeneuve's shocking pink, Nicolas Reverdy's Sancerre, which was the colour of a setting sun, and then a bounty of local pale wines from Provence. With the early-morning light reflecting long shadows in our wine and three or four bottles bobbing in a transparent ice bucket, it was hard to imagine how shoppers could resist.

As we put the final touches to our stand, we regarded the trail of miserable would-be traders following Sébastian, looking for a place. By mid-April a snake of people had developed, winding its way through the stalls, mimicking Sébastian's every move. Looking at the uncertain eyes of the followers, and how they elbowed past each other to catch the *placier*'s eye, I was suddenly very grateful for our winter's work. Without a word being said on the matter, our status in the market had changed. With the help of the other traders, we were allowed to find our own place. It meant that we were in command of our own destiny and not subject to the whim of a policeman.

Nevertheless, we still had to worry about being given a permanent place for the summer. At the moment we were in the privileged position of filling in for absentee traders. Soon no one would dare to be absent. All winter we'd heard whispers of the day when Sébastian confirmed everyone's place, but as yet we'd been unable to find out when this was happening. Easter, the official start of the tourist season, was approaching and yet still there was no word. The simple thing to do would have been to ask Sébastian, but since his nature was so unpredictable, it might have resulted in a confrontation, and because the day in question had no official status, I shied away from forcing the issue.

Already Julien, the thirsty leather-goods merchant with the fast line in market patter, was taking steps to protect our position. Every Friday he urged us to move next to him into the secondary line of stalls that was gradually evolving. But keen to keep our sales going, Tanya and I stayed put, moving from position to position in the primary aisle, taking the place of absentees. Julien, quite correctly as it turned out, told us we were making a mistake.

On the penultimate Friday in April, over one of his increasingly frequent morning glasses of rosé, he insisted that we move immediately and stake a claim to a couple of empty square metres next to him. I assumed he was just trying to secure his summer's supply of cold wine. Our current position was a little inconvenient for him, with no direct line of sight to his stall. Much better to place us on his right-hand side and guarantee uninterrupted access. When we once again declined the offer, he shook his head and declared us to be fools.

Later the same morning a rumour went around. 'Make sure you are here next week – that's when Sébastian's going to confirm the places.'

Tanya and I spent the next half an hour chatting with our supporters in the market. The consensus of opinion seemed to be that we would be OK. We'd been ever present during the winter and were clearly higher up the pecking order than the raft of new faces who'd just appeared.

With my confidence bolstered, I said a loud *bonjour* to Sébastian as he did his rounds to collect the money. He glanced up at me, ticket in his hand. We hadn't spoken since the truffle market – was this to be the moment when the silence between us was broken? Would he tell me about the importance of next Friday? He hugged and kissed the other traders, and if we really had risen up the market hierarchy, surely we merited some sort of acknowledgement. I took the ticket and waited for a response. Nothing but a dark-eyed stare and a click of the heels as Sébastian whirled and showed me his back.

We tried not to discuss what would happen if we didn't get placed. Undoubtedly it would mean long hours of driving to other large markets and plenty of wasted mornings getting up at dawn only to be sent home because our chosen substitute market was full. It was no way to conduct a wine business. To succeed, we needed to be in the same place and for word of mouth to pass around the news of us.

Keeping our minds off Lourmarin, we concentrated on our round of other markets. Sunday in Ansouis and Monday in Cadenet passed without incident, but the rest of the week was disastrous.

Every Tuesday in Cucuron more and more traders whom we'd never seen before returned to claim their places, and while we still set up next to Martine, the charming honey saleswoman, we knew our time was limited. As was usual now, Olivier, the *placier*, made us wait until 8 a.m., just to check that the potter hadn't returned to claim his summer place – our current pitch.

The *étang* was already wearing its high-season wardrobe – a rippling image of cafés, parasols and the fresh green canopy overhead. Tanya and I sat on the surrounding low brick wall and contemplated the disaster that would be losing both markets in Lourmarin and Cucuron in the same week. For the last month we'd waited like this, watching the gently expanding circles in the water until the chime of the hour. Our greatest fear was the sound of approaching vans. Any one of them might be the potter, and the throaty cough of his decrepit engine would herald the end of our time in Cucuron.

The heavy hand of the village clock lurched closer to the hour, and anxious to get started, I began shifting boxes of wine. In the last few weeks a more permanent structure had been erected around the flagstone over which the old lady had tripped. Plastic barriers rather than tape now encircled it, and a warning sign sat proudly on top of the piece of stone. In such a pretty market it was a real eyesore and also an inconvenience. Each time I returned to the car to retrieve bottles of wine I had to edge past the barriers. In my opinion it was more dangerous now than it had been before. As I hefted a case on to my shoulders, Tanya placed a cautionary hand on my wrist. 'Listen.'

At first there was nothing unusual, just the clatter of goods as they were stacked on to stands, the raspy morning greetings of the traders as they forced out a few words between puffs on their smouldering cigarettes and the wind fanning the branches of the plane trees, creating a whispering hush of air, which swept across the surface of the *étang*. Distinguishable among these familiar sounds, however, was the faint echo of a jarring, bumping passage, which was funnelled down the narrow village streets towards us. For a second the noise disappeared and we relaxed, reassuring ourselves that we'd imagined it or that the guilty vehicle was heading in the other direction. But there it was again, closer this time, the pleading whine of an old engine. A red van swung into sight and came to a juddering clutch-wrecking halt right next to our pitch. Swinging open the door, a young man jumped down and began unloading pottery. He didn't even look at us. Why should he?

Olivier tried to find us another place, but in the end he had to send us home.

On Wednesday we busied ourselves around the house, doing the domestic chores – mopping the floor, changing the sheets, weeding the garden – with as much vigour as possible to keep our minds from the reality of our situation. Having places in the two small non-touristy markets of Ansouis and Cadenet was no way to make a living. At six we sat together on the terrace in the terracotta glow of the early-evening sun, staring silently at the gentle shadowy hills. Whatever happened to us, the view would always be imprinted in our minds. Despite over eight months in the house, we still found our gaze drawn deep into the Luberon. Even the most engrossing of books got cast aside and forgotten, its story replaced by a fifteen-minute daydream filled with images of the ramshackle *cochonnière* with its exposed beams and cracked tiles, the ancient olive tree that grew in the middle of our drive, forming a natural roundabout for us to turn the car, the angular row of cypresses arranged in height order like a family photograph and the crumbling weathered brick of the *mas*.

The following day we drove to L'Isle-sur-la-Sorgue. The trip in the early-morning half-light took about an hour. All winter we'd been chopping and changing between this market and Apt. Both were big, belligerent beasts where traders fought the narrow streets and the intransigence of their colleagues to somehow manoeuvre their vans in and out. The beginning and end of such markets were stressful experiences for us, as we sought to tiptoe around the fragile temperaments of the regulars, who regarded any interruption to their usual routine with an irrational anger. Because of the size and the fame of the markets, we'd rarely been well placed, but somehow the *police municipale* had always found a pitch for us. On occasions we'd made good money, but mostly we'd been left questioning whether our meagre profit was worth the petrol and the aggravation.

As usual, on arrival in L'Isle-sur-la-Sorgue we made our way to the main square. Many of the regular traders had already set up and were gathered outside the shabbily chic Café de Paris.

Five ramshackle tables were spread at uneven intervals across the pavement, and trails of smoke rose from each. Inside, the silver bar was lined with beers and cloudy yellow pastis. Nobody spoke; instead they drank, smoked and waited. The scene belonged, freeze-framed in black and white, hanging in a frame in cheap student digs.

The *placier* recognised us as we approached. '*Bonjour.*'

'*Ça va?*' we enquired.

'*En forme, merci.*'

'*Vous avez deux metres?*'

He shook his head. '*Aujord'hui c'est déjà complet. J'ai aucune place.*'

Tanya and I complained that we'd come every other week in the winter and that we'd supported the market when others hadn't, but the *placier* just spread his hands, to illustrate that there was nothing he could do.

'Try again next week,' he urged.

We stood still for a while, as if the passage of time would somehow remedy the situation, but in the end there was nothing to do but get back in the car, which was crammed with our redundant stock.

For the second time in a week we drove home disconsolately. While we'd been marvelling at the changing colours of the landscape – the poppies, the rape and the blossom – something much more important had been happening in the markets. The season had finally arrived. Whether it was from bad luck or just not picking up on the nuances of life in the market, we were being elbowed aside. The more experienced vendors, people who'd known the *placiers* for decades, were returning, and in the bigger markets, where the proper money was to be made, there was nowhere for us to go. All that we now awaited was for our fate to be confirmed in Lourmarin.

Without a pitch there, our rosé business was finished before it had ever really got started.

16

The Placing

When I opened the window early the following morning, the mistral almost slammed the shutter back in my face. As I struggled with the latch, a squall of heavy rain lashed in cold slugs across my forearm. The mountains opposite were obscured by thick cloud, and only the outline of the *cochonnière*, barely 20 metres away, was visible. Normally I would have closed the shutter and returned to bed. Very few traders were foolish enough to attempt to set up in such high winds, and even fewer shoppers ventured out in torrential rain. But this morning was different. It was absolutely essential that we traded in Lourmarin, and it was even possible that the weather might put some of the other vendors off and that we would secure a better pitch as a result.

Our hearts thudded in time with the windscreen wipers as we arrived in the village just before seven. Usually at this time there would only be a scattering of traders, and with the intemperate weather I half expected to see an empty square. Instead, stretching across the *place* stall after stall was set up, and apart from the almost ghostly lack of people, everyone was ready to trade. Unloading our wine and table on the corner of the square, I walked down the main aisle looking for a place. Our pitch from the previous week was now filled by a lady selling jewellery and from the week before that by another returnee, a woman selling novelty French street signs such as 'Place de Pastis'. Reaching the end of the row, we'd said fifteen or so *bonjours* but had yet to find the spare 2 metres we needed.

We tried the secondary aisle, panic now creeping into our stride and carrying us quickly onwards, so that shouted greetings trailed unanswered in our wake. I was bemused – where had all these people come from, and why were they able to set up so confidently? Did they not fear Sébastian's wrath?

The weather rolled relentlessly in. The traders clung to their parasols like sailors fighting to stay aboard a storm-tossed ship, and it looked like the only chance of us securing a spot was the wind sweeping someone's stand away. Clothes and handbags were getting ruined by the wet dirt being fired into the air by the unforgiving mistral.

Tanya and I must have looked pathetic. While the rest of our friends from the winter months were busy trying to protect their goods from the elements, we stood sodden and purpose-less. Occasionally Tanya would walk back down the aisle to check we hadn't somehow missed a possible spot, but she always returned glum-faced. The clock struck half past seven, and the itinerant traders, who were too low in the market hierarchy to claim a permanent place, arrived. These were the people whom we'd watched for the last two weeks, trailing the *placier* like supplicants a religious leader. The lucky few would be granted a pitch for the summer; the remainder would not be seen again. Already, on the far side of the square, I could see Sébastian marching officiously up to the various stalls and with a quick nod confirming the position.

'I can't believe it's come to this,' said Tanya, clasping my hand with sympathy.

Before I could reply, I heard a shout from the other end of the aisle: '*Anglais, venez ici vite*' – 'English, come here quick.'

Tanya and I scrambled forwards into the wind. Julien, the leather-goods salesman with a weakness for rosé, was standing at the top of the steps that led down from the *place* to the tree-lined avenue. He'd tied a rope round his parasol to which he was desperately clinging. Just one big gust would send the parasol pitching into the air like a kite and drag Julien off his feet. Whatever he'd found must have meant a lot for him to risk his stall in this manner. Pointing excitedly at the stairs, Julien shouted over the weather, 'The poster salesman hasn't turned up. Put your stuff there and it's yours for the summer.'

We didn't wait to discuss the matter. Shouting, '*Merci*,' over our shoulders, we raced across the *place* to retrieve our gear. I could see Sébastian approaching our prospective place, glad-handing the traders he knew well and ignoring others. Tanya grabbed the table legs and I took the board we placed over the top of them. The rest could wait; we just needed to get the bare minimum installed before the policeman reached us.

Panting back to the spare pitch, we dropped our equipment on the ground. It didn't seem correct to set up without Sébastian's nod of approval. Despite the worsening weather, we grinned foolishly at each other, and wiping her sodden hair away from her face, I gave Tanya a kiss. We had in all probability secured one of the best pitches in the market. I guessed that 90 per cent of the people who visited used the stairs at some point in their visit. Our stall would be on one of the main thoroughfares, bringing us into contact with thousands of shoppers. We'd have to buy some adjustable legs for our stand to compensate for the steps, but fate, it seemed, had given us every chance to succeed. Somehow we'd been in the right place at the right time, but I thought privately to myself, you make your own luck in this world.

Sébastian approached and we waited for the nod that would confirm our place for the year, the same perfunctory jerk of the head we'd experienced for the last month. He glanced at our drenched clothes and the water dripping from our hair into the river at our feet, said, '*Vous ne pouvez pas rester là*,' and walked off to the next stall.

I looked at Tanya to check that I'd understood. With his third ever sentence to us, Sébastian had wiped away our chances. All year we'd listened to various opinions about Lourmarin's *placier*. The generous traders, or perhaps just those with good pitches, argued that he had an exceptionally difficult job to do. It was impossible to please everyone, but Sébastian tried harder than most *placiers* to accommodate as many traders as possible. Others muttered about the favourable treatment accorded to some and recalled with horror the ensuing arguments when they'd tried to stand up to Sébastian. At this precise moment I knew whose side I was on. We stacked our equipment against the wall and took the only option available to us: we joined the rear of the trail following Sébastian around the market.

'It's just like old times,' said Tanya sardonically, as we all swayed out to the left, mirroring the movement of our mother hen, the *placier*. As a line, the pitchless traders followed down the steps, united by our need to find a space and at the same time competing to be the lucky person chosen to fill any gaps. Like everyone else, Tanya and I looked swiftly in all directions, scanning in circles around us for the barest hint of an opportunity. Some people shouted out concessions in the hope of gaining favour with Sébastian – 'Normally I need five metres, but I'll take two' – others raced on ahead of him, trying to predict his path and keep themselves permanently in his eyeline. In the next half-hour thousands of euros were at stake, and as the minutes dragged and Sébastian inspected every corner of the market, people began to push, shove and jostle.

As we obediently traipsed around, some of the regular traders called out to us.

'Haven't you got a place yet?'

'It's a disgrace – you've been here all winter.'

Or more simply: 'Sébastian, have a heart – give them a place.'

But it seemed the *placier* had mislaid his *coeur*. Pointing at various free pitches, he picked off his favourites from the following group. There were people whom we'd never seen before and others who'd only returned to the market in the last few weeks, after taking the whole winter off. Up until this point I'd always thought that our treatment in the French markets had been reasonably fair. We'd tried to understand the system and work hard to earn our places, but it seemed the rules the other traders had taught us no longer applied.

It was nearly eight thirty and there was still a crowd of twenty people gathered around the *placier*. At most there were two or three small pitches left in the market. Sébastian led us once more down the steps, and to inject some humour into our situation, I began quietly humming 'The Grand Old Duke of York'. The *placier* jerked his finger at a young tapenade vendor. 'You there, take three metres by the post office.'

The nearest traders looked incredulously at Sébastian. They whispered hurriedly with their neighbours and the news spread quickly through the market. The trader in question had first turned up at the market at the end of the last season. He'd been present in some but not all of the winter markets and for him to be given a prime spot, right next to the post office and the all-important cash machine, was unbelievable.

There were traders still up on the *place* who'd worked Lourmarin Market for a decade and who'd spent the last five years consistently lobbying for a move to the tree-lined avenue. The leafy plane trees made the summer heat bearable, and it was here that the throngs of tourists gathered and the real money was made – often up to three times more than a trader could hope to take on the *place*. With the exception of the flower seller – whose flowers all died one July morning on the *place* due to the sweltering heat and who, with the agreement of everyone, had a legitimate case to trade in the shade – all the pitches *en bas*, or below, as the traders on the *place* referred to the area, had earned their right by length of service. Until now.

A gang of angry traders quickly arrived from the *place*. They swarmed around Sébastian like footballers protesting a poor penalty decision, waving their arms and forcing him backwards with every step. I think it was only his police uniform that kept them from pushing him over.

'I've been waiting for ten years.'

'I've only got three metres – what about me?'

Sébastian responded to the commotion by ducking under the mesh of angry waving arms and scuttling away to the opposite end of the market. We followed. Back up the stairs we went, prompting another rendition of 'The Grand Old Duke of York' from me, and around the *place* in a zigzag until Sébastian reached his car and clambered in. The clock struck nine, and a few brave locals prepared to ignore the weather started arriving to do their shopping. Shivering with cold, Tanya and I realised that we'd been wasting our time. The *placier* started his engine, flicked on his indicator and turned the car round. His face was as dark as the weather as he squeezed his car between the encircling vans. Winding down the window to check he wasn't going to scrape the bodywork, he suddenly looked up, almost as if he noticed us for the first time that morning.'*Il y a une petite place à côté du magasin – c'est pour vous.*'

Before we could reply or ask for specifics, he'd disappeared. We gathered our equipment and looked around. One thing was certain. The pitch he was referring to would be on the *place*. One of the prime aisles ran opposite the long line of shops that stretched across a side of the square. Dodging shoppers, we walked the length of it twice, but there was not even a spare half-metre. We crossed to the other side of the *place*. Here, there was a slip road, which all the traders used to get their goods in and out of the market. It ran past an ugly stained concrete wall, which had the delivery door for a restaurant and a large puncture hole for an extractor fan cut into it. A couple of metres along from the restaurant door was a set of steps leading up to a small clothes shop. We'd be isolated from the rest of the market, assaulted by the odours of cooked food and unlikely to encounter a shopper unless they were lost, but we had to assume that this was our place for the summer. We dropped our table into the sodden earth and began to set up.

Within minutes there were problems. A fruit trader with wild staring eyes came and pushed at our gear. 'You can't leave this here. How will I get my van back in the market?'

He was joined by the nearest clothes seller. 'Who told you to set up here? This pitch doesn't even exist.'

'Sébastian,' I replied, hefting wine on to the table.

'Idiot,' muttered the clothes trader, apparently satisfied we had some sort of authorisation.

The fruit seller angrily rocked our table once more and then stalked away.

Tanya and I were exhausted from the tension of the morning. We'd spent two hours nervously wondering whether we'd get a place at all. When we'd finally been assigned to the fag end of the market, we'd actually been grateful that at least we had somewhere, but the bullying attitude of the nearest traders had quickly dispersed any joy. We put the ice bucket on the table, neatly arranged our bottles and waited for the miracle that, in such an out-of-the-way location, would be our first customer. At least there was one positive: although it was still raining, I could see patches of blue sky over the hills. It was still early and there was a chance the sun would break through.

We spent most of the remainder of the morning trying to work out what was being served for lunch. Hemmed against the back wall of the restaurant, sitting on our high stools, we discovered the extractor-fan outlet was exactly at head height. To begin with, we identified the crushed garlic and frying mince of a spaghetti bolognese, which on an empty stomach was mildly nauseating, but just about acceptable. Things quickly became worse, however, as a malodorous stench of fish started being churned towards us. The extractor fan was obviously on full blast because the rotten air threatened to blow our parasol away. I assumed that the restaurant staff were having their lunch and that the cooking had to stop soon, but half an hour later the smell was still being pumped out. Tanya, looking quite white, disappeared to the front of the restaurant to try and identify the dish.

She returned shaking her head. 'Bouillabaisse.'

'Is it a special?' I asked hopefully.

'No, it's on the menu – they'll be making it every week.'

Customers refer to bouillabaisse as the 'golden soup' and pay extortionate prices for this fish broth which began life as a humble dish for fishermen made from the leftover catch. While the restaurant's clients could enjoy the final version of this rich soup with its accompanying croutons and garlic dip, Tanya and I would have to suffer its creation every week – an interminable process of boiling down old fish heads and innards to create a stock, before adding tomatoes and some choicer cuts of fish. A speedy chef could probably create a passable bouillabaisse in four hours – exactly the length of the market.

I shook my head. 'No wonder nobody wants this pitch.'

'Our clothes are going to stink,' said Tanya, wrinkling her nose.

Mid-morning Julien, the leather-goods salesman, strolled over. He winked at us, plucked a bottle of wine from the ice bucket and poured himself a glass. 'Have you had any customers?'

We shook our heads.

'But look at the rest of the market – it's packed.' He was right. The rain had stopped at about 10 a.m., and the sky had cleared to a rich blue. Many of the tourists now ambling around the market probably didn't even realise there had been a mini tempest. The sun had sucked the moisture from the earth, and the cicadas were singing happily in the pine trees. A constant stream of shoppers wound their way around the *place* before disappearing down the steps.

'It's not fair. You have to ask Sébastian to move,' said Julien, helping himself to another tipple.

'But where to?'

'That's the problem,' he said, pitching the rest of his wine down his throat and immediately heading back to his stall. 'There's nowhere left.'

Just before midday a curious thing happened. The smell of fish was still churning out of the restaurant, our stall looked as unattractive as possible with a concrete wall as a background, but in spite of these handicaps, various customers began to find us. More and more shoppers became snagged in the group around the ice bucket. Often they spotted us from a distance and, curious about the commotion, made their way over, only to become trapped by the offer of a glass of free wine. The majority of them were English. Despite its fame, Lourmarin remained essentially a French village, and over the winter Tanya and I had become so used to selling to French customers that it was strange suddenly to hear so many English voices.

Many of our new clients trailed little children from their hands. They were dressed better than the campers we'd become used to dealing with, and after about five minutes of conversation most of them confessed to having a second home in the region. To our delight, they all ordered wine. French customers felt not the slightest embarrassment at tasting all of our wines and then sauntering off without parting with a euro, so this new relaxed attitude to spending came as a shock. Nobody checked a price or queried the value of what we were selling; instead they happily bought their wine for the week.

'What do you think we need for tonight and tomorrow, dear?'

'Ten bottles should do it.'

There was no sense of shame, no mumbled excuse that the wine was for someone else; there was just a frank acceptance that they were going to drink a lot of wine and have a good time. If a Frenchman had needed a case for a party, he would have bought a couple of bottles from us, a couple from another source and so on, lest village tongues wag about his descent into alcoholism. It was a relief finally to have discovered some drinkers, and in the hour before lunch we sold fifty bottles of wine. Other than the Christmas market, this had been the first time our sales had exceeded our target per market.

'Where have all the English come from?' I asked in one of our rare breaks.

We both realised the truth at the same time. We'd been so wrapped up with worry about the placing that we'd forgotten the date. Claire, Neil, Rosie and Tristan were coming over to see us on Sunday for an Easter-egg hunt and today was Good Friday, the official start of the tourist season.

'If it continues like this, we might just survive in business,' said Tanya, as she served another prospective customer.

At a quarter past one I was so happy contemplating our new successful future that I didn't notice the queue of trucks forming at the entrance to the market. Tanya and I were serving our last customers and working out how much money we could make if every market from now followed the same pattern. Meanwhile exasperated traders were wheeling their goods past us, or lugging them on their shoulders. As the minutes passed, the swear words became choicer and I gradually retreated from our dreamy prospects to the reality that we'd better pack up the stall pretty quickly or risk it being steamrollered by an impatient van driver. I dispatched Tanya to get the car and began to take down our stall, whistling happily to myself, completely unaware that I was about to put all our good work at risk.

A boy and a girl approached and studied the wine list. If I'm generous to my conscience, they were sixteen, but it's possible they were no more than twelve. They selected a bottle and handed over some money. 'It's a present for our father,' they chimed.

I simply didn't know what to do. In France the journey from nipple to grape is one of the shortest in the world. Once a child is able to walk, parents are happy to dilute water with a touch of wine. The two eager young palates before me probably knew as much about *tipicité* and *terroir* as I did. Should I serve them? Culturally was this type of transaction acceptable in France? Half my mind was on packing up as quickly as possible, and the other half was thinking about my lunch. Mechanically I took the money, gave them the wine and counted out the change.

It was only after they left, bottle in hand, that I pondered the consequences of my actions. 'A present for our father' – what type of fool was I? In a couple of hours they'd be swaying down the main street of the village singing 'La Marseillaise', and when Sébastian picked them up and asked them where they got their wine from, that would be the end of our nascent rosé empire.

And yet, perhaps I was right – perhaps French children were more honest and adult about alcohol than the English. They'd certainly showed no sign of embarrassment as I had served them. Had I refused, it could have been another Anglo-Saxon faux pas to add to a long list of embarrassing errors. I put the matter to the back of mind.

Tanya arrived back with the car. I mentioned nothing of the sale to her, and under the angry gaze of the other traders we packed away our gear as quickly as possible.

As I lugged the final box into the car, the fruit vendor with the fixed eyes, who'd been unable to get his van back into the market because of our stall, tapped his watch. 'Next week move your stand earlier,' he barked. 'That's if you're still here.'

It seemed a bizarre thing to say. Why wouldn't we still be here?

17

Easter

Easter should have been a joyful occasion. For weeks the *boulangeries* had been full of ever more extravagant chocolate creations – cars driven by bunnies, dolphins leaping from white-chocolate seas and enormous eggs – which were given away as first prizes in village lotteries. Tanya and I spent the Saturday preparing for the arrival of Claire, Neil, Tristan and Rosie. We put chocolate on the children's pillows and planned an Easter-egg hunt through the olive grove. Ever since Lourmarin Market our mood had been jubilant, and we were both looking forward to a long family weekend.

Our guests were due to arrive just before midday on Sunday, and that morning I drove down to the village to get croissants. The *place*, which was filled by the market every Friday, was empty, but I noted with pride the bare 2 metres of dirt that now belonged to us, even if it was only for five hours a week. Passing the delicatessen on my left, which as a sideline sold bread, pains au chocolats and croissants, I walked the extra 100 metres to the bakery where I knew everything was made onsite. Idle village gossip rattled around the queue – the children who were being disruptive in class, a rumour that the car park was going to have an apartment block built on it and a diatribe about the ineffectiveness of the new road–calming measures. Breakfast in hand, I whistled my way back on to the street, only to come face to face with Sébastian.

I said a cheery hello, assuming that since I was now officially placed in the market, our relationship could become a friendlier one.

Sébastian muttered a scarcely audible *bonjour* and then proceeded to ruin my day. 'The *mairie* has demanded your alcohol licence. You must deliver it first thing next week.'

'But why?'

Sébastian shrugged in response and entered the bakery.

There was only one explanation: somebody had seen me serve the young boy and the girl in the market. My mind quickly worked through the possible outcomes. A similar offence in the UK would merit a small fine and a warning that the punishment would be more severe next time. In France I had no idea what might happen, although it was quite conceivable that my licence to sell alcohol would be suspended or even revoked. But they had to have evidence first. If I'd been reported by another market trader – and I had a good idea who might be responsible – then it was simply my word against theirs. I could easily deny everything and bluff my way out of the crisis. Having said that, lying wasn't a habit of mine; at best in life I was prepared to blur the truth. By the time I'd arrived home I'd decided that if questioned at the *mairie* I would just confess to having made an honest mistake.

There was only an hour until Claire and her family were due, and given how much Tanya had been looking forward to seeing her sister, I opted to keep the events in the village to myself. While Tanya made the final preparations for the meal, I sat down and started a long-overdue job – working out how much wine we'd sold since we started in the markets. Perhaps because of the problems with Sébastian, I was suddenly fixated on finding out how much of a financial hole we'd got ourselves into. When we'd started trading, we'd set a target of selling 8,000 bottles of wine in the first year, which meant shifting thirty-five to forty bottles a market. A target that was ostensibly achievable. Making the total would demonstrate that our rosé business was viable, and year on year we could then seek to increase sales.

I knew that winter had been lean, but I hadn't quite realised how bad until I started going over the numbers. From October until the middle of April we'd managed to sell just under 1,000 bottles. If our licence was suspended for the summer months, we'd be left with a *cave* full of wine we'd paid for and couldn't sell, wiping out our small profit. Somehow I would then have to meet the rental payments on our apartment without any income. Even being positive and assuming that no action was taken against me for serving minors, we'd be left with six months to sell 7,000 bottles at an average of over fifty bottles per market. Lourmarin on Friday had shown us that it was possible, but to make the target every single market for the rest of the year was going to be more than challenging.

Tanya hummed happily to herself in the kitchen, and Claire's family arrived. The promised Easter-egg hunt turned into a race to gather the chocolate before the sun melted them. There was a large lunch of marinated lamb with roast potatoes and then a *tarte aux framboises* and more chocolate. The children screamed around the garden on a sugar high, and everybody had a great time, except, that is, for me. Try as I might to participate in conversations, I found myself drifting away into my own thoughts, so that my contributions were at best tangential to what was being discussed and at worst completely irrelevant. On several occasions Tanya covered for me, and as the afternoon dragged on, I found myself drinking more and more wine and wondering how I had made such a mess of things.

The following day I awoke with a heavy hangover. Strangely, in a country that awards its workers bank holidays for the most spurious of reasons, the day wasn't a holiday in France, but Claire and Neil didn't leave until lunchtime and of course the *mairie* was closed all afternoon, so there was no opportunity to resolve the uncertainty. I moped around supposedly organising our wine, but in reality calculating just how much we'd spent on the stock we now might not be able to sell. I phoned a friend who'd once worked in a restaurant in Paris and asked about French alcohol laws. Apparently they were even stricter than England, with surprisingly draconian penalties.

The day got worse when midway through the afternoon Tanya noticed a small mark in one of the kitchen surfaces. It was circular and at most 2 centimetres in diameter. It was something that we could have easily have covered with a kitchen mat, but since our landlords were busy in the olive grove, there was an obvious opportunity to discuss the damage with them. We approached Antoine as he was chugging through the trees high on his tractor, leaving Rose scrambling in his wake spraying pesticide.

The last time we'd really spoken was just before Christmas, when we'd organised a traditional English Sunday lunch. Rose and Antoine had laced their roast beef with horseradish sauce, not quite appreciating that we'd also made a gravy. They wiped sweat from their brows and smiled encouragingly as they munched their way through some admittedly doughy Yorkshire puddings. At the end of the meal we'd served Antoine a large tumbler full of whisky from the Isle of Skye and he'd relaxed back into his chair with a satisfied grin.

Even so, our relationship was still a curious mixture of mutual trust and distrust. Quite rightly they had no idea why a young English couple would come to France and try to make a living selling rosé. To them, we were probably just another example of crazy foreigners infected with a short-term dream of life in the sun. One day we'd return home and then they'd find some proper French tenants who wouldn't dream of serving them Yorkshire pudding.

We convened in the kitchen and examined the tiny pockmark

in the surface. I expected a conciliatory '*C'est pas grave*'; instead Rose began a lecture on how the kitchen surfaces weren't heat-proof and how we should never put anything hot on them. Waiting for the end of the storm, we restrained ourselves from pointing out that perhaps it would have been a good idea for them to tell us this at the beginning of our tenancy. But Rose was far from finished. She fussed up and down the kitchen, and then looking at Antoine for support, she declared, 'We'll have to put a new unit in and you're going to have to pay.'

Trying not to get into a fight when I didn't need to and expecting a piece of plastic that wasn't even heatproof to cost little more than €100, I asked, 'And how much will that be?'

'I'll get a quote, but about a thousand euros.'

At which stage the argument began. As usual with the French, there was plenty of arm waving and accelerated speech, which made nearly everything incomprehensible to us. We pleaded for Rose to speak slower and argued that it might be better to find another solution to such a small problem, but Rose was adamant and, telling us that she would have a quote in days, left.

'That's another two hundred bottles of wine,' I grumbled, feeling ever more sorry for myself as I headed back to the *cave* to continue the stock-take.

By the end of the day Tanya had had enough and confronted me. Wallowing in gloom, I explained that we now needed to sell inordinate quantities of wine to make a success of our first year.

'I know you love France,' I concluded, 'and I do as well, but we're no closer to being able to make a living here.'

Next I whined on about the unreasonableness of the landlords for a good ten minutes. While I'd been feeling sorry for myself, Tanya had been researching. After a couple of telephone calls she discovered we were probably in the wrong. French law had no concept of fair wear and tear, and when we left the apartment, it was our obligation to return it in the state we rented it, including a spotless kitchen surface. It might seem unfair to us, but apparently that was the law.

'So you might as well cheer up,' said Tanya. 'These things happen.'

'There's another problem as well,' I confessed, and began slowly to relate the story of how I might have sold wine to minors. I described my meeting with Sébastian in the street and the *mairie*'s demand to see our papers. What I couldn't get my head around was that such a small slip could have such dramatic consequences. Two seconds of thoughtlessness had in effect jeopardised a year of work, and finally, after two days of irrational behaviour, I did what I should have done in the first place – apologised to Tanya.

Despite my anxiety, Tanya's more rational view was that nothing would come of my mistake. The likelihood was that nobody had spotted the incident, and even if I had broken the law, culturally such behaviour was probably quite acceptable in France. We had to continue as normal, leave the visit to the *mairie* in Lourmarin to the following afternoon and try and get into Cucuron Market in the morning. Without a permanent place, this meant being the first people in the queue in the event one of the regular traders didn't turn up. At Folcaquier Market, one of the biggest in the area, we'd heard that placeless traders camped overnight, but we decided that this was a little extreme.

Instead we woke at five o'clock the next morning and I began packing the car. Recently this had felt like a futile exercise. We'd been turned away from two markets the previous week, and stacking crates of wine was back-breaking work. We arrived at 5.15 a.m. and sat in the lamplight on the wall by the side of the water, waiting for the café to open. At 6 a.m. we had a coffee and watched as a couple of other placeless traders arrived to try their luck. Gradually the regulars arrived, erecting their multicoloured village round the *étang* and joking among themselves.

We felt like a dispossessed underclass. What had been our right all winter had been taken away.

The *placier* strolled through the market, shaking hands and making the odd joke. His job at this stage was to supervise the unloading, making sure that people didn't obstruct each other. As he did so, he quizzed them about the whereabouts of the regulars who were running late. At 8 a.m., nearly three hours after we arrived, he would begin awarding any available spaces. For now we just had to wait and try not to let successive cafés crèmes eat up our morning's profit.

Our former neighbour, the honey lady, Martine, arrived. We waved from our wall and observed as she methodically set up her pitch. Alert as ever, she stopped, box in hand, seemingly staring into space. Shoving her honey to one side, Martine came running up, bright-eyed and flushed-faced. She spoke excitedly. 'Quick, quick you must see the *placier* before someone else grabs the spot.'

We were both bleary-eyed and disconcerted by the sudden commotion. Taking both our hands, Martine dragged us stumbling across the market. 'Don't you notice anything different?' she said with exasperation.

If she'd had the time, I think she would have given us a lecture about fending for ourselves in the big bad world. Instead she barked, '*Restez ici*, and don't let anyone move you.'

She zigzagged away through the market looking for the *placier*. She returned two minutes later looking delighted. 'You have a permanent place.'

'Where?' we chorused.

'Where you are standing,' replied Martine, raising her eyes at our stupidity.

We looked around. We were near the end of the *étang*, metres away from where we usually traded. Neither of us could work out why the space had suddenly become free. Certainly nobody else had ever traded from it. All winter it must just have been empty, but that still didn't explain why this morning the *placier* had suddenly changed his mind. And then Tanya realised. We'd been sitting for three hours regarding such a familiar scene that we'd failed to notice one important difference.

'The flagstone?'

'*Voilà*, the flagstone,' said Martine, finally losing patience. 'The *mairie* decided it was too much of a health and safety risk to leave it here.'

Tanya and I stood trying to fathom how we hadn't noticed.

'Quick, set up before anyone else gets interested,' urged Martine.

As Tanya thanked Martine, I crossed to the car, snapped open the table legs, hefted a piece of board on top and spread our tablecloth. Finally we had a place in Cucuron Market, and neither of us could keep the grins from our faces. Our cheerfulness and the leftover Easter tourists boosted sales. As the morning progressed, we crept towards fifty bottles of wine. The fabled season that everyone had described, when the markets teemed with people, was living up to expectations. Six more months and 120 more markets like the last two and we would be on our way to having a rosé business. Provided, that is, we survived our visit to Lourmarin *Mairie*.

The walk through Lourmarin that afternoon was a familiar one. We parked the car next to the *cave* cooperative. The manager, Bruno, was a jovial, flamboyant man who'd taken great delight in our arrival in town. He'd sampled our wines and offered us an endless supply of culinary advice as we'd struggled to master the French staple of *cuisse de canard*. There was always a problem to recount to Bruno – either we cooked the duck for too short a time or the heat was too high – and in the end despairing of us, Bruno bought a vacuum-packed jar of the dish. 'There,' he'd said, 'this can't possibly go wrong.' We glanced into the interior of the *cave* but there was no sign of anyone.

We passed Tanya's hairdressers, Elodie and Nadesh, two pretty, enterprising young girls who'd just set up their own salon. It was one of the centres of gossip in Lourmarin. If you wanted to keep a secret, you stayed out of the baker's and had your hair cut in Cadenet. We waved hello, but failed to attract their attention. Further up the street, Alex, who made beautiful lights, carving their bases from the local olive wood, was standing outside his shop, cigarette in hand, lounging against the wall with one leg bent behind him for support. He blew smoke rings into the air and greeted us. Such was Alex's cigarette habit that it was impossible for anything to happen in the village without him knowing.

In front of us was the imposing building of the *mairie*. A staircase and an iron railing divided it from the street, and the French flag fluttered proudly against the blue sky. The walk through the village had felt a bit like a spaghetti western. I'd half expected all the shutters to be bolted shut as we passed, for kids to be called in from the street by anxious mothers and for some judiciously placed tumbleweed to come sweeping towards us, as the director gradually increased the volume of the chilling background music. All that was needed for a proper climax was for our invisible tormentor – perhaps the fruit seller with the crazy eyes who'd issued the cryptic warning about not seeing us next week – to come limping round the corner, flexing his trigger finger. Instead we climbed the steps to the *mairie* wondering what fate awaited us inside.

We pushed the heavy door and entered the cool, stony shade. In front of us, a large staircase led up to the council chamber, but we turned right into the secretariat. Two ladies sat behind the high counter, swinging between workstations on wheeled chairs as they fought the ever-multiplying mounds of paper.

One of them glanced up over her glasses. 'Can I help you?'

I nodded and handed over an envelope containing our market

papers and alcohol licence. 'Sébastian asked for these,' I said, embarrassed that my hand was shaking slightly.

'Yes, he told me,' she said, taking the envelope and pushing herself backwards at high velocity towards the photocopier.

I just wanted the waiting to be over. I glanced at Tanya, who seemed much calmer than me. The copier churned into action and its ugly blue light scanned the papers.

The woman placed the copies in a file and then pushed herself back over to us. It was time for the verdict. She held out our envelope. '*Merci beaucoup*,' she said.

I took hold of it. '*C'est tout?*'

'*Oui, c'est tout*.' She smiled. 'There's a new law and we need copies of all the alcohol licences.'

We walked back out into the sunlight. The village looked as beautiful as ever, all old stone and bright spring flowers. We were still the proud owners of a licence to trade alcohol, and what's more we had guaranteed places in four local markets. With the night-market season coming and plenty of other day markets to try, we were ready to make money. As Peter Tate would have said had he been with us, 'Everything was marvellous, absolutely marvellous.'

18

Pre-Season

In May the cherries gradually ripened. The pale fruit deep-
ened in colour with each passing day until the orchards were
covered in a galaxy of lush red stars. Beaten-up old cars were
discarded by the roadside and stepladders rested by the sides of
the trees, but the human pickers were usually totally obscured
by the heavy foliage. When they emerged, they were so stained
with blotches of red that they looked like they had chicken-
pox.

Days after I first tasted the ruby flesh of the cherries, local
melons began to arrive. Grown under long tarpaulin covers that
stretched for hundreds of metres, I'd struggled to place the smell
of the ripening fruit for days. Like suntan lotion, it triggered
memories of blazing days and salt-kissed seaside lunches, but
it wasn't until the aroma drifted towards me as I entered the
market one morning that I associated it with ripe melons. That
lunchtime we cut open our first of the year, scooped out the
seeds and feasted on the succulent bright-orange flesh.

The melons were quickly followed by trays of nectarines and
peaches, soft to the touch with the creases in their skin grinning
at the sky. Fat tomatoes ripened just kilometres from the point
of sale dwarfed their inferior winter brethren, and in the space
of just a few days the markets donned their best summery livery.

Jewellery vendors with tiny stalls, barely half a metre wide, squeezed themselves into the last remaining spaces. Traders who'd made a steady living from selling sensible seasonal clothes suddenly shred any pretence of trying to serve local customers, revealing ranges of skimpy T-shirts bedecked with silly slogans – *'Voulez-vous coucher avec moi ce soir?'*

Shops that had long lain dormant reopened their doors. Postcard racks lined the pavements like slalom posts, prices for the *plat du jour* in restaurants rose by a surreptitious couple of euros, and everyone took a deep breath and waited. Overhead, airline jets trailing vapour wrote our fortunes in the sky – for months they'd passed hundreds of kilometres too high, heading for sun-drenched winter hotspots, but now they ducked low over Mont Sainte-Victoire and descended to Marseille, Nice and Nîmes. The roads filled with map-clutching, gawping sightseers who seemed oblivious to the fact that some people used the narrow lanes to get from A to B. Tanya and I rubbed our hands with glee; at last it had begun. Or so we thought.

Perhaps everybody had just been waiting too long. Perhaps the traders had forgotten what last summer was really like, and over the long winter months had drawn sustenance from and built upon a myth rather than reality. After all the expectation and the endless discussions, it could never have really lived up to the hype, and just a few weeks into May the moaning began.

'It's even worse than last year.'

'It'll never be the same again.'

'That's it. I'm finished. I'm going to become a barman.'

'It's the world economy.'

'It's terrorism.'

'It's all the fault of the Bordelais.'

The problem according to everyone was that the wrong sort of tourists were arriving. The markets looked impressively full. There was a steady stream of suncream-coated, straw-hat-wearing, red-kneed individuals passing by. They talked, they pointed, they picked up, they examined, and they even asked to have their photos taken behind the stalls. The one thing they didn't do was buy, justifying their behaviour with a litany of familiar excuses – the car's too far away, there's no space in the suitcase to take it home, or I must just go and ask my husband.

The traders analysed the calibre of the tourists, explaining each fluctuation in sales by the changing holiday seasons around the world – the end of the English Easter holidays (late April), the beginning of the American summer holidays (May) and the German (June). Each week they promised us that our trade would increase the following week and that the *vraie saison* would soon begin. Each week we listened to another series of complaints.

Customerless, the Provençal market trader is a verbose sort. I'd have thought the Americans would be public enemy number one. In the past I'd heard them linked to all sorts of ills. When Tanya was stung by a jellyfish two years ago, the queue of people in the local pharmacy had concluded that it was all the fault of George Bush. Global warming had led to higher sea temperatures and a proliferation of jellyfish along the Med, hence the link between the American president's actions and my wife's sting was undeniable – he was culpable. But although the Americans took a pasting for their inability to learn how to even say '*bonjour*' or '*merci*', without doubt it was the Dutch who were the least welcome tourists.

In the local imagination, Holland is little more than a massive car park for camper vans. All that flat land makes an easy marshalling point for these white tanks before they bulldoze their way south, laden with cans of Amstel and a month's supply of Edam. According to market hearsay, the last thing any self-respecting Dutch person does on holiday is buy regional produce. Instead they illegally park their vans in the municipal parking – who needs to pay for a campsite when there's a *parking* so close? And who cares if the residents can't park and have to lug their shopping and their children a couple of hundred metres to get to their houses? Camp chair in the next-door parking space, the Dutch sit under the trees munching their Dutch cheese and drinking their Dutch beer.

'They are too cheap to even buy a baguette,' grumbled one trader.

'At least they speak the language,' I argued. As always, I was impressed by anyone with a command of more than one tongue, and the Dutch I'd met spoke at least three, switching effortlessly between English, French and their native voice.

'It makes them smug,' snorted the trader. 'Never, ever spend any time serving the Dutch,' he advised. 'They'll taste absolutely everything you have on offer, they'll talk to you for hours and prevent you from engaging with other customers, and then they'll just walk off. Forget *oursins* in the pocket, the Dutch have whopping great Portuguese men of war. If their fingers so much as stray near a spare euro, they risk being stung to death. No wonder they don't spend anything.'

In my experience the French were just as bad. Rather than the locals, the markets began to fill with tourists from across France. Inevitably, holidaying vignerons and a seemingly endless legion of amateur sommeliers were drawn to our stand. They studied the labels meticulously and then pounced.

'I see you have a Sancerre.'

'We've got rosé from across France.'

At this point Tanya would normally walk graciously to the front of the stall and run her hands along all the bottles, rather like the hostess of a TV game show displaying the prizes. She'd pluck an ice-cool bottle from the water and offer a taste.

'That's not good wine.'

'The Sancerre? But it's excellent. It's a hundred per cent Pinot Noir and made by a friend of ours, Nicolas Reverdy, in Maimbray.'

'Exactly – Maimbray. It's too far from Sancerre. The *terroir* is no good, no good at all.'

'But it's only a couple of kilometres from town, and every resident of the village is a vigneron. Nicolas Reverdy specialises in rosé.'

'Bah.'

The wine was tossed to the ground in disgust.

And so it continued, with tourists from Bordeaux being as disparaging as possible about our Bordeaux, and from Burgundy all too damning about our Marsannay. In the month of May hundreds of glasses of good wine were tipped on to the gravel. I tried to analyse why our wine was provoking such a negative reaction. It certainly wasn't because of its quality. There was doubtless an element of one-upmanship with the English, but there was something else as well. I noticed that the French, like the Dutch, weren't buying anything at all, but their circumspection had nothing to do with being suspicious of local products. Once again I consulted the other traders for an explanation.

'C'est la France,' they said, and shrugged their shoulders.

Little by little and market by market I coaxed more information. I'd heard plenty of vignerons moan about France's economic problems before – they told stories of having to call labourers in from the field during the *vendange*, or harvest, for fear of contravening working hours legislation – but I didn't expect the traders to have a similar right-wing perspective on the country's ills. But they did, telling me how it was almost impossible to make money in France. The moment you made it, the state took it back. The base for pension and healthcare contributions started at nearly €3,000, and for most traders it represented nearly 30 per cent of their annual income before they even paid tax. Any employer thinking of taking on a new staff member immediately had to pay their yearly contributions. The result was that businesses refused to employ people and the whole economy ground to a halt.

'Nobody has any money in France, apart from the Parisians,'

my sources concluded with plenty of spits for good measure as they mentioned the Parisians.

For us, this was problematic. Tasting wine is a national pastime in France. Even the French who claim not to drink will happily idle away fifteen minutes at a free *dégustation*. And for people with no money in their pockets and the holiday hours to fill, our stand was a natural destination. Inevitably we were lectured about the poverty and high price of our wines, and in the end rather than argue back Tanya and I nodded, poured free wine and prayed for that rarity, a paying customer.

We had high expectations of the English, but in mid-May with the children back at school, the demographic hurtled upwards and the price expectations of our aged clientele appeared rooted in the 1950s. It was dispiriting to sit and listen to interminable discussions between couples about whether it was a good idea to save 50 centimes and buy the wine from the *cave* instead.

Our worst experience with the English was with a lady who appeared to think that she owned the Luberon. Her hair was tied high on her head and fixed firmly in place by spray and webbing. She wore a floral dress cinched so tight round the waist that the pressure of flesh on fabric looked like it might become too much at any moment. As she circled our stall, we had plenty of time to observe her bright-red lipstick and puffed cheeks layered with make-up. Finally she moved in for the kill.

'What are you doing here?'

'Selling rosé.'

'It's not your wine?'

'No. We're wine merchants.'

'I think it's a disgrace. Every year there's more English. This isn't the Dordogne, you know. People like you are ruining the Luberon.' She clicked her heels and turned her back, stalking off to the café to have a drink among the French, except the tables around her were actually filled with the Dutch, and the Germans and Scandinavians and of course the English. For the duration of her coffee I fought to stop myself going over and asking where she'd been while Tanya and I stood in the freezing cold in January, when the lions carved on the fountains had icicles for teeth. We both could have understood if she was French, but instead she appeared to want the Luberon to be enjoyed by her and her alone.

Amid the English pensioners, the Dutch skinflints and the French free *dégusteurs*, it was a joy to serve Americans. They were gleeful when they discovered people who spoke the same language as them and indulged in long discourses about the merits of American blush wines versus dry Provençal rosés. They inevitably left our stand with bags of wine to add to the other purchases that were swinging from either arm. Some delightful gay New Yorkers even described rosé as 'juice plus'.

May rolled into June and the markets became busier still, but people continued to window-shop. The situation was so bad that Tanya and I even learnt the irregular Provençal verb to describe this behaviour. The word was so local that if we'd said it to a trader in Avignon or further south on the Côte d'Azur, they'd have struggled to understand, and for once the lack of comprehension would have nothing to do with our accents. '*Badar*' was a word that specifically applied to the markets and it tried to express in its harsh syllables all the effort the traders put into their stalls only to see people fingering merchandise and then moving on. The traders would look at each other and spit, '*Il bad.*'

The anxiety engendered by a continuing lack of profits began to creep into people's behaviour. Neurotic as ever, the traders started to blame their pitches. They saw someone else make a couple of sales and immediately assumed that the centre of shopping gravity had shifted elsewhere in the markets. Early-morning delegations beseeched the *placiers* of all the markets, arguing that their pitches should be moved. To me, it seemed futile – the cricketing equivalent of plugging a hole at second slip after a couple of wild slashes had rifled through at catchable height.

We noticed that those traders with the most influence changed position on a weekly basis, trying to feel their way into the minds of the richer tourists. Where would they tarry? What would they buy? And without exception everyone's stall expanded. The growth was so gradual it almost went unnoticed, but traders began to grab an extra couple of inches each week, convincing themselves that profits would rise just by dint of this increase. In the larger markets we visited where we didn't have a permanent place – Apt and L'Isle-sur-la-Sorgue – this behaviour made it almost impossible for us to find a space. Whereas before the *placier* had the gaps between people's stands to play with and could cajole people into making room, now the traders had to duck under their tables to get out. The result for us was distant pitches surrounded by crowds of stray dogs rather than people.

In Cucuron, our newly created pitch was disappearing with the same inevitability as the polar icecaps. Every week the traders on either side took a nibble at the space, planting the stands for their parasols where our table leg had rested the previous week. Our table consisted of two wooden boards resting on collapsible legs and by mid-June we were having to slide one board underneath the other to squeeze ourselves in. We protested and our neighbours agreed to change their behaviour the following week, but instead they turned up at the market even earlier and grabbed another couple of inches. Eventually the *placier* came to our rescue, chalking the dimensions of our pitch clearly on the ground. This solution worked until we arrived one morning to find the markings washed away. Since there had been no rainfall that week, we had to assume human intervention. The only option was to beat our competitors to the market and set up ever earlier.

Our biggest dispute took place in a surprise location. The markets we did came in all shapes and sizes – aggressive animals like Apt, where there was a snarl of traffic at six in the morning as everyone tried to cram into narrow streets, and genteel villages like Cucuron, where speaking in a whisper sometimes seemed too loud.

Out of them all the last place we expected any trouble was Ansouis. The more we turned up, the more convinced I became that it must be one of the most relaxed markets in Provence. Possibly it was the environment – the square shaded by two plane trees, covered in the type of loose earth that was perfect for a game of boules, and the peaceful accompaniment of the soothing sound of water flowing through the adjacent ancient baths. The traders trickled along later week by week. Setting up was done at a leisurely pace. Tanya and I were usually the last to arrive and light-hearted banter started immediately.

Sunday after Sunday Stefan, the cured-ham seller, grinned and called out, 'Where is Brian?'

The rest of the traders giggled and responded with the by now familiar, 'In the pub with Peggy.'

These exchanges were regarded as hilarious by everyone. The joke for the French was that Brian and Peggy were the characters from their English textbooks at school. The joke for us was that no matter how hard they tried, the French just couldn't pronounce 'Peggy'; instead they kept asking about the whereabouts of 'Piggy'.

The gentle teasing typically continued for the rest of the morning. Between customers there was time to laugh at one topic or another – the biscuit maker's new line in marzipan – as he cut off pieces of the uncoloured almond paste for people to taste, the other traders called out, *'Faites attention, c'est le boudin blanc'* – 'Pay attention, it's white pudding.' And whenever there was a lull, one of the traders shouted out, 'Where is Piggy?' and laughter rolled around the stalls.

But one Sunday in mid-June the smell of tourists and money was in the air. As usual we put up our stand and crossed to the *poulet rôti* van, where the owner, Barbara, doled out turbo-charged shots of espresso, and we stood in a thick fog of Gauloise smoke, pretending to ignore the entrails and innards visible through her glass counter as we sipped the bitter black liquid.

'Stefan, your ham is more expensive than Harrods,' I joked, stirring in sugar, which sank slowly through the viscous surface. Pata negra retailed at €100 a kilo and for just a few slices customers could expect to pay €20. Sometimes I wondered how he managed to keep a straight face when tourists with no concept of prices a kilo enthusiastically encouraged him to keep cutting.

In response Stefan pretended to look offended. Did we not know that the pata negra pigs grazed on a diet consisting exclusively of acorns and that it was then hung for two years before coming to the market? 'In Barcelona you can easily pay a hundred and sixty euros a kilo,' he insisted with a grin. 'I sell a whole leg a morning in the summer in Lourmarin.'

We returned to our stand, and just as I was uncorking our bottles of wine, I noticed problems on the other side of the square. An old man with an elegantly pruned handlebar moustache had set up a small table and chair. Under a cloth was an enormous paella cooked and ready to serve in plastic takeaway dishes. The price was €5 a portion, conveniently undercutting his rival, who, like us, had been in Ansouis since it reopened after the winter break.

A lynch mob of gesturing French market traders quickly surrounded the interloper, almost driving him from his seat with the draught created by their whirling arms. Ruefully fingering his moustache, the paella vendor headed home for what must have been a large lunch.

Turning back to my stall, I was accosted by a young Frenchman. His eyes were dark, his hair short and his accent heavy with the local twang. The pantomime of a conversation we had went something like this.

'You're in my place.'

'But we've been here all spring.'

'No you haven't.'

'Oh yes we have.'

'Oh no you haven't.'

Our challenger turned out to be a local vigneron trying to bully us from our pitch – under the plane trees with an ancient wall to sit on, it was right in the centre of the market and the dappled sunlight made an excellent location to sell wine. He must have scented blood. We were English and therefore vulnerable. Did we have permission from the local *mairie*? Did we have an alcohol licence? The aggressive questioning continued and gradually I began to weaken. I had an alcohol licence but didn't know that we needed permission from the *mairie* as well. Each French village appeared to have its own rules and I was on uncertain ground.

Quite soon we were surrounded by the same whirling mob who'd driven the paella vendor away. We were fighting against a man who grew his wine no more than 100 metres from where we stood. How could we win? Parochial interest in France always triumphed against central government, against European law and most definitely against a couple of English market traders. But there was a more powerful force at work – the law of the market. We'd been working in Provençal markets for nearly eight months. We'd turned up in the winter when customers were sparse, traders stuffed newspaper in their shoes to keep warm, and the village dogs toasted themselves by lying on the pavement in front of the *poulet rôti* van. Winter service had to triumph over summer opportunism, otherwise there would be chaos.

Stefan, the ham seller, took control. 'Of course they have permission from the *mairie*,' he lied, and leading the angry interloper away, he showed him a less favourable pitch on the far side of the market. Our place was safe, at least for another week.

The jostling for position continued in all our markets and

somehow the sales situation got worse. The last two weeks in June were dreadful. This was a time of year when I budgeted we would be selling over fifty bottles of wine per market. Nearly all the villas in the region were full, and if we captured the tourists at the right moment at the beginning of their holiday, I hoped to supply them with wine for their entire stay. Unfortunately instead of sunshine, the weather gods sent the mistral, and when the wind stopped, clouds cavorted across the sky, sending rain dancing across the market squares. The tourists stayed inside, read books, watched videos and cursed their bad luck, while the market traders shivered and talked about taking up new occupations.

Each day of bad weather sent the average number of bottles we needed to sell per market creeping upwards. Soon it was nudging sixty and then sixty-five, and even on the rare sunny days there was no sign of the *vrai* tourist; instead there was endless '*badding*' and our sales fluctuated around the twenty-bottle mark. 'Maybe next week' became our motto, but it was hard not to conclude that our year was going to end in failure. The sense of despair we felt was shared by many of the other traders. Slowly they were going out of business.

The only positive development was our improving relationship with Sébastian in Lourmarin. From our arrival in the market we'd presented him with a problem – how should he treat us? We were foreign, spoke enough French to survive in everyday life but barely understood the market patois. Doubtless the other traders would expect him to place us at the bottom of the market hierarchy. To begin with this was an easy solution, but as we'd turned up at market after market throughout the winter, he'd had to adapt his attitude. At the unofficial placing he'd probably been totally confused – on the one hand it was undeniably his duty to place all the French people who wanted a place, however recently they'd turned up, before foreigners like us; on the other hand this didn't seem fair given our devotion to the market. Only at the very end of the placing had he caved in and given us a place. Admittedly it was in a dreadful position, but no doubt Sébastian rationalised that we were lucky to have a pitch at all. And now as long as we didn't moan about our location, we were no longer a problem, and he could begin to have some fun with us.

'I told the shopkeeper you'd give him a bottle every morning as a thank-you for having you outside his store.'

We'd learnt from observation that Sébastian's humour revolved around his authority. He assumed he was all-powerful and that the traders believed 100 per cent in whatever he said, even when he was joking. To allow Sébastian to have his fun, we nodded along and promised to give the shopkeeper a bottle. 'Make sure it's good wine, not your cheapest, and you'd better give the waiters in the restaurant some as well.' His face eased into a smile as we were finally permitted to know he'd been teasing us.

One week I'd made the mistake of paying Sébastian with a mishmash of change, including the miniscule 5- and 10-cent bits. 'I am not a bank, you know,' he'd declared in a mock huff.

The following Friday as we set up, he came over, trailed obsequiously by some hopefuls still looking for a place. 'If you don't have the right money this week, I am going to split your pitch up – five centimetres here, twenty there and then you'll see what it's like.' He smiled as he turned away, but I still made sure I had the correct large change to pay him later that morning.

At least we were now talking, and at least some time in the future – if we survived our first season, that is – we might get a decent place, away from the pervading stench of bouillabaisse, which permeated our clothes every Friday morning and made our apartment stink like a fishmonger's.

19

The *Vraie* Season – Part I

July was supposed to be the month when it all came together. Finally we would be rewarded for the bitter winter mornings when we had struggled to lift cases of wine with our cold, brittle fingers. We'd reap the benefits of our patience in dealing with the French bureaucracy and the tireless shuttling between the *sous-préfecture* in Apt and the Chambre de Commerce in Cavaillon. Summer was here and the season of plenty was upon us. Like the other traders, we'd waited all year for July and August. These two months had dominated market conversations from the narrow alleyways of L'Isle-sur-la-Sorgue to the broad *place* in Lourmarin. We'd effectively been training for this moment for the last nine months, honing our skills as salesmen, perfecting our market patter until the punters believed that the only rosé they could possibly drink was ours. Yet within four weeks, despite the markets teeming with tourists, I was ready to call time on our nascent business.

The month began with a riot of purple. Day by day the laven-der had been baking in the sun and slowly deepening in colour, with each new shade only subtly different from the last. Then, one morning, the Luberon was transformed as nature unveiled the deep, luscious purple of the postcards. From high in the hills near Bonnieux looking north towards Mont Ventoux, a patchwork of fields was visible across the valley – some planted with vines, others sown with golden wheat – and dotted amid them was this brilliant purple pageant. Up close, the fields of lavender stretched in long regal lines, curving over the crest of hills, dipping and rising in giddying waves. Photographers crouched low in the earth, swishing away the bees, checking the light, adjusting their aperture and clicking away, searching for the ideal shot that could be syndicated to travel editors worldwide – the lavender breaking around an old stone *borrie*, or sweeping upwards towards the white peak of Mont Ventoux.

The countryside was alive with smells and activity. Aromatic lavender drifted on the warm wind, mixing with the sticky scent of pine and herbs – rich rosemary and the prolific bushes of wild lemon thyme. Wild boars scuttled down from the mountains, the noise of their hyperactive noses divining for water sometimes waking us in the depths of night. Spiders the size of our hands crept into the showers, and scorpions hurried from stone to stone. Tiny green olives swelled on swaying branches, and ruby grapes peeked from beneath the bushy foliage of rows of vines.

Bright posters for village *fêtes* appeared on lamp-posts, stages were constructed in squares, and at night the strains of the old English pop music the French love so much could be heard blaring into the starlit sky – 'Life Is Life', 'Another Brick in the Wall' and of course 'Sunday, Bloody Sunday'. Bumper-car rides were shifted from village to village, and tigers surprisingly materialised in roadside cages as big tops were constructed overnight. Signs the size of London advertising hoardings appeared every 5 kilometres or so on the major roads proclaiming, '*Melons, jus de fruits, fraises*,' and enterprising villagers opened up their front doors and sold courgettes and tomatoes from small foldaway tables. A trip to the supermarket became a dreaded experience as pink-fleshed tourists battled with uncontrollable trolleys laden with a week's worth of beer and wine. The privileges of life in the Luberon – an early-evening aperitif in a shady cobbled street or a quick coffee and croissant while studying the *météo* page of *La Provence* – were subsumed by the mass of people hogging our favoured spots.

Market day – in whichever village – was chaos. The municipal police called in reinforcements from the gendarmerie, but the new officers were more interested in preening and strutting – adjusting stray stands of gelled hair and admiring the resulting sleek look in their colleagues' reflective sunglasses – than dealing with the unfolding traffic chaos. The French ditched their cars, riding kerbs, blocking drives, balancing precariously on the edge of drainage channels, and traffic jams throttled the roads. The more considerate tourists parked miles from the villages and performed feats of endurance as they panted back to their cars laden with bags of goods.

Inside the markets, there were almost too many people. The moment anyone stopped, a press developed behind them. The crowd reminded me of a Tube station at rush hour or football fans surging to get through the turnstiles before kick-off. Elbows jarred against chests, shopping was dropped scattering to the floor, and the traders battled to stem the flow near their stands, creating bottlenecks of punters to relieve of euros.

Our stand had never looked so pretty. At one end we had the darker rosés, and bottle by bottle, in a painter's palate of pinks, we edged towards the extremely pale rosé we loved. We used old wine boxes to raise some of the bottles on to different levels and interspersed magnums and jeroboams across the length of the table. The centrepiece was an enormous transparent ice bucket, which we crammed with bricks of ice and as many multicoloured bottles as possible. By midday, with the heat building, water running in fresh beads of perspiration down the bottles, and the bright sunshine creating a pink prism inside the ice blocks, it should have looked like a vision of nirvana to the passing hordes.

But for the first week of July it didn't. The tourists jostled past the stall, joking, pointing and taking pictures but not really buying. The other traders cautioned us to wait just a few more days and then the *vrais* tourists would arrive. I'd been assured of this so many times that I was beginning to lose faith that the *vrai* tourist – the creature with the bottomless pockets – actually existed.

As the month progressed, in some markets we sold fifty bottles; in others we sold practically nothing. In Lourmarin, Julien, the leather salesman, came over to us and explained that we were 'experiencing the deep breath before the storm', and over another glass of rosé passed on the imponderable wisdom that 'markets are like the first flush of love – you never know from week to week how the relationship will develop and whether your beau will wrap you in a passionate embrace or slap you in the face'. But even he, the eternal market optimist, sounded a little downbeat.

Then finally it happened. We began to work. For a frantic two hours between eleven and one every day we sold case after case of wine. We would finish serving one customer only to find a queue of potential tasters. There was barely time to wash out the glasses. Even under our parasol we sweated in the heat. The constant movement of replacing the wine on the stand, topping up glasses and keeping a conversation going with three or four people at the same time sapped our energy, so that by the time we returned home we were exhausted. Each market was an exhilarating performance as we choreographed customers into buying as much wine as possible. The buzz of finally seeing the business succeed drove us from bed in the morning, and for a fleeting week it seemed possible that we could make enough money in the season to see us through the following winter.

But in the middle of July, on the weekend of the *grand départ*, when Paris decants itself on to the *autoroutes* and heads south, our fortunes suddenly turned. On Thursday night we set the alarm and went to bed early, aware that while we slept, the first sun-seekers from the north would be racing through a caffeine-filled night ready to break with a rush of holiday high spirits on Lourmarin Market. At first light I stretched out in bed, only to feel a throbbing pain in my foot.

Rehearsing the previous day in my mind, I ascertained I hadn't bumped into anything or stubbed my foot accidentally loading and unloading for the markets. Was it possible I'd kicked out in the night and badly bruised my big toe? Shifting my position, the weight of the moving duvet cover made me wince. Only a vicious karate kick could have done this much damage, and anyway, what sort of crazed dream would make me lash out at the wall? Stumbling from bed to load the wine, I immediately fell back on to the mattress in agony. Tanya tried to help with shoving our equipment into the back of the car, but with me a complete invalid it wasn't possible.

Instead of a morning selling wine to the Parisians, I spent most of Friday with my foot up and a glass of rosé in my hand bemoaning our misfortune. By early evening if possible the swelling had increased. Had I been bitten by a large ant or a spider, or had some infection crept through broken skin? I barely slept that evening and we missed Apt Market the following morning.

The Provençal countryside is liberally scattered with herbs, and in the age before there was a pharmacy in every village, local hypochondriacs had to make do with homemade remedies. In our time in France well-wishers had advised me to treat my eczema by daily soaking my feet in a bath of first-press olive oil, and to cure a common cold by hunkering under a tea towel and inhaling a hot-water infusion of lemon and thyme. Undoubtedly the most popular panacea was lavender. According to folklore, a little lavender essence added to wine would banish a head-ache quicker than paracetomol. Its other applications included nausea, vertigo and flatulence. It was no surprise, then, when a neighbour suggested a footbath of lavender essence to draw out any infection. Temporarily I noticed an improvement, and unwilling to waste the precious extract, we used the remainder to swab the floor – lavender helps to ward off scorpions – and soaked a little into sponges, which we placed by the doors and windows to repel the flies.

Our house smelt like a Provençal giftshop and overnight by a process of osmosis I felt I must be cured, but on Sunday the pain was worse and we were forced absentees from Ansouis Market. By Monday morning I could barely walk and I needed a stick to support me as I hobbled through Lourmarin to the doctor.

Easing myself on to the couch, I explained that I thought I had an infection. The doctor took one look. He barely even examined the affected area and asked with something approaching glee, 'Do you like good wine?'

I nodded my head, enjoying the sympathetic repartee.

'And plenty of charcuterie?'

Another nod, another understanding smile from the doctor. Although it was only mid-morning he was already sweating. His line of questioning was intriguing given that his eyes were glazed with the memory of an indulgent night and the skin under his chin was sagging under the weight of too many good lunches.

'And of course blue cheese?'

Well, I might be English, but I am as partial to Roquefort as a native.

Clapping his hands together and helping me from the couch, the doctor pronounced his verdict. I was about to be offered membership of a privileged club. It was one which I was convinced my doctor had himself joined many years ago. '*C'est une crise de goutte*,' he proclaimed, beaming as he wrote out the prescription, reciting the complicated dosage without any difficulty. As I left, he vigorously shook my hand. If only there had been a prize for the best patient of the day, I am sure I would have won.

I limped into the pharmacy and was greeted with garlands.

'Take a seat, monsieur. Put your foot up, monsieur, and we'll get the prescription right away.'

It was the same in the village. I'd never had an illness that drew so much sympathy before. As I made my way back to the car, people patted me on the back and wished me, '*Bon courage.*' A free baguette and some goat's cheese were even pressed into my hand by a well-wisher.

Back home, I explained the strange reaction to Tanya. In England, gout sufferers are afforded little consideration. The illness might be painful but it's seen as self-inflicted. Why the difference?

'Blue cheese, wine, charcuterie,' said Tanya, 'you've caught the French equivalent of the common cold.'

It was all becoming clear. Every man in the village had doubtless suffered *une crise de goutte*. My limp had probably been instantly diagnosed. It was almost a badge of honour. I wanted to protest that all I'd been drinking was a little rosé and that my blue-cheese intake was very limited, but Tanya wasn't having any of it.

'You're an honorary Frenchman now. I shall call you "Gouttier".'

The pills the doctor gave me took a couple of days to work and it wasn't until Thursday morning that we were ready to start in the markets again. One key week had been wiped from our yearly profits, but our sales had been so healthy before my *crise de goutte* that we were confident we could quickly make up for the losses. Our friend Peter Tate's car – the old BMW that ferried us from market to market – had other ideas.

The car had a long history of electrical faults, which can sometimes seemingly be rectified by a couple of softly spoken words. Examples of past misdemeanours include the locks refusing to work or on hot days with the hood down the wiper-fluid reservoir inexplicably emptying, giving us an impromptu shower. In our heads these problems had imbued the car with a whimsical personality, which always seemed to materialise at the worst possible moment. On Thursday morning I'd been up at five loading the car as light crept over the landscape. We snatched a quick breakfast and Tanya and I hurriedly clambered into the BMW. I turned the key. Nothing. It was six in the morning and far too early to call the local mechanic. Instead we emptied the car, drank tea and waited for the clock to tick round to a more reasonable hour.

Both of us were worried. As a result of my gout, we'd missed a week of markets in the peak season. If we failed to turn up again, then it was possible that on our eventual return we would find another trader in our place. All the hard work over the winter months securing our positions would have been futile. Then there was the lost revenue to consider. If we couldn't get the car up and running quickly, we'd lose another crucial week of sales. Before calling the mechanic, Tanya tried the car one last time. The engine grumbled to life. It was too late to rush to L'Isle-sur-la-Sorgue Market, particularly since we had no guaranteed place and needed to arrive before the other itinerant traders, and so instead we drove straight to the local garage.

In Lourmarin, there is a Corsican restaurant, a Corsican bar and also a Corsican garage. It's run by Bruno, a dark-haired mechanic with a reputation for being '*correct*' and fixing just about any problem you may have. While he's at it, he'll try to sell you mechanical olive-harvesting machines, enormous lawnmowers and the type of vicious chainsaws usually wielded by the villain in a horror movie, but if you can manage to resist, you usually leave with a fixed car and a small bill.

When we arrived, Bruno extricated himself from beneath a Jeep – he's unusually large for a Corsican and so the process took a couple of minutes. We explained the problem and poured out our worries about losing our place in the market. 'We need the car fixed and we need it fixed quickly,' we concluded, aware that in Provence 'quick' meant 'within a week or so'.

The average UK garage mechanic in a situation similar to this would recognise a gift horse. They'd scratch their heads, mutter something technical and promise to get right on to the problem. A couple of days later with the fault supposedly rectified we'd be presented with a bill in excess of the value of the car. Not Bruno. Instead he looked confused.

'The car works?'

We nodded.

'You drove it here and you can drive it home?'

We nodded.

'What's there to repair?' He shrugged.

We pleaded for him to at least have a look.

'Next time it happens, call me and I'll come straight away.'

For a couple of days everything was fine. Business returned to normal, and despite the markets we'd missed, sales were so good that Tanya and I both reverted to optimism. Then on the Tuesday morning the same fault occurred again. Once more it was first thing in the morning, but this time I was armed with Bruno's mobile number and his vow to be with us the moment the fault reoccurred. I dialled and went straight through to answer phone. What I heard didn't surprise me.

Summer in the south of France is the busiest time of year. The roads are rammed full with cars, and *autoroute* slip roads are lined with overheating casualties of the relentless rush south. It should be a fantastic time of year for the garages of Provence. Bruno – according to his recorded message – just like all the other Provençal entrepreneurs, the plumbers and electricians, who leave overcrowded hotels to fend for themselves, and the doctors in the village, who desert the swelling population – had gone on holiday for a month.

During the next week I investigated hiring a reserve car, which was prohibitively expensive in the tourist season, long-leasing a car – there's a fantastic tax loophole for non-Europeans that makes this possible for three-month periods and really cheap, but not unfortunately for us – and buying a clapped-out van from a local, but in the end we both decided that we just had to swallow the cost of the occasional missed market and get the car fixed on Bruno's return. We were lucky: the car only broke down on a further two occasions, wiping out more profits, but certainly not justifying the expense of hiring or buying a replacement.

More misfortune was on its way, though. We turned up in Ansouis Market having missed two out of the last three Sundays (gout and car). Our place under the plane tree was free and so we began to set up, saying a cheery hello to the other traders. One of them took an order for croissants as he headed off to the *boulangerie*, while Barbara in the butcher's van began to make shots of her extra-strong coffee. Within half an hour our rosé was glinting in the ice bucket. Tanya was busy brushing away the breakfast crumbs from the table, while I flicked through *La Provence*.

Neither of us noted the crowd of people gathering around our stall. Eventually we looked up. Our view of the château, perched on the rocky outcrop above the village, had been obliterated by a bunch (I am not sure of the correct collective noun) of vignerons. Their elected leader, the one who'd gesticulated at us nearly a month back, explained that they'd all gathered to ask us not to come back to Ansouis Market. Our stand was preventing them from selling their local wine and we had no official approval from the *mairie*.

Stefan, the ham seller, who'd supported us so vociferously before, came to our aid once again. To him, our continued presence in Ansouis Market was a matter of little more than personal pride, but he argued – as only the French can – as if feeding his family depended on the outcome. Showing an agility of mind to match that of a Sciences postgraduate, he explained that the vignerons had no case – they were selling local wines, whereas we were selling rosé from across France. If customers wanted local produce, then they would surely purchase from the vignerons; if they wanted wine from elsewhere, then they should be able to purchase from us. The more stalls and the more choice for the customer, the better the market would become and the more profitable each individual local trader. Adam Smith would have been proud.

This time, though, Stefan was outnumbered and the clamouring for our removal – forcible if necessary – became louder. Discovering my inner Frenchman, I began a long and impassioned rant about our right to sell wine. My arms flailed and I jabbed my finger aggressively towards our tormentors as I grappled to make my French intelligible despite my anger. Splinter groups of vignerons broke off to discuss the matter with other market traders and eventually an official from the *mairie* was called for – a reasonable solution for us, considering the more extreme factions had been in favour of having the local gendarmerie take us away.

The official was a demure man with white hair and a soft voice. We'd met him on a number of occasions before and helped promote local events by handing out his flyers from our stand. Taking us aside, he explained that in our absence a rota had been drawn up allocating different Sundays to different vignerons. It had been agreed that there should be no more than two wine sellers in the market at any one time. If we'd like to participate in this arrangement, we were of course more than welcome. We nodded eagerly, foreseeing an equitable end to our problems. However, he continued, we would have to wait until at least October, because every slot was currently booked.

I'd run out of argumentative French vocabulary, so I stood sullenly silent, refusing to take down our stall. The vignerons were still muttering about calling the gendarmes when I spotted a customer approaching. Perhaps my mind was elsewhere, perhaps I was just clumsy. Ignoring the ill will floating in the air, I swiftly, too swiftly as it turned out, circled round to pour some wine.

My foot caught the leg of our table, dragging it off the ground, and for a second I stood entranced, not realising the significance of what was happening. The wine began a slow slide towards me. Had I not been off balance, I could have opened my arms and caught most of it, I might have even managed to right the table, but as I un-snared my foot, the tilt became vertiginous and everything came down. Bottle after bottle smashed in a series of sharp cracks, which ricocheted off the mountains. People in the village would have been forgiven for thinking that the hunting season had started prematurely. Our ice bucket lay upended and a stream of rosé flowed away into the gutter.

For the next half-hour Tanya and I very publicly packed up and left. We picked shards of glass from the dusty ground, squeezed the water and the wine from our sodden tablecloths and loaded the municipal rubbish bin with the jagged-edged bottles. The people who'd bought wine from us over the preceding weeks stood and watched, gossiping away about our downfall. Every trader spared five minutes to help with the clear-up, but despite this show of support it was a humiliating way to leave.

Back at home, we agreed not to go back to Ansouis. We'd put up a fight, but ultimately neither of us wanted to work in a market where our arrival sparked such antagonism. After my ill health and the problems with the car, it began to seem that luck was conspiring against us. While all around us other traders had been busy raking in the cash, we'd spent much of July confined to our house, and when we'd made it to the market, we'd lost a couple of hundred euros worth of stock in a freak accident.

Looking at the figures, I became quite morose. With only one good month of the season left and with one less market a week, we still had nearly 3,000 bottles to sell to meet our conservative first-year target of 8,000. And when the mistral wiped out the final three markets of July, I was ready to concede defeat.

20

The *Vraie* Season – Part II

O ne afternoon at the beginning of August we spotted a
most peculiar sight at the bottom of our garden. First
there was a rustling in the bushes, suggesting the presence of a
wild boar or one of the large local hares. Then we heard gravel
crunch underfoot and a bellow of laughter.

'Took a wrong turning in the village and ended up behind
these trees.'

We would have both rushed to embrace our old friend Peter
Tate were it not for his curious attire. He held a lit cigar in one
hand, a couple of boules in the other and was dressed in what
can best be described as a weightlifting outfit. Made from one
piece of skintight Lycra, it was cut just above the knee and was
almost indecently revealing around the crotch before splitting
into two at waist height, baring Peter's hairy chest, and rising in
two spandex braces over his shoulders.

'It's what we used to swim in at school,' said Peter, clearly
enjoying the impression he'd created.

'But why now?' said Tanya, as she gave him a tentative welcoming hug.

Peter grinned. 'Remember Saint-Rémy?'

Two years ago, when we first came to France together, we'd
been turned away from the municipal pool in Saint-Rémy-de-

Provence. The reason – both Peter and I had swimming shorts, rather than the requisite Speedos. At the time I'd attributed the prohibition to the thong fetish of the local mayor, but subsequently I'd learnt that municipal pools across France all had the same hygiene regulations. Men were required to swim in something that they couldn't possibly wear when out for lunch. Glancing once again at Peter, there was no doubt he'd be admitted to Lourmarin pool.

'I thought we'd have a game of boules and then go for a swim,' said Peter, laughing infectiously.

Grabbing a bottle of rosé, we prepared to play, and in the spirit of ridiculousness that Peter had suddenly introduced into the day, I joined him in my recently purchased Speedos, which can best be described as exceptionally brief.

Games of boules with Peter sometimes take unexpected turns and he has patented what he calls an extreme version of the game. Rather than just play on the flattest stretch of available gravel, he likes to go round bends, over the corners of houses and even play aquatically on the bottom of pools. That afternoon the most readily available obstacle was the large olive tree that stood in the centre of the drive. Chucking the *cochonnet* over the branches, he followed up with an arcing pitch. As it fell, the boule just clipped the branches of the olive tree and came to rest adjacent to its target.

Taking my throwing stance, I tried to block out the fact I was dressed in practically nothing. Glancing back towards the house for a little support from Tanya, I noticed two figures watching us from across the field. Rose and Antoine – our landlord and landlady – were stood stock still, as if petrified by a gorgon, regarding the spectacle.

Despite my lack of clothing, the last thing I was worried about was my Speedos: Frenchmen have a strange predilection for wearing thongs in public. It happens so regularly that the hygiene rules of pools are often rendered redundant by Gallic holidaymakers nonchalantly getting their groceries in flip-flops, T-shirt and Speedos. In this respect being spotted playing boules in my briefs was actually a positive – it showed I was going native.

What I was really concerned about was that we were in the process of trying to extend our lease, which ran out in a month's time. Neither of us had any idea what fortune, or otherwise, the rest of the season would bring and we wanted to keep on trading until the last of the tourists quit the Luberon at the end of October, before evaluating our position. While our relation-ship with Rose and Antoine was typically good, there had been moments – such as the damaged kitchen (the repair bill eventu-ally came to €500 not €1,000) – when I felt that they were just waiting for our tenancy to end.

So far, despite our repeated requests, the new lease had not been forthcoming, which was making me increasingly anxious. If we did have to move house, it would come at a very dif-ficult time both for business and personal reasons. As I stood about to pitch a boule through the branches of Antoine's prized olive trees, I could see the delay in the new lease becoming a permanent state of affairs. Thankfully, Peter had also spotted the danger, and with a casual flick of his foot, he'd repositioned the *cochonnet* to the side of the tree. I rolled my boule along the ground and Rose and Antoine moved off, apparently satisfied that there was no danger to their olives.

Over the next few weeks traders and customers in the markets of Provence experienced what I came to call the 'Peter Tate effect'. At each market Tanya and I did the usual – set up, bought a pastry and waited for the rising sun to engender a thirst. Peter was having none of it. Standing in front of our stall like a sales rep at a mobile-phone conference, he accosted anyone who came near, whatever the hour.

'It's twelve o'clock somewhere in the world,' he bellowed at customers who tried to excuse themselves by pointing at their watch.

Noting the bottleneck of punters that built up on a daily basis around Peter's ample frame, one of our fellow traders commented that he was like a *bouchon*, the French word for cork or traffic jam. It was uncannily accurate. Nobody could shop unaccosted in the market until they got past Peter, who wielded our bottles of wine like a cowboy playing with his six-shooter. Conscious of our budget, we normally poured people a small sip, trying to ensure that a bottle lasted a whole morning, but Peter took the view that the bigger the glasses, the more guilty people would feel if they didn't buy anything. His sales patter was merciless.

'Buy the wine and get a free bag,' he said, proudly displaying one of our plastic carrier bags to a frail old man.

'I can't drink wine – I'm diabetic.'

'Buy it anyway,' roared Peter, 'and I'll drink it for you.'

People engaged in conversation with him at their peril. The moment Peter asked a stranger where they were from, he would casually begin to fill a bag of wine from our stall. Then as the stranger made to leave, he would hand the bag to them as if they'd made a conscious decision to order. Without a trace of embarrassment he relieved them of their money, frequently persuading them that they didn't need any change – 'It's only Monopoly money.'

Typical of this sales onslaught was the experience of a lovely French lady called Capucine. All winter we'd been cultivating a relationship with her and gradually she'd begun to buy her wine from us. Tanya and I had always been polite, charming and anxious not to offend, aware how difficult it was to gain and retain local custom. Poor Capucine didn't know what had happened when we set Peter loose with his pidgin French.

She foolishly mentioned she'd been invited for lunch, and despite her protests that she'd already baked a cake as a gift, Peter went through every course with her and selected an appropriate wine. Tanya and I looked ruefully on, wondering how many of our business relationships would survive Peter's visit, but when Capucine left the stall, she had a massive smile on her face and she told us that our friend was '*mervellieux*'. If they hadn't both been married, I think she would have seriously considered him as a future husband.

Thanks to Peter, at the end of every market our stall was practically devoid of wine, and our money belts bulging with euros. We were selling in excess of sixty bottles a day, but given our disastrous July, it still wasn't enough. One evening over a glass of pink Sancerre, Peter took a look at our yearly figures.

'You're never going to survive on that,' he said, shaking his head.

'We'll get by,' Tanya and I replied a little defensively.

'F★★★ that,' said Peter. 'You need to raise your prices.'

We patiently explained that we were trying to sell wine at the '*correct*' price and that our local customers would refuse to use us if we overcharged, but gradually Peter's logic won. We had to concede that in July and August prices in the Luberon rose – whether it was the *plat du jour* in a local restaurant, which increased by a couple of euros, or the cost of a kilo of beans in the market, everything became that little bit more expensive. Our regular customers would understand the mark-up – they knew we had to make a living – and would be grateful when we knocked a little off the price for them.

'Think about it,' said Peter, raising his glasses on to his head and fixing us both with an intense stare. 'Just add a euro a bottle to your prices. You sell nearly sixty bottles a day. That's three hundred and sixty euros a week, and over a thousand euros a month.'

Tanya and I nodded in agreement.

'People will pay, and you really need the money,' concluded Peter, pointing at our accounts book.

*

By mid-August every market was an endurance test in the heat. We supped from frozen bottles of water and watched to see which wilted first – the brittle holiday good humour of the tourists or the optimism of the flower vendor. Bouquets swooned the moment the sun hit them, and shoppers stumbled from stall to stall in a befuddled haze. I even began to feel sorry for the visitors, who'd no doubt heard about the famous markets of Provence – the wonderful linen, the fruits and the herbs. They obviously felt that a market needed to be ticked off their list like a visit to the Palais des Papes in Avignon or a glimpse of white horses in the Camargue, but in the dry August heat browsing in the markets was for the masochistic.

Thankfully there was an alternative. The hot weather meant an early harvest, and the vignerons who'd signed up for Cucuron Night Market at Christmastime were now too busy preparing for the *vendange*. As a result of their absence we were able to swap one of our morning markets for the evening market.

The atmosphere was completely different, a little like going to an open-air theatre. The play started in the cool of the day just before night fell, and there were several acts, which gradually built to a denouement. Early on smoke rose from empty grills, traders squabbled over access to electricity, and a thin stream of people took their seats in the cafés. The smell of *moules*, seasoned with parsley and cooked in wine, simmering in a drum drifted across the square. Tables of games – giant chess and miniature skittles – were set up for the children to play, and finally the punishing sun fell below the old village walls.

The crowds swelled, driven from villas and old village houses by the balmy evening air. Once again an illuminated corridor of stalls fringed the *étang*, reminding us of the Christmas market and how we'd clapped our hands for warmth, pulled our Santa hats low over our ears, and somehow managed to sell freezing cold red wine. Now we wore shorts, and the main worry was how quickly the ice for the rosé would melt.

Rickety tables and chairs emblazoned with the name of the village quickly filled with people clasping plastic plates full of food – aromatic lamb seasoned with the local herbs and served with a fragrant couscous, or spicy merguez sausages smothered in mustard and crammed between bread. We sold wine by the glass and listened to the music bouncing around the streets – the flamenco dancers twirling by the *étang*, the horn of a brass band keeping a jaunty tune together and the staccato beat of tribal drums echoing from a distant café. Small girls weaved between adults trailing nostalgia as the hems of their flowery dresses rose high in the breeze.

Meals were finished, and a jazz band was launched floating on to the water as men in linen trousers and pressed flowing shirts clasped their partners' hand and strolled amid the spotlit stalls – examining leather handbags and sparkling jewellery – unaware that they'd become part of the show. And then as midnight approached, the crowds thinned, leaving a last gaggle of inebriated clients clamouring for the final wine from our stall. Islands of light remained around the *étang*, but with a final clunk the power was pulled and the vans moved out.

On a summer evening Cucuron Night Market, which took place every Friday in August, was the best show in the south and it quickly became our most profitable excursion of the week. The crowds were so large that all the bars were permanently overstretched, and none of the owners had any objections to their customers buying wine to accompany their meal from our stall. We marked up our prices from the daytime rates, and because our overhead was simply the paltry amount we paid for the stall, and the clientele was virtually limitless, we made exceptionally good money. The only limit on our takings was the amount of wine we could fit in the back of the car, but as always Peter turned this apparent disadvantage into profit, auctioning off the last ten bottles of wine to the highest bidders.

'You'll not go to bed thirsty,' he said at midnight every Friday, bidding our swaying clientele good night.

I'd thought I used to work hard when I was a lawyer, getting to the office at seven in the morning and leaving after dark, barely seeing daylight for months on end, but the exhaustion I felt by the middle of August exceeded anything the City of London had thrown at me. We were working in six, sometimes seven markets a week, and the job was both physically and mentally demanding. Every client had to feel special and we often spent over twenty minutes talking about our wines to individual holidaymakers. The majority of our customers were interesting, but some droned on about the leaking tap in their villa and the difficulty of finding Provençal workmen to fix it. Throughout these stories we could never switch off; instead we had to be gently encouraging, allowing our clients – an equal mix of holidaying Brits and Americans, and wealthy Parisians – to rehearse their prejudices until they felt we shared them.

After four hours in the gruelling heat, we packed up, often having to carry the wine hundreds of metres, through a traffic jam of white vans, to the car. By the time we'd then unloaded the wine back at home, my shirt was damp with sweat and my brain befuddled by a morning of hard selling. Inevitably there were then deliveries to do or wine to pick up from suppliers.

Our days were so busy I lost track of how many bottles we'd sold. Jotting the details of each market down on the torn-off corners of wine boxes, I placed them in a drawer, always resolving to add them to my yearly spreadsheets, but somehow never quite finding the time. By nightfall the three of us were listless, barely able to mutter a word to each other, as we stared at the sun setting behind the hills. And it was this final view of the Luberon – the olive trees, the sentinel cypresses and the rows of vines – that made all the day's efforts make sense. In the summer we earned our right to live in this *coin de paradis*.

Without Peter our sales onslaught would have been impossible.

Ironically, Lourmarin Market, where we'd fought so hard for a permanent place, was among our worst of the week. The *place* was dusty, and the concrete wall behind us absorbed the sun's heat, getting hotter and hotter as the summer progressed until it felt like working next to a radiator. The numerous visitors to the market were primarily window-shoppers and we wasted infuriating minutes explaining about our wines to people who never had any intention of purchasing.

By contrast Cucuron Market on Tuesday morning was always a pleasure. Martine, the honey lady who worked next to us, was so busy that she arrived with her mother and eight-year-old son. The two of them spent the morning struggling to reload the stall with jars as quickly as Martine could sell them. The proximity of the water lent the market an atmosphere of serenity, and despite the heat and the crowds, the numerous shoppers were so relaxed that the market was still enjoyable. People bought rather than looked, and for us, it was our most successful market.

In Cadenet, the atmosphere changed in August. Smart Provençal linen replaced replica swords as the vendors moved their wares upmarket to match the new clientele. Shiny people carriers from Paris rather than battered vans rode the kerbs, and money that had fallen like an intermittent drip in the preceding months now flowed freely. It wasn't quite Cucuron or Lourmarin, and there was a certain wariness among shoppers and traders, who both clasped their purses tightly, but even so it worked.

With no pitch in Ansouis, we spent the rest of the days of the week travelling to the large tourist markets, hoping to get a space. We left early, waking up at five thirty and leaving by six to arrive in Apt, L'Isle-sur-la-Sorgue, Cavaillon or Gordes before seven. Usually we were rewarded with a pitch, but on other occasions we drove back home, picking up croissants to eat a disconsolate breakfast on the terrace.

Nearing the end of August, we were all flagging. The

excitement had gone from our voices as we explained for the thousandth time how the colour of a rosé depended on the amount of time the juice of a red grape was left on its skin. After hours in the car we knew every twist and turn of the sinuous *combe*, or coombe, of Lourmarin, and every *mas* hidden in the hills on our way to Cucuron. Like us, our equipment was worn through. Our parasol had had one of its limbs ripped off by the mistral and a spike of wood now jutted at an irregular angle, threatening to poke unwary customers in the eye. The wooden boards that formed the tops of our tables had to be handled with gloves to prevent a forest of splinters lodging themselves in our fingers. Even the wine was showing signs of age – we were forced to stop selling one of the 2005 rosés we still had in stock because it was slowly turning to vinegar in the heat. We were overstretched and desperately in need of time to regroup and reinvest, but with the season so short, we slogged ever onwards, patching up our gear and ourselves.

Then, and for us not a moment too soon, the Luberon sighed with relief, smiles returned to traders' faces, and we all looked around in disbelief, questioning whether it had really happened. Where once waves of people had rushed through the aisles and charging white breakers of shoppers had rolled relentlessly to the far corner of markets, there was now only a lazy and receding tide of foreign voices, their accents a muted echo of the storm that had just passed.

In response stallholders began to pull out, leaving patches of bare gravel, churned by the passing of so many feet. During this last week in August the markets existed in a curious limbo. Standing looking at the traders around us, and noting those who'd already disappeared, it felt like the set of a play had been partially dismantled. The missing parasols and intermittent spare spaces allowed us to look right through markets from one side to another. The illusion of a permanent tented village, even a community, created by squeezing so many stalls into such a small place, had vanished. The magic of the summer was lost, and those who were staying had to regroup, abandon the poorer pitches and huddle together in a tighter group, but this process would take weeks, and for now everything was out of kilter.

For us, like everyone else, it was time to count the money, then divide the total by the ten long months we had to wait until the season returned and work out whether our business could survive. Part of me was too scared to start. I knew that for the first time we'd made real money in August. There was a pot in the house with thick wads of €50 and €100 notes curled inside. Our *cave* was full of wine, which had all been paid for in cash, and my bank statement, which came through just before the end of the month, showed an impressive row of credits and not a single debit. Added to the year-round totals, there was a chance that we'd made enough for a viable business, and for a couple of days this possibility made me light-hearted. Had we at last conquered the dilemma of how and where to live our lives?

A couple of times I sat down at my desk and began to do our yearly accounts. On each occasion I dragged myself reluctantly away, knowing that I needed a day rather than a grasped hour to get a complete picture. Yet often I found myself drawn back to my study, absent-mindedly fingering the accounts book as I gazed out of the window at the hills. The markets still dominated our week, eating away at any spare time and forcing further delays, but I was happy. For the first time since the beginning of the tourist season, there was a reason to hope and dream again.

Finally, at the beginning of September, I had a free week-end. But before I could start the calculations, it was time to say goodbye to Peter. On his last night we drove the old BMW to Lourmarin. The village was *en fête*. A row of fairground attractions had been set up on the tree-lined avenue where the market was normally situated. There were bumper cars, candyfloss machines, shooting galleries and a twirling carousel of painted horses trotting in time. An assortment of mismatched tables and chairs were scattered beneath the plane trees, and as darkness fell, the village ate together, applauding the live band between courses.

Fairy lights looped in silvery waves from the branches above us, and we sipped on warm rosé from plastic beakers. Friends from the village passed, stooping to kiss us on both cheeks and wish us *bonne fête*. Peter puffed contentedly on his cigar, leaning back on his chair, with both his hands clasped comfortably behind his head. Mopeds rattled through the streets. Their riders were young and helmetless, and usually there was a pillion passenger chatting on a mobile rather than clinging on.

After the meal a carnival of fireworks erupted, illuminating the towers of the château and the Protestant and Catholic churches. Galaxies of multicoloured stars exploded, threatening to engulf the village before finally raining from the sky. Shrill whistles corkscrewed towards us, and explosive bangs rippled into the mountains, echoing down the narrow valleys. Despite the late hour, there was still a comforting warmth in the air. Children chased between the mottled trunks of the plane trees, while parents and grandparents sipped from beakers of wine. New groups of people arrived and there was a brief carnival of kissing as seats were pulled up and drinks offered around.

Back in England, September evenings are spent huddled around the TV, rather than dancing in the scented southern air. Tanya and I swayed gently to a couple of songs, while Peter danced several energetic foxtrots with startled and only just complicit French ladies. The village clock struck midnight, and Tanya and I rested at an abandoned table. Looking across the dance floor, we realised that Peter had chanced upon Capucine, the woman who'd described him as 'marvellous' in the market. The two of them were whirling relentlessly round, careering into other couples and scattering them like bowling pins.

In the early hours of the morning, when the music had

slowed, Peter stubbed out his cigar and finished his rosé with a satisfied sigh. The dance floor was still full of couples waltzing in the evening air, but it was time for bed. As we left, Tanya pulled on my arm and pointed at a pair of dancers. The man was steering his partner precisely round while puffing occasionally from a pipe, which hung unsupported from his lower lip. It was then I realised. Amid the heat and hubbub of August, one very important date had crept up unnoticed. The waltzing pipe and the immaculately straight back were the same I'd noted on our very first night in Lourmarin, at the village *fête* exactly a year ago, on 1 September.

'Happy anniversary,' said Peter, clapping me on the back and engulfing Tanya in a bear hug.

And then he strode quickly on, leaving us wondering to whom he was talking when he shook his head and said a loud 'Marvellous, absolutely marvellous'.

21

Another French Government Course

O ur lives have a strange repetitive quality at the moment. We find ourselves returning precisely a year on to the same *vides-greniers*, or car-boot sales, where we purchased the paintings, chairs and beds that fill our rooms. This September we are looking for the finishing touches, an old clock to go on the wall, some heavy weights to prevent the mistral slamming shut the front door and a big wooden chest to sweep up the imminent clutter.

The same families man the stalls and because our senses were so alive last year, taking in every detail of the scenery around us, the feeling as we walk around is of a life already lived. I can see us in the past pausing for coffee or marvelling at a set of rusty boules complete with leather carry-case, and yesterday on my way home from the *vide-grenier* in Ansouis, I did just for a second feel as if my shadow and I had become one. It happened when I stopped at the roadside to collect a selection of the bright-orange berries that populate the hedgerows, thinking they would make a nice present for Tanya. As I snipped away, a thorn gashed my finger. Raising it to my mouth, I was suddenly transplanted by the taste of blood to twelve months ago, crouching near a similar bush and absent-mindedly shredding my thumb as I worried about getting our market licence and whether we could finally make a living from rosé.

The sense of déjà-vu faded quickly, but today it has returned. It's unsurprising really, because somehow we have found ourselves sitting in another seminar room looking at a whiteboard chalked up with confusing acronyms. A battered leather briefcase rests on the front desk, and a rare storm has just broken the weeks of drought. Our clothes are sodden from a frantic chase through the streets trying to find the right building, and outside the raindrops are energetically chasing each other down the glass window. The air is heavy and soporific, and the lights are dimmed as a DVD is placed in the machine at the front. As the programme begins, I look around the room and realise that I am the only man.

To ease my sense of insecurity and because I am bored (given the nature of the course, this is a dreadful confession), I begin making these notes, trying to sum up everything that has happened to us, not just this year, but since we left England. It's difficult to know where to start and how to incorporate everything, because I know this is likely to be the end of our story as it appears on the pages of a book.

The familiar is the easiest place to begin. Each morning Tanya and I get up and go to the markets. These days for Lourmarin and Cucuron she occasionally tarries beneath the sheets and I return to collect her later. The school buses are back on the road, and groups of children huddle at irregular intervals on the verges. As we arrive at a market, the streetlights cast a pallid glow in the half-light.

The sun, when it arrives, is no longer the blazing beast of August, which swallowed the savaged earth in a baking shroud. Instead there's a painter's light. The sky is a lighter, less threatening blue, illuminating rather than dominating the landscape, and on fine days we can trace the path of individual crevices running down the side of Mont Sainte-Victoire, some 50 kilometres away, near Aix. The fields are full of pumpkins rather than melons, and the wine harvest has just begun. Tractors chug from the rows of vines to the local cooperative five or six times in a morning. In the bars the talk is of the continuing *sécheresse*, or drought, and the lack of juice in the grapes. The wine will be good this year, but there will be little of it.

This September is just over three years since we sat down for a lunch in Provence, consumed a little too much pink wine and ended up accepting a challenge to find the palest rosé in France. Looking back, neither of us expected our lives to have changed so drastically. We assumed the trip would mean a six-month sabbatical from London and that we would return refreshed to our careers, but travelling around France that summer made me realise I had a choice – I could continue on the pre-mapped city existence or I could set out into the unknown. The decision was easy. Like Tanya, I'd become captivated by the dream of a different life away from the dreary London streets and the confines of an office.

Since we've left England and made our life in France, the most common phrase contemporaries use to describe Tanya and myself is 'very brave'. It's a compliment, but at times there's a veiled pleasure in the fact that bravery leads to disaster more often than success. In fact we were more naïve than brave, in that we had no idea of the difficulties that we would face. Plenty of people retire abroad, perhaps dividing their time equally between home and their new sunshine retreat, but precious few leave when they are young and commit to living full-time in a foreign country.

Even in France, so geographically close to England, the barriers to success can seem insurmountable. There's the language – the better I get, the more mistakes I realise I am making. Fluency is for me unattainable, and all I aspire to is a degree of acceptable competence, or some might just say incompetence.

Then there's the continual day-to-day misunderstandings. Culturally I used to think that the French and the English couldn't be that different. The garlic-eating, baguette-carrying, beret-wearing Frenchman was just a convenient stereotype wheeled out by the papers to explain every cross-Channel dispute, whether diplomatic or sporting. A Frenchman of my age would have grown up with the same Western European world view as my own, and we should understand and sympathise with each other. Or so I believed.

In fact the longer I have lived in France, the less I understand the French. At the moment I see them as unfailingly polite, gracious and generous, but also genetically incapable of saying what they actually want, despite the flow of words with which they greet you. Even in the face of incontrovertible evidence, they are absolutely unwilling to admit they are wrong. No doubt my views are prejudiced and they certainly change on a monthly basis, as I am alternatively outraged by some new bureaucratic hurdle or pleasantly surprised by the lack of one. And this is the face of French society I am allowed to see.

There is also a second level of society, whose secrets will never be revealed to me. The closest comparison in the UK is probably freemasonry. In any area of France there will be people who seemingly exist outside the law. To give a few examples, they can build houses on national park land without planning permission, they can waltz into the market and immediately be granted the prime pitch, and if they are a vigneron, their wines are automatically stocked by all restaurants in the area.

Given that we will never fully understand the language or even the rules of the first open level of French society, I am sometimes troubled by what we are doing here. It's something the locals who split open our rubbish and daubed our car with paint midway through the year want to know. Recently there's been a further spate of incidents. Driving home from a market, a young driver, still with his 'P', or just passed, plates on the car, followed us for fifteen minutes, repeatedly overtaking us and then stopping to let us pass. Each time he came by he stuck two fingers up and yelled something derogatory about the English. On another occasion just as we turned on to the small road that leads to our house, another youngster drove so close to our rear bumper he ended up ramming us. Perhaps his car was just feeling amorous and want to touch number plates with an English counterpart. Our consolation, other than the sheer idiocy of the behaviour, is that it's not just us being targeted. Anyone from outside the region can suffer similar treatment.

It's harder and harder to deal with such events, because as far as outsiders can, we are beginning to feel we belong. There's a small community of young French people who invite us out for drinks. Some evenings we speak in English, others in French, but mostly we mix languages, switching from one to the other. Surprisingly for such a florid language, it is often easier to express some concepts in French – particularly where food and wine are concerned.

In the village, most people know us by name, and while they are never going to become our best friends, we kiss and swap gossip in the street. My biggest fear, that our landlords wouldn't renew our lease, has also not come to pass. The much-asked-for document eventually materialised in true south of France fashion at the very end of August. The *immobilier* responsible had, of course, been on holiday and Rose and Antoine had not appreciated our twitchy London urgency to get the paperwork done.

So we are back on a rolling three-month notice period, watching as the seasons turn again and the leaves of the vines slowly shift to a ripe gold. Thankfully the question of what we are doing here no longer pops so frequently into my head. Growing up, I would never have put 'Provençal market trader' on my list of possible careers, but now I love getting up for the markets, chatting with the other traders, sourcing and explaining about our wines, and in the morning just one glance at the sky and the gently folding green landscape reassures me we made the right choice. Right now, neither Tanya nor I could picture what we would do if we went back to London, and therein lies the problem. A determination to follow our dreams has led us to our rented *mas* in the lee of the Luberon hills, but for how long can we continue?

One of our friends from Lourmarin Market has already given up. On the first Friday of September a morose Julien – the leather-goods salesman who started trading on the same day as us – shared a post-market drink. As he sipped on his complimentary rosé, he explained that he was closing his business at the end of the month. Both Tanya and I were shocked. While plenty of traders sold goods of inferior quality and dubious provenance, Julien was a craftsman, an artisan, as the French would say. He designed his goods, drove hundreds of miles to the south's largest leather market to ensure they were manufactured from the best material and then hand-stitched them. Every article on his stall was a beautiful piece, and one of my favourite possessions is a leather wallet I purchased from Julien during our first market. It is still as supple and soft as the day I bought it.

Reflecting on Julien's decision, I am no longer so surprised. As far as I can see, there are two business models that work in the market. The first is the traders who are providing a year-round service. In the depths of winter, when fingers of ice creep across the Cucuron *étang*, they will still be there, selling seasonal vegetables, clothes to keep people warm and the local olive oil. There will be a bed salesman with his mattresses propped up against the tree and furniture makers, weaving reed into the back of battered old sets of chairs to ensure another decade of service. There might even be the odd vigneron selling his wine or even an artisan *pâtisserie* maker offering delectable tarts. The goods will be high quality and all the prices *correct*, and the locals will visit the same traders year round, so the profit level on each sale doesn't need to be too high.

Despite the workmanship, Julien could never be one of these traders – his handbags and wallets are simply too expensive.

Unfortunately he also doesn't fit into the second category – the merchants who arrive in spring. For these traders, the winter has been largely idle, hunting trips, pastis and, to break the monotony, one or two trips to China to load up with produce.

The market that is unveiled on Easter weekend may look quintessentially Provençal, with the multicoloured linen and tableware, the trays loaded with lavender essence, the pretty pink soaps and the rows of *saucissons*, but in reality it's just a powerful mirage that none of the tourists want to see through. The utopia of Provence, as a rural landscape where people work the land and bring their produce to market, has a powerful allure. It's how the world functioned before global trade, and for holidaymakers it's worth clinging on to, at least for a couple of weeks a year.

Fortunately there's no danger of the traders dissuading them of their quaint notions, despite the fact that most of the olive oils and *saucissons* are shipped in from Spain and the linen from factories on the subcontinent. It's all about margins and mark-up, and French goods are generally too expensive. Take lavender – the products are among the most popular in the market and the countryside is awash with the plant. It stretches credibility to believe that it could come from elsewhere, but it often does. China has one of the largest and most aggressive lavender industries in the world, harvesting the flower at a fraction of the cost in France. With a cut-price workforce ready to make little sweet-smelling balls for people's clothes drawers, what self-respecting trader trying to feed his family wouldn't plump for the cheaper option?

If we wanted to succeed, we could follow one of these two paths. We could spend the winter sourcing wine at a ridiculously cheap price, buying up barrels that would otherwise be converted into petrol. We could then stick a pretty label on the bottle, count the cash and not worry about villa-loads of tourists waking up with a sledgehammer of a hangover. Repeat custom is unusual in the summer anyway, and by making this simple choice, we could quickly treble our profits. The alternative, and more palatable, option was to continue to slowly build our business. Work the markets year round, expand our range of wines and sell everything at the *'correct'* price – apart from the odd Peter-induced summer hike.

Looking at our accounts book for the year – particularly before August – only an eternal optimist would have thought this latter option possible. I've circled the final figure repeatedly with my pen and underlined it several times, as if the added emphasis of the little extra ink on the paper would solve the conundrum. Since November, when we finally got our licence, we've worked in just over 200 markets. In Cucuron, on 16 August we recorded our highest sales ever of 110 bottles, but that was more wine than we sold in the whole month of January. Our total to date is short of our first-year target of 8,000 bottles but only just. Thanks to the Peter Tate effect, the night markets and the endless supply of August customers, we've sold 7,000 bottles, which given my despair at the end of July, I regard as close to a miracle.

Yet it's only a start. For anything more than a subsistence existence, we need to double our sales. Thankfully there are already signs of improvement. Some of our French customers have taken our mobile number and are ordering wine direct from us rather than buying in the market. September sales are also unexpectedly high. Our new clientele in the market still rent villas, but they are either too old or too young to have kids with them. There are no children's meals to cook, no bedtime stories, no interrupted nights' sleep and so the September tourists can concentrate on enjoying themselves. The weather is still hot, the rosé is flowing, and with each passing market the yearly figures improve. By our anniversary in the markets at the beginning of November I expect us to make the year's target.

The question now is, how much better can we do next year? Is there enough upside to convince us to keep the business going?

As the last three years have shown, neither Tanya nor I have ever been short on optimism, and numbers aside – I could never add up anyway – we've succeeded in creating a very promising small business. Our position in the various markets can only improve, and our regular clientele grow. There are plenty of other avenues for us to explore as well, such as approaching holiday companies about stocking their villas with wine. It may take time, but in a couple of years we hope to have sales of 15,000 or 20,000 bottles per annum. Particularly since there will be an added incentive driving us to succeed.

As I mentioned, I am making these notes in a lecture theatre. Tanya has been nudging me incessantly for the last half-hour, demanding I pay attention. Try as I might, I haven't been able to watch the lengthy film we've just been shown. The first five minutes were interesting and instructive, but after that it's largely been propaganda from the French government, complicated by the fact that the vocabulary is totally alien. It's no real surprise, then, that I have been dreamily reflecting on our lives.

The lady who is taking the course is dressed in a neat white dress. She crosses to the television and turns it off. The shutters are opened and I see that it has stopped raining outside. A branch from a pine tree frames the blue sky. In the distance beyond the sun terraces of the townhouses, there are olive groves and field after field of vines. I can't help thinking that it will be some first view, even if it will be forgotten in seconds.

'Well, I hope that was useful,' says the nurse in a voice so quiet it wouldn't even wake a baby. 'The rest of today's session is going to be interactive,' she declares, 'and so to begin with I'd like everybody to introduce themselves and let us know when they are due.'

I smile at Tanya, finally getting my revenge for the market-trading course in Apt, when I'd stumbled through a ten-minute explanation of our plans.

'My name is Tanya. I'm English. I'm thirty-five years old, and we are expecting our first baby at the end of October.'

'It's nice to see a husband here.' The nurse turns unexpectedly to me and a sick feeling rises in my stomach as I pray she doesn't ask me anything.

But of course she does.

'Tell me, what did you learn about breastfeeding from the video?'

I look up from these notes completely lost for words.

La Carte des Vins

Hiver

Vin blanc
Saint-Véran, Domaine des Deux Roches, 71960 Davayé
Tel: 03 85 35 86 51

Vin rosé
Château Saint-Estève de Néri, 84240 Ansouis
Tel: 04 90 09 90 16

Vin rouge
Château Constantin Chevalier, Montée du Galinier, 84160 Lourmarin
Tel: 04 90 68 38 99

Château de Roquefort, Quartier des Bastides, 13830 Roquefort-la-Bédoule
Tel: 04 42 73 20 84

Château Villars, 33141 Saillans, Bordeaux
Tel: 05 57 84 32 17

Domaine de la Brillane, 195 Route de Couteron, 13100 Aix-en-Provence
Tel: 06 80 93 55 63

Domaine Richaud, Côtes du Rhône Villages, Route de Rasteau, 84290 Cairanne
Tel: 04 90 30 85 25

Eté

Vin rosé

Bordeaux

Vignoble Despagne, 33420 Naujan-et-Postiac, Branne
Tel: 05 57 84 55 08

Burgundy

Laurent Fournier, Domaine Jean Fournier, 34 Rue du Château, 21160 Marsannay-la-Côte, Côte d'Or
Tel: 03 80 52 24 38

Corsica

Jean-Laurent Bernardi, Clos de Bernardi, 20253 Patrimonio, Corse
Tel: 04 95 37 01 09

Mark Giovannetti, Domaine Pastricciola, 20253 Patrimonio, Corse
Tel: 04 95 37 18 31

Loire

Domaine Pascal and Nicolas Reverdy, Maimbray, 18300 Sury-en-Vaux
Tel: 02 48 79 37 31

Provence

Château Blanc, Quartier Grimaud, Route de Saint Saturnin, 84220 Rousillon
Tel: 04 90 05 64 56

Château Constantin Chevalier, Montée du Galinier, 84160 Lourmarin
Tel: 04 90 68 38 99

Château Saint-André de Figuière, Quartier Saint-Honoré, 83250 La Londe-les-Maures
Tel: 04 94 00 44 70

Château Saint-Estève de Néri, 84240 Ansouis
Tel: 04 90 09 90 16

Domaine de Sulauze, Route Nationale 569, Chemin du Vieux Sulauze, 13140 Miramas
Tel: 04 90 58 04 37

Some of Our Favourite Market Stands

Barbara and Christophe's *Poulet Rôti*

Ansouis, Cucuron, Lourmarin

Quite simply the best *poulet rôti* you will ever taste. The skin is cooked to crackling perfection and dusted with delectable Provençal herbs. If you ever do tire of the chicken, then move on to the *pintade*, or guinea fowl, which, if possible, is even more delicious. From the counter Barbara also sells uncooked poultry, but it's not as simple as just choosing a bird: there are over five different varieties of chicken. The secret is to tell Barbara your recipe and let her select.

Didier the Vegetable Man

Cadenet, Lourmarin

While most of the other vegetable sellers make a twice-weekly trip to the wholesale market, Didier is busy in his garden, pulling up carrots, parsnips, potatoes and turnips. Everything is fresh on the day of sale. With his twinkling blue eyes and infectious laugh, Didier is the local housewives' favourite, so be prepared for a long queue.

Eva's Tapenades
Apt, L'Isle-sur-la-Sorgue, Lourmarin

Sundried tomato, aubergine, olive, garlic – there's a tapenade for everyone. They are just perfection spread on French bread and enjoyed with a glass of rosé before a long Provençal lunch.

Stefan's Hams
Ansouis, Cucuron, Lourmarin

Unlike some of the other traders, Stefan flies a Spanish flag to let you know where his produce is from. He's proud of its Catalan origins, which is lucky because that is where his wife comes from. The first thing you need to know about Stefan's ham is that it is expensive. The second thing is that it's absolutely delicious. Plump for the pata negra – just don't order too much! There's also a range of Spanish cheeses, olives and peppers.

Stefan's Biscuits
Ansouis

If you ever forget the name of a Provençal, just guess and call him Stefan. The likelihood is that you will be right. We've met hundreds of them. The popularity of the name is probably only exceeded by Martine for women. But I digress ... This Stefan is an artisan biscuit maker and sells everything from chunky cookies to brittle sugar biscuits. He supplies *boulangeries* across the Luberon and I suspect he only really comes to Ansouis on Sunday for the banter with the other traders.

Vincent's Tarts
Lourmarin

Sorry – more food! Vincent runs a catering business and makes the most delicious tarts I have ever tasted. Sweet and savoury, the quality is as high as any Michelin restaurant. And his chocolate pudding is sumptuous. Find him at the bottom of the steps leading from the *place* to the tree-lined avenue.

Acknowledgements

As always, Tanya and I would like to thank both of our families for their help and support. We have had a long stream of visitors this year, all of whom have assisted on the market stall and so many thanks in no particular order to the following people: Amanda, Philippa, Izzie, Lisa, John, PJ, Charmian, Adrian, Ashara, Jilly, Martine, Michelle, Wendy, Owen, Duncan, Ed, Beth, Alan, Liz, Nick, Kate, Claire, Neil, Rosie, Tristan, Freya, Pat, John, Pamela, Catherine, Faiza, Pierre, Sara, Stuart, Isla, Chippie, Malcolm, Ian, Sue, Anna, Tom and Paul. Additional thanks to Alan for his excellent proofreading, which always spares my blushes.

At Orion, Alan Samson for his continued and determined support of this series of books, Lucinda McNeile for being a good friend and Kate Shearman for all her hard work on the paperback side.

Tanya and I are also very grateful to our agent, John Saddler, who has worked tirelessly to ensure the books are as successful as they can possibly be, and all the residents of the Luberon who have supported us on our market stall and made us feel so welcome, particularly Peter and Jenny.

Finally a special mention must go to Jamie Aarvold (sales assistant) and Stuart Southgate (sales director), who almost managed to achieve the impossible and sell more wine than Peter Tate.

Index

Château de Roquefort, 164, 165–
166, 167–169, 173
Château la Dorgonne, 29–30,
31–32
Château Villars, 50–54
Châteauneuf-du-Pape, 56, 159, 160
Cheval Blanc, 51, 134
children, French, and wine, 189,
192, 196
Chilean wine, 27
Christmas
markets, 109, 114–121
preparations in Provence for,
113–114
seasonal delicacies, 113–114, 127
Christmas Day, 132–134
civil servants, French, 37–38
Claire (author's sister-in-law), 127,
132, 188, 191, 192, 193
clairet, Bordeaux, 26, 173, 205
Claude (customer), 137–138, 139,
140
Col de Lourmarin, 87
concours, 160
Concours Mondial du Vin Rosé,
160–161, 162–164, 165, 166,
167, 169
confrérie, Pertuis potato, 147, 153
confrèries, Corsican, 65–67, 69
corruption in markets, 101
Corsica, 60, 61–71
symbols of, 62–63
Corsican confrèries, 65–67, 69
Corsican rosé, 68, 69
Corsicans, 62–63
Côte d'Azur, 5
Côtes du Rhône, 26, 54
crocodiles, African, 102
Cucuron, 56, 58–59, 149
café, 58–59, 136

étang (water basin), 56–57, 109,
117, 119, 136, 149, 150, 153–
154, 175–176, 196, 197, 245
Cucuron Market, 56–57, 88, 107,
109, 147–154, 158, 175–176,
196–198, 208, 209, 235, 247
Christmas Market, 116–121
flagstone incident, 152–153,
154–155, 176, 198
Night Market, 233
old lady in, 152–153, 154
placier, 109, 151, 153, 154, 175,
176, 197, 198, 208
Cuvée Flora, 35
cycle enthusiasts, 44, 45

daube (stew), 142
Didier (vegetable seller), 157
dogs, Scruffy and Gentle, 16, 73
dogs, truffle-hunting, 125–126,
134–135
Domaine de la Brillane, 33, 34–35,
36, 47, 77–78, 138
Domaine Ott, 159
donkey, Céleste, 165, 167, 168–169
Dorking rugby club, 48
drink-driving in France, 28
Durance, river, 13, 87, 90
Dutch, the, 203–204, 205

Easter, 188, 191–196
Elodie (hairdresser), 199
English customers, 141, 187–188,
206–207, 234
English dinner-party circuit,
140–143

Fabrice (Cannes concours organiser),
162, 163, 164
Farinole, Corsica, 64